A HISTORY OF THE PANZER TROOPS
1916-1945

Werner Haupt

Werner Haupt

A HISTORY OF THE PANZER TROOPS

1916-1945

1469 Morstein Road, West Chester, Pennsylvania 19380

List of Waffen-SS Ranks and their World War II German and US Equivalents

Waffen-SS	German WWII Army	U.S. WWII Army
General Officers		
-No equivalent-	Generalfeldmarschall	General of the Army
Oberstgruppenführer	Generaloberst	General
Obergruppenführer	General	Lieutenant General
Gruppenführer	Generalleutnant	Major General
Brigadeführer	Generalmajor	Brigadier General
Staff Officers		
Oberführer	-No equivalent- **(Wore the shoulder strap of a Colonel)**	-No equivalent-
Standartenführer	Oberst	Colonel
Obersturmführer	Oberstleutnant	Lieutenant Colonel
Sturmbannführer	Major	Major
Company Officers		
Hauptsturmführer	Hauptmann	Captain
Obersturmführer	Oberleutnant	1st Lieutenant
Untersturmführer	Leutnant	2nd Lieutenant
Officer Candidates *(Basically equal to Oberfeldwebel & Feldwebel)*		
Oberjunker	Oberfähnrich	-No equivalent-
Junker	Fähnrich	-No equivalent-
Noncommissioned Officers		
Sturmscharführer	Stabsfeldwebel	Sergeant Major
Hauptscharführer	Oberfeldwebel	Master Sergeant
Oberscharführer	Feldwebel	Technical Sergeant
Scharführer	Unterfeldwebel	Staff Sergeant
Unterscharführer	Unterofficier	Sergeant
Enlisted Men		
-No equivalent-	Stabsgefreiter	Admin. Corporal
Rottenführer	Obergefreiter	Corporal
Sturmmann	Gefreiter	Corporal
SS-Obersoldat*	Obersoldat*	Private 1st Class
SS-Soldat*	Soldat*	Private

*Note: *Soldat* is a general term. Other words used here are Schütze, Grenadier, Füsilier, depending upon the combat arm to which the soldier belonged.

Source of U.S. World War II army equivalents: War Department Technical Manual TM-E 30-451 *Handbook on German Military Forces*, 15 March 1945.

Translated from the German by Dr. Edward Force,
Central Connecticut State University.

Library of Congress Catalog Number: 90-60469.

Printed in the United States of America.
ISBN: 0-88740-244-5

This book originally published under the title,
Das Buch der Panzertruppe 1916-1945,
by Podzun-Pallas Verlag, Markt 9, 6360 Friedberg,
© 1989. ISBN: 3-7909-0374-4.

We are interested in hearing from authors with
book ideas on related subjects.

Published by Schiffer Publishing, Ltd.
1469 Morstein Road
West Chester, Pennsylvania 19380
Please write for a free catalog.
This book may be purchased from the publisher.
Please include $2.00 postage.
Try your bookstore first.

CONTENTS

Introduction 7

Prelude 9
German Tanks in World War I, 1916-1918

Intermezzo 16
The Secret Rearmament, 1919-1934

The Drama 27
Wehrmacht Armored Weapons, 1935-1939

Climax 48
Early War Years, 1939-1943

Finale 111
Late War Years, 1944-1945

Appendices 140

Introduction

A *History of the Panzer Troops* joins *A History of the Infantry*, published by Podzun-Pallas Verlag in 1982, and presents in compact form the organizational history of the newest service arm of the German Wehrmacht.

This work is not a history book dealing with the history of battles in World Wars I and II, nor is it a purely technical volume dedicated exclusively to the very complex technology of the tank; rather it is intended primarily to present a history of the organization of these troops, enriched with photographs and documents. The scope extends from the development of tanks in World War I, through the secret rearmament during the Weimar Republic era to the last service of the Panzer troops in May 1945.

Although there are already numerous publications, inside and outside Germany alike, on this service arm, still in all the author is closing a gap, for this book will address every former soldier of the Panzer troops as well as every reader who is interested in this chapter of German military history, its ups and downs, its failures as well as its great successes, or its organization — practically "out of nothing."

The author, who was licensed to drive tanks from the P-I to the P-V, would like to dedicate this book to the former soldiers of the German Panzer troops who never returned home.

Waiblingen, Summer 1989 — Werner Haupt

Die Panzer sind die Waffe
des Angriffs. Sie müssen mit
hinreißendem Schwung geführt
werden und ihren Stoß unauf-
haltsam tief in das Herz der
feindlichen Stellung tragen.
Ich bin gewiß, daß der Panzer-
offiziersnachwuchs sich seiner stolzen
kriegerischen Überlieferung aus
den verflossenen 4 Jahren stets
erinnern und in aller Zukunft
ebenso handeln wird.

Guderian

Handwritten message from the Inspector General of the Panzer Troops, Generaloberst Guderian, for a book published in 1944 on the service of the tank in the eastern campaign.

Prelude

German Tanks in World War I, 1916-1918

It was on September 15, 1916, when gray clouds hung deep over the devastated landscape of the Somme and steady rain made the ground, with its funnel-like shell craters, wetter and wetter. For weeks the murderous summer battle raged in this area, and the Allied General Staff awaited a decisive turning point.

Then — after the British artillery fire slowly turned to the rearward area of the German front, the noise of motors and the rattle of heavy chains broke through the drumming of gunfire and the whistling of machine-gun bullets. When the smoke of the fire lifted a bit, the dirty, hungry soldiers of the 28th German Reserve Infantry Regiment saw grayish-yellow monsters that moved slowly through the cratered landscape toward their trenches.

They stared, horrified and almost in despair, at these steel giants that seemed to move forward undisturbed, robot-like. The few officers, non-commissioned officers and men of this Rhenish regiment were the first Germans to witness the arrival of a new weapon on the battlefield.

When British tanks rolled toward the German positions near Flers on the Somme on September 15, 1916, the history of the Panzer troops began.

It was the tanks of the British Royal Tank Corps that led the first tank attack in the history of war on this autumn day in 1916. Yet the anticipated surprise did not succeed. Of the 49 British tanks that were deployed, only 32 reached the battlefield; the others had already broken down in transport or during the advance. Five more tanks were stuck in the numerous shell craters and could not get out under their own power; nine more had to be abandoned because of engine trouble. The rest of them, which broke into the German positions, came under the fire of the German guns. Eight of these tanks took direct hits and exploded, and another was put out of action by hand grenades.

After the first tank attack had run its course here in the vicinity of the French city of Flers, German officers inspected the British steel monsters with amazement. They were tanks of the "Big Willie" type — later designated "Mark I" — that weighed 28 tons, were armed with two 57mm guns and four machine guns, and carried a crew of one officer and seven men.

The term "tank" was originally meant as a disguise for this new weapon. After the manufacture of these steel vehicles could no longer be kept secret, the British gave out the information that these giants with chains were mobile water tanks for the army. This is how the new weapon got its name. (The German term "Panzer" came into being only in the postwar years.) On the basis of the experience gained at Fiers, and following a secret conference of the Transport Technical Testing Commission of the Military High Command and the Transport Division of the General War Department on October 30, the Prussian War Ministry gave the order for the development and construction of their own tanks on November 13, 1916. After initial intensive talks with representatives of the industrial firms of Daimler, Knoop, Dürkopp, Lohrmann-Benz, Bosch, Büssing and Hansa-Lloyd, the appropriate contracts were given.

The guidelines for designing, which was to be done under the direction of Oberingenieur Vollmer of the Transport Technical Testing Commission, were as follows:

Performance:
Cross-country travel over any terrain,
Crossing of ditches up to 1.5 meters wide,
Cross-country climbing capability of 1:10, 1:4 on pavement,
Forward and reverse propulsion,
Cross-country speed 6 kph, on pavement 12 kph,
Minimum payload 4 tons,
Armor plate corresponding to payload.

Equipment:
Front and rear rapid-firing guns,
several machine guns,
80- to 100-HP motor,
Ammunition 300-500 rounds per gun, 6000 per machine gun,
Cost of construction 250,000 Marks.

Well-known engineers of the Büssing, Opel, Daimler, Audi and Knoop went to work at once. As their basis they used captured British tanks and the Austrian "caterpillar" trucks. As early as December 22, 1916 the drawings for a German tank reached the Military High Command (OHL); the tank bore the designation "A7V." (A7V was the official designation for the Transport Department of the General War Department in peacetime.)

But as is always the case with new constructions, the opinions of the OHL and the constructors and firms involved diverged widely — and costly time was thus lost. (Twenty-five years later the very same thing happened, when the OKW (High Command of the Wehrmacht), Armament Ministry and industry could never agree as to when, how and why a new tank should be built!)

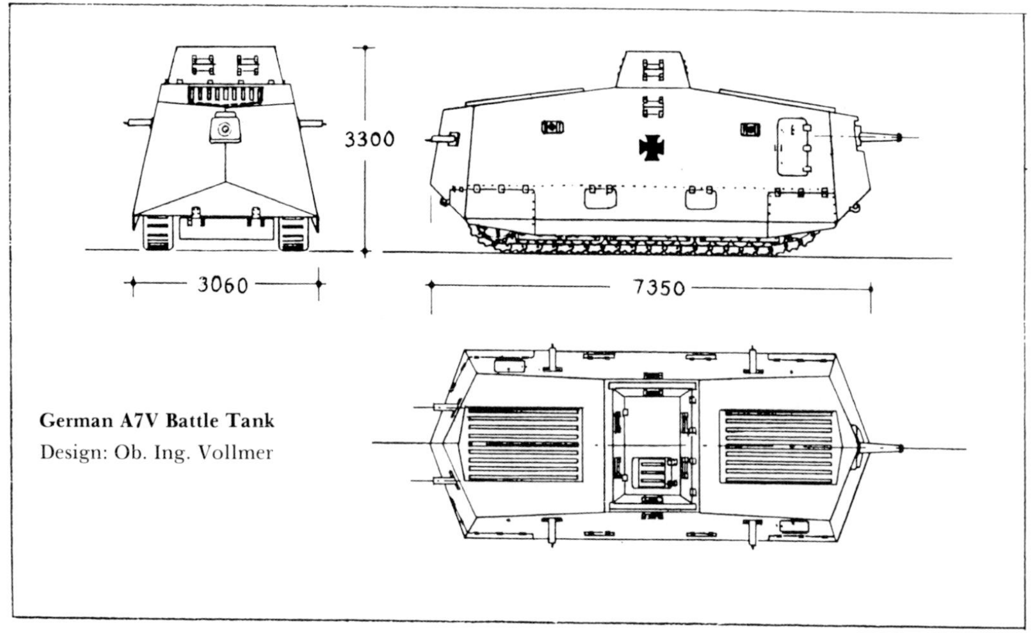

German A7V Battle Tank
Design: Ob. Ing. Vollmer

It took months of work before the interior and exterior of the "A7V" finally took shape. The construction time was also disturbed considerably by the shortage of coal at the factories and the lack of trained workers. But on April 30, 1917, the first chassis, with a wooden superstructure, was introduced at Berlin-Marienfelde. The Guard Engineer Replacement Battalion had prepared a terrain here with shell craters, ditches, barbed-wire barriers and the like, and also played the role of the "enemy." The OHL was not satisfied. Only after a further demonstration in Mainz on May 14, 1917, this time with an armored body, was the construction of tanks given the first priority level by the OHL.

Meanwhile the Allies, particularly the British Army, deployed their tanks on the battlefield more and more. On April 9, 1917, about 5:30 A.M., packs of tanks rolled toward German positions near Arras. Three days later the attack was repeated by eleven tanks, nine of which were left burning on the battlefield. The last large-scale attack of British "Mark I" tanks, near Ypres, likewise came to grief in the trenches.

Now the construction of German tanks and the training of their crews had begun. The "A7V" measured 7.35 meters long, 3.06 meters wide and 3.30 meters high. The weight added up to nine tons, the front and rear armor plate was three centimeters thick, that on the sides one and a half to two cm. The armament consisted of a 57mm gun (captured Belgian guns) and six machine guns. At a speed of 16 kph, the tank's range on the road was 80 kilometers. The crew usually consisted of one officer or sergeant and ten men.

During training it was learned that, among other things, the two 100-HP motors often did not start and easily overheated, the transmissions broke and the treads ran off the track during cross-country travel. After these problems were solved, the first German tank was ready for combat at the end of October 1917. Meanwhile a driving school for "A7V" tanks had been established in Berlin-Marienfelde.

A German tank crew and their battle tank, painted with a death's-head. The men wore asbestos suits, leather helmets and shrapnel masks.

The Chief of Field Motor Vehicles, Oberst Meyer, ordered the establishment of *Sturmwagenabteilungen* 1 and 2 (Hauptmann Greiff, Hauptmann Steinhardt) on September 29, 1917. These units were formed in Berlin-Marienfelde; each of them received five tanks.

Meanwhile, though, the war at the front had proceeded. The British General Staff decided in November of 1917 on a major offensive against the German front at Cambrai. After day-long artillery preparation, numerous infantry and cavalry divisions, supported by hundreds of warplanes and 378 (!) tanks, attacked on November 20, 1917.

The result was bitter fighting, in which the British were able on the first day to break the German front to a width of 13 kilometers and a depth of 9 kilometers. Cavalry had advanced to the suburbs of Cambrai — and the bells of victory were already ringing at St. Paul's Cathedral in London. But then the German troops struck back. After two weeks the British troops had been driven back to their original positions and lost sixty tanks.

This "Tank Battle of Cambrai" finally inspired the OHL to accelerate the construction of their own tanks and the development of this new weapon type. The first *Sturmwagenabteilung* was ready to march on January 5, 1918 and was transferred to Sedan, on the western front, a week later. Meanwhile the 2nd and 3rd (Hauptmann Uihlein) units were established at home. In February of 1918 Kaiser Wilhelm II inspected these units and their tanks. Two additional units were simultaneously established in Charleroi, using captured British tanks. Hauptmann Bornschlegel of the Royal Bavarian Air and Motorized Battalion became the commander of all tank units.

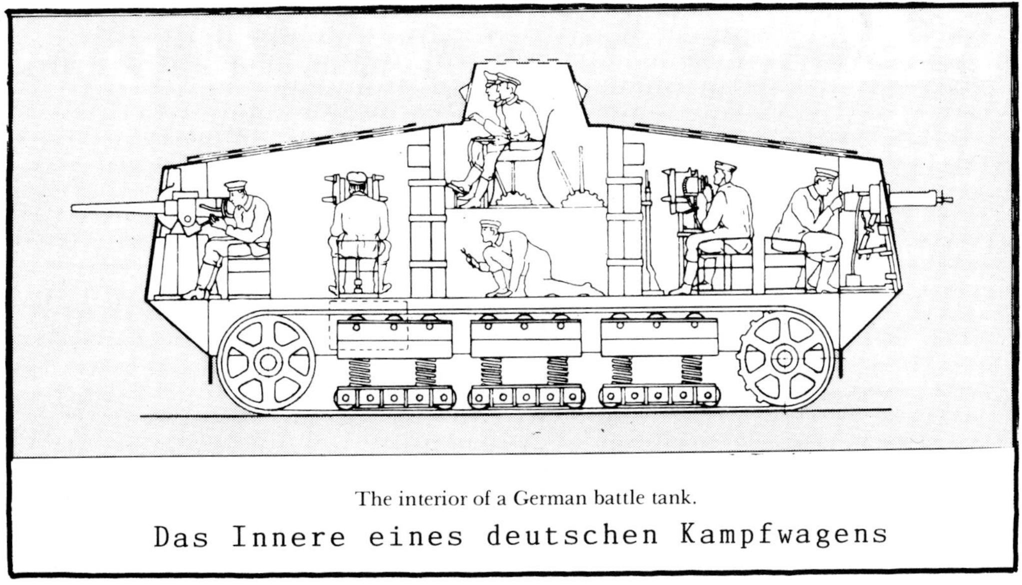

The interior of a German battle tank.

Das Innere eines deutschen Kampfwagens

Meanwhile the first deployment of five German tanks took place at St. Quentin, with partial success. The second action at Villers-Bretonneux on April 24, 1918, involving all three units, showed successes and weaknesses. The tanks were completely on their own, as there was no means of communication. Tests of this kind had meanwhile been given up, and carrier pigeons were used for the time being. The unit staffs remained behind and used messengers to contact the vehicles. After these actions the following lessons were learned:

1. Equipping the tanks with heavy guns is best,
2. Rate of fire is sufficient,
3. Ammunition quantities are sufficient,
4. Aiming with a scope is unsatisfactory, as the vehicle is constantly in motion.

On the basis of this experience, the OHL had contracted for 100 tanks, and at the same time the development of a larger and heavier tank was urged. This tank, designated "A7VU", was to weigh 40 tons, measure 8.38 meters long, 4.69 meters wide and 3.14 meters high, but it was not successful, even though it had been equipped — like the British tanks — with chain treads. The construction of this type was halted on September 12, 1918.

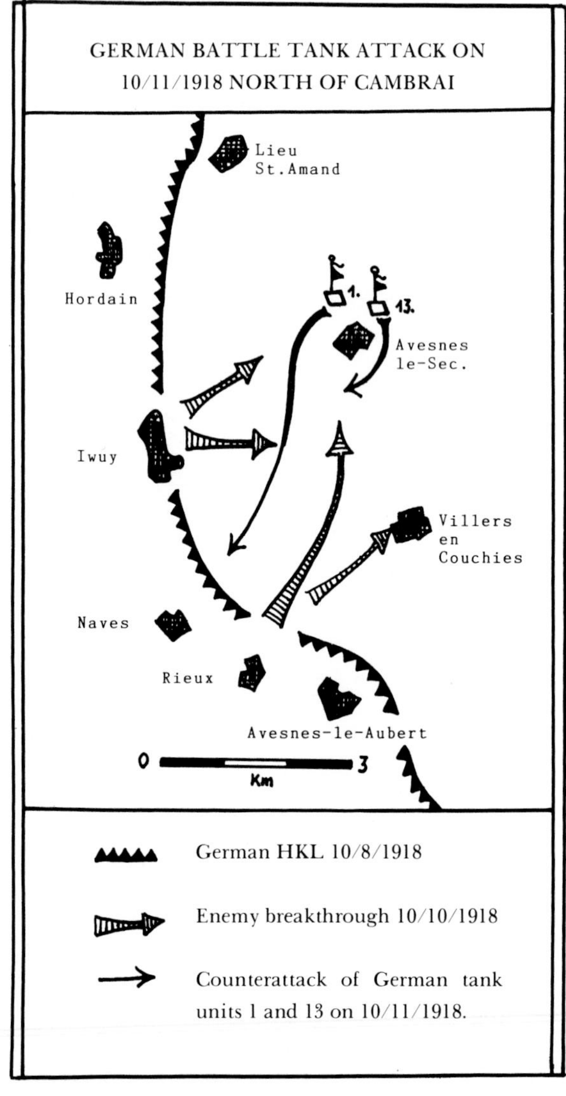

GERMAN BATTLE TANK ATTACK ON 10/11/1918 NORTH OF CAMBRAI

At this time nine units with 45 tanks were at the front. At the command of the OHL as of July 1918, the tanks were painted a uniform gray-green-brown and bore painted Iron Crosses on the front, sides and rear.

The units saw scattered service. Units 1 and 13, for example, were deployed north of Cambrai early in October, where four of the ten attacking tanks were lost. The deployment of the British "Royal Tank Corps" turned out very different. On July 18, 1918 the British attacked at Chateau-Thierry with 600 tanks, and early in October they deployed 400 at Villers-Cotterét!

In these battles the first tank-versus-tank duels took place. Leutnant Bittner and Leutnant Blitz of the 3rd *Sturmwagenabteilung* set the first three British tanks afire with gunfire. Yet with all their eagerness to fight and willingness to sacrifice themselves — the German tanks became fewer and fewer. What with the shortage of materials and coal and the continuing strikes, industry could provide no more armor plate or motors.

For this reason the OHL had decided to build light tanks in order to save materials. Thus the 17-ton "LK I" and "LK II" tank types came into existence. (LK simply meant *Leichter Kampfwagen*: light tank.) Six hundred of them were contracted for, to be sure, but only a few had been produced when the war ended.

On November 1, 1918 there were nine German *Sturmwagenabteilungen* with 45 tanks at the front. (On the same day, the Allies had more than 3500 tanks!) The last German units were transferred to Wiesbaden after the armistice and demobilized there.

The Treaty of Versailles later ordered the delivery of the last usable "A7V" tanks to Poland. Here the German tanks saw service again in the Polish-Russian War of 1920. The few "LK I" and "LK II" tanks were taken over by the Swedish Army, where they saw service until the mid-Twenties.

Intermezzo

The Secret Rearmament, 1919-1934

General of the Infantry Ludendorff wrote: "The tank won . . . an unholy influence . . . The war was to be ended." Thus the new weapon was recognized as a decisive means of making war. Naturally, according to the will and the decisions of the Allies, German troops were not to have any tanks.

But there were still a few; they were captured British light tanks and German training vehicles. These were turned over to the volunteer units organized in Berlin at the end of 1918, which saw action as the *Kampfwagenabteilung Vetter* in street fighting against the Spartacists, which lasted until the end of January 1919. Only at the urgent insistence of the Allied officials did this command have to be disbanded and the last German tanks surrendered.

A captured British tank and a soldier of the *Sturmwagenabteilung Vetter* in Berlin, 1919.

There was as yet no Reichswehr. The army units that returned from the field and had not yet been demobilized occupied the old barracks. In the autumn of 1920 the Defense Ministry of the Reich set up service positions among the two group commands in Berlin and Kassel that worked on the establishment of a so-called motorized troop. Thus a new service arm came into being in the German Army; to be sure, it was not supposed to be a battle troop; rather it was intended to handle supply service. Oberstleutnant Hannemann (Kassel) and Major Grundtmann (Berlin) were the first responsible officers of these troops.

With the establishment of the Reichswehr in 1921 on the basis of the regulations in the Treaty of Versailles — Army 100,000, Navy 15,000 men — the *Inspektion der Kraftfahrtruppen* was formed in the Defense Ministry of the Reich. This now became responsible for the establishment and training of the motor vehicle units to be formed in the seven infantry divisions. The Inspector, Generalmajor von Tschischwitz, and his chief of staff, Major Petter, understood that it was their job to create a light motorized troop that could provide necessary supplies to the fighting forces.

Inspektion der Verkehrstruppen (In 6).

Kraftfahrtruppen — In6 (K) und Fahrtruppen — In6 (F).

Inspekteur: Oberst von Natzmer (Pr.Gen.St.) 1.10.20 (24)
Chef des Stabes der Fahrtruppen: Oberstlt. Adam (GTrA) 1. 1.23 (2)
Chef des Stabes der Kraftfahrtruppen: Oberstlt. Petter (Militärtechnische Akademie) 1. 2.23 (3)

Maj. Brettner (TrA6)	18. 5.20	(10)	Hptm. Guderian (JägB10)	18.12.15	(22)
„ Feßmann (Adj.d.B.2.Kav.Br)	1. 3.23	(1)	„ Löweneck (B.GB)	18. 4.16	(35)
Hptm. Woerler (B.2.TrA)	28.11.14	(67)			

5. Kraftfahr-Abteilung.

Gr. Kdo. 2.
5. Div.

St u. 1. (Württemb.) K.: Stuttgart-Cannstatt, 2. (Württemb.) K.: Ulm, 3. (Preuß.) K.: Cassel.

Stammtruppenteile: 1. K.: Württemb. Luftsch. u. Kraftf.Tr.

Kommandeur: Maj. Knox (JR67) 15. 7.18 (6)

Hauptleute:

von Hartlieb genannt Walsporn (JR127)	27. 1.15	(34)	St	Stahl (LB5)	18. 4.18	(7)	3
Austmann (Fuß-AR13)	18. 4.17	(11)	2	Schroeder (JR116)	20. 9.18	(12)	1

Oberleutnant

Hupfeld (GR1) 18.10.17 (12) 1

Leutnante:

Runge (GB4)	22. 6.14	(7)	Adj	von Schoenebeck (GrR109)	1. 5.16	(8)	3
König (JR125)	1.12.15	(4)	2	Haarde (JR78)	1. 2.17	(6)	3

From the Army List of the Reichsheer, 1923.

Aus der Rangliste des Reichsheeres - 1923

On July 15, 1921 the Reich Defense Minister established the "Battle Tank Emblem" for officers, non-commissioned officers and enlisted men, who (to quote directly) "have taken part in at least three combat missions in German "A7V" tanks or captured British tanks in the field or were wounded on one of these missions." The tank emblem could be worn on the left breast pocket of the uniform. It consisted of an oval shield encircled with oak leaves and laurel. This wreath, with a bow at the bottom, ended in a death's head — the emblem of the former German tanks. An "A7V" tank was portrayed in the emblem itself, with three shrapnel shells exploding over it. The emblem was awarded 99 times in all.

In the same year in which this emblem was created, no officer expected the establishment of a subsequent German tank troop — but the situation was to change just a year later!

A hitherto unknown officer, Hauptmann Guderian, was transferred to the Inspection of Motorized Troops in 1922 and ordered first to serve in the 7th *Kraftfahrabteilung* (Commander Major Lutz), stationed in Munich. In the same year the German and Russian foreign ministers signed the Treaty of Rapallo. Now the German representatives, Generalmajor Hasse and Oberst von Schleicher, could hold discussions with Russian diplomats about mutual military training. (This was also the year in which German and Russian passenger planes established regular air traffic between Berlin and Moscow, before a German commercial plane was allowed to fly to any western capital!) The two states that could be said to have lost the most in World War I had agreed on military cooperation!

The German Reich Defense Ministry set up Section "R" under the direction of Oberst Nicolai (Chief of German Defense in World War I), which established a branch in Moscow (Oberst von Lieth-Thomsen, Major Ritter von Niedermayer). The cooperation between German and Russian military agencies was a great success, unlike that of the two countries' economic offices. After the treaty, German officers could be sent to the (since 1922) Soviet Union for training, and Russian officers in turn could take courses at German military schools. The German officers sent to Russia were legally required to give up their positions in Germany but were still carried on the army lists and returned to their units when they came back. The Reichswehr maintained three training centers: a gas attack school in Saratov, a pilot and observer school in Lipetsk and an armored troop school near Kazan on the Kama River; for reasons of secrecy it was called "Panzertruppenschule Kama."

The Red Army set up training facilities and barracks, supplied equipment and service personnel. The tanks used were the light "MS I" and "MS II" types, the latter already armed with a 37mm gun. After completing the appropriate preliminary training, it was chiefly officers of the motorized troops who were, as of the mid-Twenties, sent to Kazan for training lasting up to two years. At the same time, the firms of Daimler, Krupp and Rheinmetall sent engineers and technicians to Kazan. There they were able to work on new designs — such as those for the chassis of the later "P-I" and "P-II." The German directors of this training were Director Mahlbrand, Major Ritter von Radlmaier and Major Harpe (the later Generaloberst and commander of several armored armies).

The Soviet agencies supported the training of nine to twelve German officers at a time splendidly. Generalmajor von Blomberg, the later Minister of War, Generalmajor Lutz, Oberstleutnant Guderian, Oberstleutnant Model and other high-ranking German officers visited the school as observers. The good re-

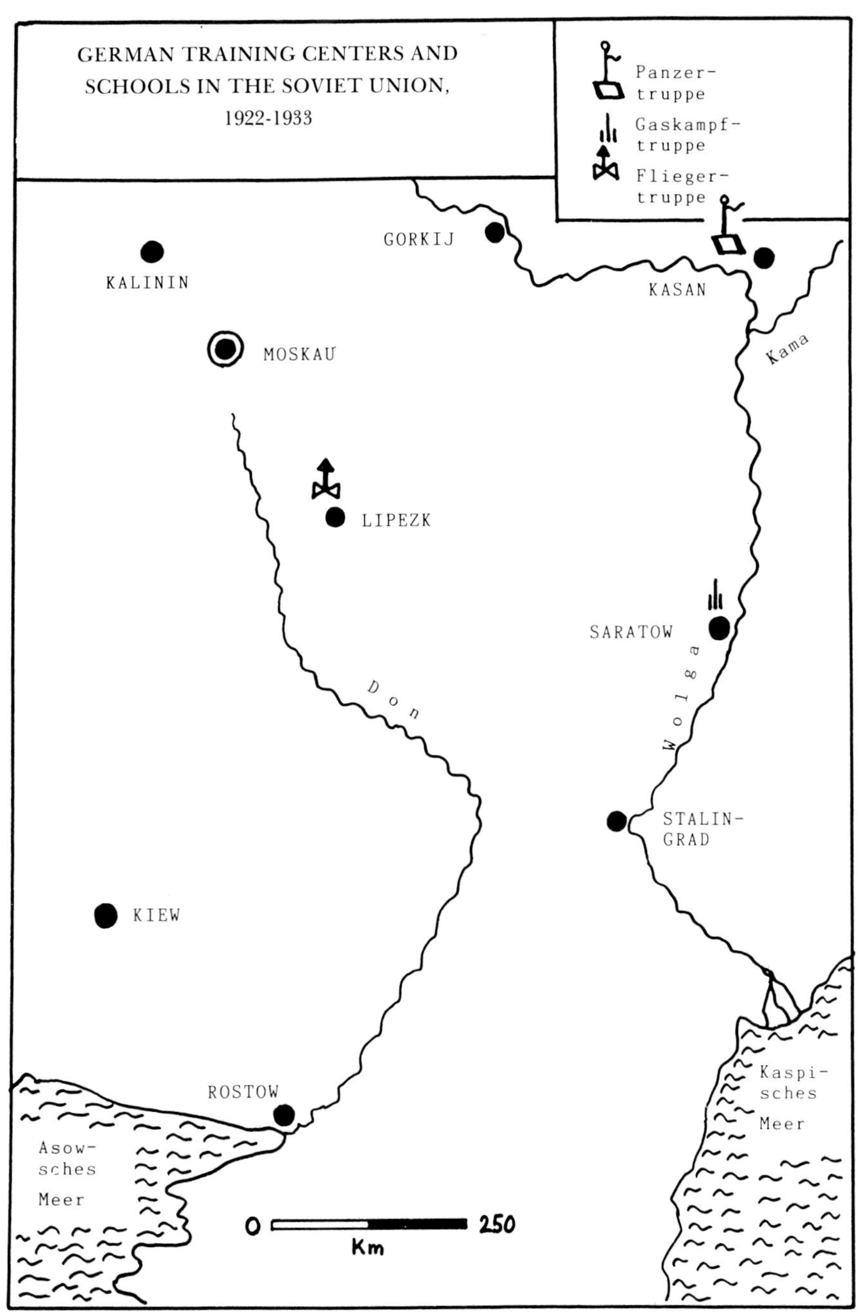

lationship between German and Russian officers was disturbed only in the summer of 1933, when strict orders came from Berlin to close the Panzer troop school. The command of the Red Army saw no reason for this abrupt breakoff.

It was finally possible, though difficult, to bring the German tanks, referred to there as light towing tractors, back over the border and establish them at the gunnery school in Altgarz-Wustrow.

Inspektion der Verkehrstruppen (In 6)

Kraftfahrtruppen — In6 (K) und Fahrtruppen — In6 (F)

Inspekteur: Gen. Maj. von Vollard Bockelberg	1.11.27	(3)
Chef des Stabes der Fahrtruppen: Oberst Adam	1.11.27	(6)
Chef des Stabes der Kraftfahrtruppen: Oberst Petter	1.11.27	(7)

Maj. Busch	1. 4.25	(6)	Hptm. Ritter von Radlmaier	18.12.15	(14)
= Kaempfe	1. 5.25	(4)	= Kühn	27. 1.18	(3)
= Krafft	1. 4.26	(10)	= Harpe	18. 4.18	(5)
= Dörffer	1. 2.28	(2)	= Schwartz	20. 9.18	(24)
= Müller	1. 2.28	(17)			

Gr. Kdo. 1
1. Div.

1. (Preußische) Kraftfahr-Abteilung

St 1. u. 3. K.: Königsberg (Pr.), 2. K.: Allenstein.

Kommandeur: Oberstlt. Mencke 1. 2.27 (25)

Hauptleute

Kempf	27. 1.16	(2a)	2	Blankenstein	1. 2.24	(10)	3
Meyer	18. 8.18	(27)	St	Breith	1. 3.24	(8)	1

Oberleutnante

Dittmann	1. 4.25	(121)	1	von Hülsen	1. 3.27	(5)	3
Brüning	1. 4.25	(569)	Adj	Teege	1. 2.28	(27)	1

Leutnante

Heyna	1.12.26	(163)	3	von Amsberg	1. 2.28	(16)	1

Gr. Kdo. 1
2. Div.

2. (Preußische) Kraftfahr-Abteilung

St u. 1. K.: Stettin, 2. K.: Schwerin (Mecklb.), 3. K.: Kolberg.

Stammtruppenteil: 3. K.: Preuß. FliegTr.

Kommandeur: Maj. von Puttkamer	1. 3.26	(2)	
Maj. Böhmer	1. 5.28	(2)	St

Hauptleute

Streich	1. 2.23	(1)	1	Werner	1. 2.26	(25)	2
von Bismarck	1. 5.24	(2)	3				

Oberleutnante

Dühring	1. 4.25	(5)	1	Koll	1. 4.25	(232)	Adj

Leutnante

Herschel	1.12.25	(90)	1	Weber	1. 3.28	(8)	3
Wolff	1.12.26	(162)	2				

List of officers of the Inspection of Motorized Troops and two transport units: 1928 Army List.

Meanwhile, in the higher command echelons of the army, tactical considerations were also taken up concerning the use of the transport units not only as supply trains but also, when possible, as front-line troops. In 1923 and 1924 the first plans involving tanks and warplanes were made by the Reich Defense Ministry. One of these plans, under the direction of Oberstleutnant von Brauchitsch, later the Commander of the Army, made it clear that armored vehicles — thus tanks — were planned for now. The first tactical maneuvers in the field thus took place, using armored personnel carriers with four-wheel drive. On the basis of this experience, in 1925 the Army Weapons Office empowered the three firms of Rheinmetall, Krupp and Daimler-Benz to design light tanks, naturally under the strictest secrecy. The development of these planned tanks was, to be sure, severely hindered by differences of opinion among the individual inspection units in the Reich Defense Ministry. Here there was no agreement — practically until 1935 — as to whether armored vehicles were to be used in the future in an offensive role or only as support for infantry and cavalry.

The subsequent Inspectors of the Motorized Troops, Generalmajor von Natzmer and Oberst von Vollard-Bockelberg, could not reconcile themselves to the use of tanks. The young Hauptmann Guderian, meanwhile transferred to the Transport Division of the Reich Defense Ministry, had his own ideas about the use of tanks in the future. He was able to develop these plans from 1928 on as a tank tactics instructor.

So it was under his encouragement that, in the same year, the first exercises took place with wooden dummies that represented tanks. Soldiers of the III./Infantry Regiment 9 (Spandau) pushed these dummy tanks and thus played the role of the first German tank soldiers on foot. The Commander of this battalion, Major Busch (the later Field Marshal), and his adjutant, Hauptmann Wenck (the later General of the Panzer Troops), were eager participants in these maneuvers.

Drills with dummy tanks by the 9th Infantry Regiment (Potsdam).

Major Guderian, who was detailed for a time to the II. Battalion Guard of the Swedish Army, got to know his first tank there. It was a light German World War I tank of the "LK II" type. On his return from Sweden, Major Guderian shared his ideas on the establishment of a German Panzer division with the new Inspector of the Motorized Troops, Generalmajor von Stülpnagel. Naturally, his plans were rejected; only the new Chief of Staff, Oberst Lutz, Guderian's former commander in Munich, showed any enthusiasm for his plan. The "insistent" Guderian thus had to be given a new position. He took command of the 3rd (Prussian) Motor Vehicle Unit in Berlin-Lankwitz. He had his 2nd Company, stationed in Döberitz, "rearmed" with dummy tanks in order to start gathering practical experience.

Inspektion der Kraftfahrtruppen (In 6)

Inspekteur: Gen. Maj. Lutz — 1. 4.31 (1)

Chef des Stabes: Obstlt. Guderian — 1. 2.31 (41)

Maj. Nehring	1. 4.31 (14a)	Hptm. Ritter von Hauenschild	1.10.28	(2)
Hptm. Irmisch	1. 5.22 (11)	Oblt. Chales de Beaulieu	1. 4.25	(420)
" Breith	1. 3.24 (8)			
" Werner	1. 2.26 (25)			

Kraftfahr-Lehrstab (Stab F. 4)

Berlin

Kommandeur: Oberst Feßmann — 1. 4.31 (12)

Abg. Ausgesch.: Oberst Genée.

Gru. Kdo. 2
7. Div.

7. (Bayerische) Kraftfahr-Abteilung

St. u. 1. Kp.: München, 2. Kp.: Würzburg, 3. Kp.: Fürth (Bayern).

Stammtruppenteile: 1. Kp.: B.FliegTr, 2. Kp.: B.LuftschTr,
3. Kp.: B.KraftfTr.

Kommandeur: Maj. Kempf — 1. 2.29 (11)

Hauptleute

Fichtner	1. 5.26 (4)	1	Cuno	1. 2.29 (12)	3
Rüger	1. 6.26 (7)	2			

Oberleutnante

Höfle	1. 4.25 (607)	1	Hansen	1. 4.31 (1)	3
Görgmaier	1.11.28 (37)	2	Stoeckl	1. 4.32 (20)	1
Pasquay	1. 2.30 (35)	Adj			

Leutnante

Gradl	1. 2.31 (63)	2	Schreyögg	Ern. 1. 3.31	3
Ott	1. 5.31 (10)	2			

Abg. Ausgesch.: H Müller.

Excerpt from the Reichsheer Army List of 1932.

Meanwhile, though, three industrial firms had been entrusted with the development of a light and a medium tank. The firms of Rheinmetall, Krupp and Daimler-Benz built two prototypes of the medium tank — called a "heavy tractor" for purposes of concealment — at the Unterlüss Works in 1928-29. This vehicle was already armed with a 75mm cannon and three machine guns, had 13-mm armor and a fighting weight of about 19 tons. Its top speed was 20 kph on land and 4 kph in water. Propulsion in water was provided by two ships' propellers. The motor produced 250 HP. This "heavy tractor" developed at Daimler by Chief Engineer Porsche even had a 300 HP aircraft motor of 1918 vintage. Both prototypes were taken by "roundabout routes" to the Panzer Troop School of Kama in the Soviet Union, but owing to mistakes in design, they were not usable.

The light tank — called a "light tractor" — built by the Krupp and Rheinmetall firms as of 1929 was more or less a full-track armored car. A 37mm rapid-fire gun was mounted in its turning turret. The weight of the "light tractor", still made of soft steel, added up to 9.5 tons. It attained a top speed of 18 kph.

From 1931 on the technical development could be speeded up. In that year Generalmajor Lutz became the new Inspector of the Motorized Troops. In the same year he appointed Oberst Guderian as his Chief of Staff. Officers who served in the Inspection during the next two years became well-known Panzer leaders a few years later: Majors Kampf and Nehring and Captains Châles de Beaulieu and von Hünersdorff.

The new Inspection now gave high priority to the further development of earlier plans for tanks. The Army Weapons Office gave the established firms new contracts to design and develop a light and a medium tank, in which the experience gained with the earlier "tractors" was to be of use.

Thus the firm of Rheinmetall, in cooperation with that of Krupp, developed the so-called "new vehicle type", of which five examples were made. One tank was equipped with a 105mm gun, others with 75 or 37mm guns, and each with a machine gun. These vehicles did not prove to be practical, and their construction was halted in 1933.

The firms of MAN, Krupp, Henschel, Daimler-Benz and Rheinmetall-Borsig were given new developmental contracts in 1932. This new tank — disguised as an "agricultural tractor" — was designed by Krupp and built by Henschel. Three prototypes were finished by the end of the year.

At this time a new era of German history had already begun. Reich President von Hindenburg, with the full agreement of the new Reich Chancellor Hitler, named Generaloberst von Blomberg to be Reich War Minister, Generalleutnant von Reichenau Chief of the Ministerial Office, and General of the Infantry von Fritsch Commander of the Army. Shortly after assuming their offices, all three officers promoted further and more intensive testing and training exercises for the motorized troops.

The first drills in Silesia as well as at the troop training centers of Jüterbog and Grafenwöhr had clearly shown the mobility of a motorized troop — here still equipped with dummies.

The new Commander of the Army gave the former Inspection of the Motorized Troops the new title of Command of the Motorized Combat Troops on June 1, 1934, naming Generalleutnant Lutz its Commander and Oberst Guderian its Chief of Staff.

Even before that. the first German Panzer unit had been created by the Inspection of the Motorized Troops on November 1, 1933! The history of German Panzer troops began on that day.

The officers and technicians returning from Kama in the Soviet Union, and the non-commissioned officers and enlisted men of the Motor Vehicle Training Staff and the 3rd Motor Vehicle Unit (Berlin Lankwitz), were combined to form the Motor Vehicle Training Command Zossen. The predecessors of this training command were the previous technical training courses of the Inspection of the Motorized Troops, from which the Motor Vehicle Training Staff had been formed in 1929. The Commander of this Training Staff, Oberst Fessmann, became the first Commander of the Motor Vehicle Training Command Zossen.

H. Dv. 300/1

Truppenführung

(T. F.)

I. Teil

(Abschnitt I—XIII)

Vom 17. 10. 33

133

Artillerie für Einzelheiten des Infanteriekampfes nicht genügt.

339. Kampfwagen und Infanterie, die zusammenarbeiten, sollen im allgemeinen dasselbe Angriffsziel haben, nach Möglichkeit die feindliche Artillerie. In der Regel werden die Kampfwagen dort eingesetzt, wo die Entscheidung im Angriff gesucht wird.

Der Angriff der Kampfwagen erfolgt entweder in der gleichen Richtung wie derjenige, der Infanterie oder aus einer anderen Richtung. Ausschlaggebend ist das Gelände. Enges Binden an die Infanterie beraubt die Kampfwagen des Vorteils ihrer Schnelligkeit und läßt sie unter Umständen ein Opfer der feindlichen Abwehr werden. Sie sind jedoch so anzusetzen, daß ihr Vorgehen die den Angriff der Infanterie hemmenden feindlichen Waffen, vor allem die feindliche Artillerie, ausschaltet oder daß sie zusammen mit der Infanterie in den Feind einbrechen. In letzterem Fall ist es geboten, sie dem Führer der Infanterie, in dessen Bereich sie angreifen, zu unterstellen.

Gelegentlich kann der Angriff der Kampfwagen die in der letzten Zeitspanne des Infanterieangriffs schwieriger werdende Artillerieunterstützung ergänzen, oder er kann den Stellungswechsel der Artillerie überbrücken, wenn sie zur weiteren Unterstützung des Angriffs vorgehen muß.

340. Der Truppenführer bringt die Gefechtstätigkeit der Kampfwagen und die Mitwirkung der übrigen Waffen in Einklang. Das Gefecht der übrigen Waffen muß sich im Angriffsbereich der Kampfwagen nach diesen richten.

Infanterie muß die Wirkung der angreifenden Kampfwagen zum schnellen Vorgehen ausnutzen.

(Excerpt from Army instructions concerning the use of tanks.)

The new command began during the winter of 1933-34 to set up a first Panzer unit, which was to be equipped with 55 light tanks. The tanks, though, were only available as of the summer of 1934. Series production of the so-called "agricultural tractor" took place at Krupp, Henschel and later MAN, and this "towing tractor" was introduced to the troops at the end of 1934 as "Battle Tank (MG) Special Vehicle 101." The first usable German tank — the P-1 — was in existence!

The first usable German tank — P-1 — which was introduced to the army at the end of 1934. It was intended originally as a mere training vehicle to bridge the gap until enough Pz-III tanks were available.

The Motor Vehicle Training Command Zossen — its members wearing the uniform of Motor Vehicle Unit 3 (rose pipings) — consisted as of April 1, 1934 of a staff, four companies and a gunnery training course.

Commander:	Major Harpe
Chief, Training Troop 1:	Hauptmann Conze
Chief, Training Troop 2:	Hauptmann von Köppen
Chief, Training Troop 3:	Hauptmann Thomale
Chief, Gunnery School:	Hauptmann Baumgart

Just a few weeks later, another Motor Vehicle Training Command was formed, this one at the Ohrdruf training site in Thuringia. Both training commands were now expanded by two units. The leadership of the two commands as of July 1, 1934 was:

Motor Vehicle Training Command Zossen:

Commander:	Oberstleutnant Zukertort
Commander, 1st Unit:	Oberstleutnant Harpe
Commander, 2nd Unit:	Major Breith

Motor Vehicle Training Command Ohrdruf:

Commander:	Oberstleutnant Ritter von Radlmaier
Commander, 1st Unit:	Oberstleutnant Kühn
Commander, 2nd Unit:	Major Ritter von Thoma

The four units were still equipped exclusively with the P-I battle tank until the end of 1934. These tanks, painted gray, green and brown, bore different identifying marks on their turrets. Playing-card symbols represented columns, circles stood for companies. The first military march for the new troops was the melody of the "Circassian Tattoo", brought along from the Kama training school in the Soviet Union.

A further development was seen on October 1, 1934. The Command of the Motorized Troops, on command of the Commander of the Army, gave the order to form the 1st Panzer Brigade, which was to be subordinate to the General Command of the Motorized Cavalry Corps.

Cavalry Regiment 12, stationed in Dresden and Kammenz, had to dismount and become the first Motorized Infantry Regiment of the Army, which together with the 1st and 2nd Panzer Regiments formed the 1st Panzer Brigade.

The seven previous motor vehicle units — renamed Motorized Combat Units since May 1, 1933 — formed the two Panzer Regiments along with reconnaissance and antitank units. The former Cavalry Regiment 12 (mot.) was meanwhile retrained for tanks, in order to form the 3rd Panzer Regiment subsequently. While these three units were training with the P-I tank, developmental work for a ten-ton tank was proceeding at MAN, Henschel and Krupp. This type, known as "Agricultural Tractor 100", was delivered to the troops in 1935, armed with a 20mm gun, as Special Vehicle 121 or P-II. The very short developmental time resulted from the rearmament that had begun in 1935. The P-II type underwent several stages of development and reached the troops only in version IIc, after 200 tanks of this type had already been built. The IIc version could be recognized by its five medium-size road wheels and quarter springs.

German Battle Tank P-II. (Picture from the British Tank Museum in Dorchester.)

The Drama

Wehrmacht Armored Weapons

1935-1939

"The Government of the Reich has enacted the following law, which is proclaimed herewith:

1

(1) Military service is an honorable service to the German people.
(2) Every German man is obligated for military service.
(3) In war, above and beyond that, every German man and every German woman is obligated for service to the Fatherland.

2

The Wehrmacht is the bearer of arms and the military training school of the German Reich.
It consists of:
the Army
the Navy
The Luftwaffe

3

(1) The Supreme Commander of the Wehrmacht is the Führer and Chancellor of the Reich.
(2) Under him, the War Minister of the Reich, as Commander of the Wehrmacht, has the power to command the Wehrmacht."

The text of this "Defense Law" enacted on May 21, 1935 now authorized the buildup of the Wehrmacht without international political considerations. At the same time, rearmament in terms of weapons, materials and vehicles could be carried out in a big way.

The first official appearance of the *Kraftfahrkampftruppe* — the term *Panzertruppe* was introduced only in the autumn of 1935 — took place at the parade of an armored unit of the *Kraftfahrlehrkommando Zossen* in June of 1935. Oberstleutnant Harpe drove the P-I tank past Generalleutnant Lutz in Potsdam. The second appearance of the newest service arm took place a few weeks later at the Munsterlager training facility. Here all the existing units as well as the reconnaissance and antitank companies formed by the motorized units were united to form a tank training division. Generalleutnant Freiherr von Weichs was the first Commander of this troop unit. The four-week training session gave the command of the motorized combat troops the opportunity to establish the organizational and tactical capability of such a large unit. Plans, guidelines and instructions were prepared and proclaimed for the armored divisions that were to be established in the autumn.

The manufacture of P-I type tanks could go on at top speed as of the summer of 1935. After the Krupp firm had introduced the first chassis of the new tank from England, German development took over. The firm of MAN, which was also involved in P-I production, was called on to develop the P-II tank. This tank, formerly disguised as an "agricultural tractor", could now bear its official designation.

The vehicle built by Krupp was used without a superstructure as a training vehicle and ammunition tractor.

The further development of the P-I was upgraded with a 100 HP six-cylinder Maybach engine as of March 1936. Since this motor needed more space, the armored hull and the running gear had to be lengthened. This vehicle was now known as the P-I Type B. (In all, 2000 of these tanks were built before the war broke out.)

The P-I tank, seen from the front.

The Army High Command gave developmental contracts, through the Army Weapons Office, to the firms of Daimler-Benz, Krupp, MAN and Rheinmetall-Borsig for the production of a tank weighing up to 15 tons. On the basis of the developed prototypes, the firm of Daimler-Benz was contracted to manufacture the tank. This vehicle, known by the disguised designation of "ZW" (*Zugführerwagen*), was given the designation of P-III until the outbreak of the war. The Army High Command decided in 1935 what colors the tanks should be. Thereafter the armored surface was painted 2/3 dark gray and 1/3 brown.

The Army Motor Vehicle School in Berlin, in existence since 1934, was transferred to Wünsdorf in 1935. The new barracks were given the name "Cambrai Barracks." In the same year the school was subordinated to a motor vehicle training and testing unit in Döberitz, which was moved to Wünstorf in 1936. The two units formed the *Kraftfahrkampftruppen-Lehrabteilung* and the *Kraftfahrkampftruppen-Versuchsabteilung*. The first unit included the 4th Company of the Tank Company and the 5th Armored Infantry Company.

The latter company was placed under the command of the tank gunnery school, which had been transferred to Putlos at the end of July 1935 (and commanded by Oberstleutnant Baumgart).

October 15, 1935 became the most decisive day in the short history of the tank service arm.

The command of the armored troops had finally prevailed against the Chief of the General Staff — who remained true — then as before, to the concept that tanks were to be regarded only as support for infantry and cavalry. Now, on October 15, 1935, three tank divisions came into being simultaneously as independent major units of the Army. Each division included two tank regiments, an infantry regiment, an artillery regiment, an engineer battalion, a reconnaissance unit, an antitank unit and (in some cases) an intelligence unit.

The staff of the 1st Tank Division (now called Panzer Division: Panzerdivision) was assembled in Weimar under Generalleutnant von Weichs. The staff of the 2nd Panzer Division was formed in Würzburg under Oberst Guderian, and that of 3rd Panzer Division in Berlin under Generalleutnant Fessmann.

The former Tank Regiment 1 (*Kraftfahrlehrkommando Zossen*) was renamed Tank Regiment (now Panzer Regiment) 5. Tank Regiment 2 (*Kraftfahrlehrkommando Ohrdruf*) was given number 1. The other four regiments were new formations. Cavalry Regiments 4, 7 and 12 contributed all their officers and men. Cavalry Regiment 12 was already motorized as of May 15, 1935 and set up as the disguised "Cavalry Regiment Dresden." Similarly, Cavalry Regiment 4 in Potsdam had given up its horses for tanks in the spring of 1935.

The last regiment that still carried on the tradition of the old Prussian guard regiments now passed it on to the new tank regiments. For example, the First Unit of Panzer Regiment took over the tradition of the *Gardes du Corps* Regiment.

The 1st Panzer Division consisted of Panzer Regiments 1 (Erfurt) and 2 (Eisenach), the 2nd Panzer Division of Panzer Regiments 3 (Kamenz) and 4 (Ohrdruf), and the 3rd Panzer Division of Panzer Regiments 5 (Wünstorf) and 6 (Zossen). Regiments 3, 4 and 6 remained where they were for barely a year, then they were transferred to new garrisons in Bamberg, Schweinfurt and Neuruppin.

Arrival of the 6th Panzer Regiment at its garrison town, Neuruppin.

Arrival of Tank Unit 1./10, equipped with P-I and P-II tanks, at Zinten, East Prussia.

The recruits of all the regiments, who arrived in October of 1936, were sworn in formally in the first week of November before their service with weapons and vehicles began. The young Panzer troop was to experience its first tactical operations just a few months later. the Command of the Panzer Troops, surprisingly, assembled individual regiments for large-scale maneuvers at the Staumühlen camp of the Senne training facility in late February and early March 1936. The first day and night drills, combat procedures, armored reconnaissance and firing on the move were on the schedule.

The tank regiments and all the units gathered there were prepared to serve as an operational reserve. This circumstance became clear when, on March 7, the first infantry units marched into the formerly demilitarized Rheinland.

Maneuvers with P-I tanks at the Senne training base in the spring of 1936.

The regiments still remained back in the Senne district; only when the political situation had been smoothed out in the next four weeks did the units return to their garrisons.

The coming summer months had to be used for intensive training. The individual regiments — (the companies at first consisted of only eight tanks; only from 1936 on did each company receive 22 P-I tanks) — were gradually transferred to the Putlos Gunnery School or drilled as a unit at the various drill facilities in the Reich.

The former Command of the Panzer Troops became an equal-ranking Inspection (In 6) in the Army High Command. The officers as of June 1, 1936 were as follows:

Inspector:	General of the Panzer Troops Lutz
Chief of Staff:	Oberst i.G. Nehring
Colleagues:	Oberst Kempf, Oberstleutnant Breith, Irmisch, Werner, Major Châles de Beaulieu, Ritter von Hauenschild, Nedtwig, von Schell.

The Inspection formed two additional regiments in the autumn. They were the 7th Panzer Regiment (Vaihingen), made of men from the 1st, 2nd and 4th Regiments, and the 8th Panzer Regiment (Böblingen), of men from the 3rd, 5th and 6th Regiments. The older regiments contributed entire companies to the new ones; they were replaced by personnel sent from replacement offices. The new 7th Panzer Regiment was part of the 1st Panzer Division, while the 8th Panzer Regiment belonged to the 3rd Panzer Division. At the same time as these regiments, a 4th Panzer Brigade was formed (at first consisting only of a staff).

A Panzer unit on parade in their new uniforms.

Marching to take part in the parade.

The staffs of the older Panzer brigades, which had already been formed on October 15, 1936, had the task of serving as command staffs for the two regiments.

Sonderbekleidung der Panzertruppen

Zum Dienst mit Panzerwagen wird von den Panzertruppen und den sonstigen mit gepanzerten Fahrzeugen ausgestatteten Truppen eine Sonderbekleidung aus schwarzem Tuch: Schutzmütze, Feldjacke und Feldhose getragen.

Schutzmütze:

Das Hoheitsabzeichen zur Schutzmütze entspricht dem der Feldmütze, ist also für Unteroffiziere und Mannschaften aus silbergrauem Baumwollgarn, für Offiziere aus hellem

Aluminiumgespinst. Eichenlaubkranz für Mannschaften, Unteroffiziere und Offiziere aus silbergrauem Baumwollgarn.

Feldjacke:

Grundtuch schwarz; Vorstöße am Kragen und um die Kragenpatten in Waffenfarbe; Kragenpatten schwarz mit Totenkopf aus Aluminium. Schulterklappen mit Vorstößen in der Waffenfarbe, Grundtuch schwarz. Schulterklappen für Unteroffiziere mit entsprechendem

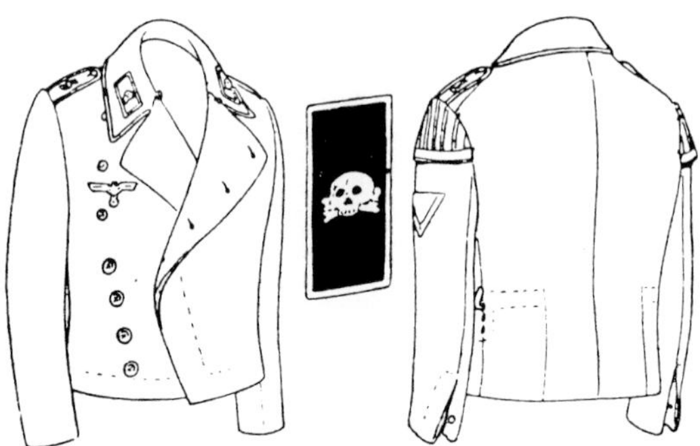

Tressenbesatz usw., für Offiziere Schulterstücke der Feldbluse. Abzeichen für Mannschaftsdienstgrade, Spielleute, Musiker wie zur Feldbluse. Keine Kragentressen für Unteroffiziere, jedoch doppelte Ärmeltresse für Hauptfeldwebel. Hoheitsabzeichen für alle Dienstgrade aus silbergrauem Baumwollgarn auf schwarzer Unterlage, gewebt.

Schwarze Feldhose ohne Vorstöße.

Zur schwarzen Sonderkleidung wird Koppel ohne Seitenwaffe getragen; zu Paraden von Offizieren Feldbinde mit Achselband, von Unteroffizieren und Mannschaften Schützenschnur, soweit verliehen. Schuhwerk: leichte Schnürschuhe.

The expansion of Panzer troop personnel was paralleled by an increase in tank construction. While 3000 light tanks had already been delivered by the end of 1936 and the construction or design of the P-II and P-III continued, the Army Weapons Office had given the Krupp firm a contract at the beginning of 1936 to build an even better tank than the P-III. This tank, originally referred to by the disguised name "BW" (Battalion Leader's Vehicle) was to carry a five-man crew and a medium gun.

Stoffgliederung 21	**Geheime Kommandosache!** Pz Kpfw II (2cm) Sd Kfz 121 Ausf. A-C und F (F= Sd. Kfz. 122)	Blatt G 300

Dringl.-St.: -

Technische Daten:

Gesamtgewicht des Fahrzeuges (Gefechtsgewicht) 9,5 t
Motor Maybach HL 62TR 140 PS
Spez. Leistung 14,75 PS/t
Höchstgeschwindigkeit 40 km/Std.
Mitgeführte Kraftstoffmenge 170 l (einschl. Reservetank)
Fahrbereich mit einer Kraftstoff-Füllung:
Straße ~ 190 km; mittl. Gelände ~ 125 km
Grabenüberschreitfähigkeit 1,7 m, Klettervermögen 0,42 m
Watfähigkeit 0,925 m, Steigvermögen 30°
Bodenfreiheit 0,345 m
Besatzung 1 Pz. Führer zugl. Pz. Schütze, 1 Pz. Funker, 1 Pz. Fahrer

Länge 4,810 m, Breite 2,280 m
Höhe mit Aufbau Ausf. A-C 2,020 m, Ausf. F 2,150 m
Feuerhöhe: 1,595 m
Bordmunition 180 Schuß 2cm Kw.K.
1425 " M.G.
Bestückung: a) Turmwaffen 1 2cm Kw.K. 38, 1 M.G. 34 in Walzenblende
b) Bugwaffen —
Abfeuerung Kw.K. u. MG: mech. Handabfeuerung
Optisches Gerät: a) Turmoptik 1 TZF 4, Zielschiene "2cm u. MG 34"
b) Kugeloptik —
c) Fahreroptik KFF 1
Funkgerät (normale Ausstattung) 2 UKW-Empf., 1 UKW-Sender
Panzerung: Front 35 mm Seite 14,5 mm
Turm 30 mm Dach 10 mm
Bug 30 mm

Kette 108 Glieder, Kettengewicht 385 kg

Rohstoffbedarf f. 1 Stck. i. kg ohne Waffe, Optik u. Funk	Fe	Mo	Cr	W	Mg	Sn	Cu	Ni	Al	Kautschuk Reifen u.s.w.	Pb	Zn

Preis RM 49.228.- ohne Waffe	Durchschn. Fertigungszeit ~ 12 Monate	Arbeitsstunden

Since the P-III was regarded as the main weapon of the Panzer regiments, the new tank with its larger gun was to be merely a support tank for the other tanks. This new tank, of which the first 35 examples were delivered by the end of 1936, was later used by the troops as the P-IV tank.

The term *Kampfwagen* — or usually *Kampfpanzer* from 1941 on — referred only to the tanks with turning turrets. They belonged to the Panzer troops; they included P-I to P-VI with their various versions.

The year of 1936 was to bring these new weapons — or at least a small number of them — their first serious use and baptism of fire. The Spanish Civil War had, in its first few months, led to a commanding position for the left-wing liberal and communistic forces, so that the leadership of the Nationalists (which included the army in particular) asked the governments of Italy and Germany for military and economic support.

The Army High Command (OKH for short) established a "Führer Herr" command in Berlin in September of 1936. It was responsible for the transfer of military units to Spain to provide training and field support for the Spanish nationalist volunteers.

The Army High Command establisher a Panzer unit which was given the camouflage name *Abteilung Drohne* but was officially called *Panzerabteilung* (Pz.Abt. for short) 88. The Commander of this unit was Major Ritter von Thoma. The 4th and 6th Panzer Regiments each had to contribute enough volunteer officers, non-commissioned officers and enlisted men to form a company, plus a repair shop column, which was at that time the most modern column in the German Army; shortly thereafter it was expanded to a company.

The first 300 volunteers in this new Panzer troop embarked on the Woermann Line's passenger ships as civilian members of the Union Travel Organization and sailed to Spain under the flag of the National Socialist "Kraft durch Freude" (Strength Through Joy) organization. Below decks the ships naturally carried the P-I tanks. The destination was Seville.

The staff of Pz.Abt.88 first set up its headquarters there; in the following years it moved several times, to Toledo, Burgos, etc. The German soldiers had to do the job of training Spanish nationalist soldiers as tank crews. The unit's camp was originally in a small desert town called Cubas, not far from Toledo.

Officers and NCO's of Panzer Unit 88 in Spain. At the far left is Leutnant Buchterkirch, later the Panzer troops' first member to receive the Oak Leaves.

German volunteers under the hot sun in Seville.

A damaged P-I tank at the workshop in Cubas.

After the Spanish National troops, especially the Moroccan units, had succeeded in capturing the first Spanish communist tanks — usually the Russian Type "T-26 B" — the first tank companies of the Spanish National Army could be established. The German volunteers' baptism of fire took place in October of 1936. A few P-I tanks were deployed to support the Nationalist attack on Madrid.

After Panzer Unit 88 received further reinforcements — adding up now to three combat or training companies, one transport and one repair company — the German tanks could be used for the first time on May 11, 1937 in a concerted attack on the Spanish Communist positions near Eremita in the Teruel area; they functioned as part of the 5th Navarra Division.

After the battle the first three German officers, a sergeant, a non-commissioned officer and a corporal were decorated with the highest Spanish medal for bravery.

The volunteers remained in the Spanish theater of war for a year and were then replaced. Only in February of 1939 did the last volunteers of the Panzer troop return home. Oberst Ritter von Thoma was honored by General Franco with Spain's highest honor for his leadership of Panzer Abteilung 88. The colonel himself had introduced the "Panzer Troop Medal of the *Legion Condor*" at the end of 1936; it was awarded to the former members of Panzer Unit 88 on July 10, 1939. Ten non-commissioned officers and four soldiers did not return from this service. They were the first soldiers of the Panzer troops who fell to the enemy.

The development of the troop at home proceeded energetically during 1937. Intensive training for all units was on the schedule. Regiments of various Panzer divisions trained at the Jüterbog and Bergen (Lüneburg Heath) training camps for the first time in the summer. In the process, the new P-II tanks could be tested in the country.

On the occasion of the Italian Chief of State's visit, the so-called "Mussolini Maneuvers" took place in the Neustrelitz area of Mecklenburg from September 14-29, 1937. Here the 3rd Panzer Division and 1st Panzer Brigade (Pz.Br. for short) took part together, with 800 P-I type tanks.

After the subsequent Wehrmacht maneuvers at German training camps, new Panzer units were formed. On October 12, 1937 there came into being:

11th Panzer Regiment (originally at the Senne training camp, later at Paderborn), of the I./1st Panzer Regiment, II./4th Panzer Regiment and men from Military Zone VI (Münster);

15th Panzer Regiment (Sagan), of the I./5th Panzer Regiment, I./2nd Panzer Regiment and men from Military Zone VII (Breslau);

I./10th Panzer Regiment (originally at the Stablack training camp, later at Zinten, East Prussia), of men from the 1st, 6th and 7th Panzer Regiments;

Pz.Abt.25 (originally at the Grafenwöhr training camp, later Erlangen), of men from the 3rd Panzer Regiment and Military Zone XIII (Nürnberg);

Pz.Abt.65 (originally at the Senne training camp, later Iserlohn), of the 7th Panzer Regiment.

The last unit listed was the first Panzer unit that was not subordinate to a Panzer division. In a constant disagreement between the Inspection of the Panzer Troops and the Chief of the General Staff, the latter had insisted that, instead of additional Panzer divisions, light divisions must now be formed. Thus units were to be established that would take the place of the cavalry, meaning that these light divisions had the task of carrying on combat reconnaissance and securing the flanks of the attacking infantry.

For that purpose, each one was given a unit of tanks carried on low loaders, which were never able to live up to the slogan of General Guderian: "Clobber — don't slobber!"

At the same time as the new Panzer units were being assembled, the renaming of the former Motorized Troop School at Wünsdorf took place; now called *Panzertruppenschule,* it consisted of four (later five) sections:

1. Tactical training,
2. Technical training,
3. Regulations office,
4. Panzer Gunnery School Putlos,
5. Panzer training unit.

This last section was formed in October of 1937 of the mass of the former 8th Panzer Regiment, which was reconstituted at Böblingen, Württemberg, as well as men of various ranks transferred from all the other Panzer regiments.

In addition, the Inspection of the Panzer Troops had begun on January 1, 1937 to publish the periodical *Die Kraftfahrkampftruppe*, which was intended not only to further the training of members of this service arm, but also to inform the public.

Turning over the colors in November of 1937, when new recruits were sworn in. At left is General of the Artillery von Küchler, later Field Marshal.

A new barracks building for the Panzer troops — 1938.

A further upgrading of the Panzer troops took place on February 4, 1938. The OKH created three new General Commands on that day: the XIV. Army Corps (AK) for all motorized infantry divisions, the XV. AK for all light divisions, and the XVI. AK for all Panzer divisions.

The Commanding General of the XVI. AK was Generalleutnant Guderian; the Chief of the General Staff was Oberst i.G. Paulus (the subsequent Field Marshal). The three Panzer divisions were now commanded by:

1st Panzer Division: Generelleutnant Schmidt,
2nd Panzer Division: Generalmajor Veiel,
3rd Panzer Division: Generalleutnant Baron Geyr von Schweppenburg.

In addition to the three Panzer divisions and the Panzer units set up independently within the light divisions, the Panzer Lehr Unit was founded in 1937. This unit, commanded by Major von Lewinski and based at the Panzer Troop School in Wünsdorf, was meant above all to test the new tanks. The unit was made up chiefly by transfers from the 8th Panzer Regiment and was able to test not only the new production types of the P-II (the D and E versions) in the country, but in 1938 received the first prototypes of the new P-III and even P-IV types for testing.

The Tactical Numbers of Armored Vehicles

In order to afford the leaders of armored units an overview of their groups, all armored vehicles operating in closed units were equipped with tactical numbers. They were as follows: armored battle tanks of Panzer regiments and Panzer units, self-propelled guns of the armored grenadier regiments and armored engineer battalions, as well as the armored vehicles of the unit staffs, the reconnaissance companies and the heavy companies of the armored reconnaissance units. Not as a rule equipped with tactical numbers were: the armored vehicles of the higher staffs, armored scout cars, assault guns, self-propelled guns of the Panzerjäger, armored observation vehicles and self-propelled guns of the armored artillery and observation batteries.

The tactical number consisted basically of three digits. The first digit always indicated the company, the second the column and the third the position of the vehicle within the column. For example, an armored vehicle with the tactical number 324 was the 4th vehicle in the 2nd column of the 3rd company, or one with the number 5412 was the 2nd vehicle in the 1st column of the 5th company.

The vehicles of the unit or battalion staffs carried, in place of the company number, the number of the unit in Roman numerals; those of the regimental staffs bore the letter R. The following list provides information as to the commanders' vehicles:

Tactical Number	Armored vehicle of the
R01	Regimental Commander
R02	Regimental Adjutant
R03	Assistant Adjutant or Intelligence Officer
R04 etc.	Regimental Staff
I01	Commander, I. Unit (Battalion)
I02	Adjutant, I. Unit
I03	Assistant Adjutant, I. Unit
I04 etc.	Staff, I. Unit
II01	Commander, II. Unit
101	Chief, 1st Company
102	Company Troop Leader, 1st Company
111	Leader, 1st Column, 1st Company
131	Leader, 3rd Column, 1st Company

Unit staffs of independent armored units, such as Tiger units, bore the tactical numbers I01 etc. In the event that Panzer regiments with two units were given a Tiger company, these bore the tactical numbers 901 etc., according to their company number.

If conditions required, four-digit tactical numbers could also appear when the companies bore numbers over 10. This occurred in Panzer regiments with 3 units, and particularly in the 10th company of the armored grenadier regiments, the armored grenadier engineer companies. The numbers were then:

1001	Company Chief
1023	3rd Vehicle, 2nd Column, 10th Company.

The tactical numbers originally consisted of small white numerals on diamond-shaped panels. These panels could then be attached to the armored vehicles. Later somewhat larger white numerals were painted on the walls of the armored vehicles themselves. In the French campaign, the large red numerals with white borders, which later came into general use, were used for the first time. The smaller white numbers could be seen clearly on a dark gray background, the larger red ones also on a khaki background. The latter could be seen clearly at short distances, but were hard to make out at medium or long distances. In the case of photographs, one must bear in mind that during the war the tactical numbers were often removed by painting over them.

The large numbers of Panzer and motorized units existing in February of 1938 that were also still divided into three different types of divisions led to the following declaration by Generalleutnant Guderian:

> "I have very much deplored the division of forces in the realm of motorized and armored units, but could not prevent the development from following this course in the beginning."

The first large-scale action of the Army's motorized units was not long in coming. The Chief of the General Staff of the OKH, Generaloberst Beck, gave the command on the evening of March 10, 1938 to the General Command of the XVI. Army Corps for the 2nd Panzer Division and the SS *Leibstandarte Adolf Hitler* unit, temporarily subordinate to it, to be ready to march immediately. Both large units were alerted during the night and joined to march into the Passau area.

The advance into Austria was about to take place.

There were no appropriate preparations. The 2nd Panzer Division as yet had absolutely no supply or maintenance units. Maps of the areas to be occupied were not available. Thus time was lost. The infantry columns had been marching over the border since the early morning of March 12, 1938; the first units of the 2nd Panzer Division reached it only around 9:00 A.M.

The advance of the flagged vehicles proceeded trouble-free despite partially icy roads, and they were greeted excitedly by the native population. The course led the 2nd Panzer Division, followed by the *Leibstandarte,* via Linz and St. Pölten to Vienna, which was reached in the early morning of March 13. In 48 hours the 2nd Panzer Division had covered a course of 700 kilometers; 30% of the tanks were left behind on account of motor, gearbox or tread damage or sliding off the road.

The experience gained in this march led to the considerable expansion and improvement, effective immediately, of the maintenance services of the armored units!

During the integration of the Austrian National Army into the German Wehrmacht, the single tank unit — called *Panzerwagen-Abteilung* — of the Austrian Army was taken over. This unit was designated *Panzerabteilung* 33 and

(List of officers of Panzerabteilung 33.)

Panzerabteilung 33

H. Gru. 5
4. leichte Div.

St Pölten

Kommandeur: Maj. **von Köppen** (Pz. Tr. Schule) 1. 4.36 (5)

Maj. **von Collani** (Pz. R. 2) 1. 8.37 (52) 1

Hptm. **Streit**	1.10.38	(77)	4	Lt. **van Gember**	1. 4.37	(398)	4
Nekola	1.10.38	(91)	2	" **Wießner**	1. 1.38	(1551)	2
Waldeck	1.10.38	(105)	Adj	" **Hafen**	1. 1.38	(1656)	3
Oblt. **Schoen** (Pz. R. 6)	1. 6.38	(43)	3	" **Mackensen**	1. 1.38	(1721)	1
Lt. **Sturm** (Pz. R. 5)	1. 4.35	(351)	St	" **Grüner** (Pz. R. 1) Ern.	1. 9.38	(735)	1
von Trotha (Pz. R. 5)	1. 3.37	(5)	3	" **Hoitz** (Pz. R. 6) Ern.	1. 9.38	(1380)	1
Kettenacker (Pz. Lehrabt.)	1. 4.37	(281)	4				

remained stationed in St. Pölten. The unit was strengthened with officers and non-commissioned officers transferred from the 1st, 2nd, 5th and 6th Panzer Regiments, as well as the Panzer Lehr Unit, while some of the former Austrian officers were transferred to those regiments in the Reich.

The staff of the 2nd Panzer Division remained in Vienna, which became its peacetime location, along with the staff of the 2nd Panzer Brigade. The two regiments of the brigade — the 3rd Panzer Regiment in Mödling, the 4th Panzer Regiment in Korneuburg —were quartered in the barracks there. *Panzerabteilung* 33, which remained in St. Pölten, was subordinated to the newly formed 4th Light Division.

The coming summer and autumn months were devoted completely to intensive training. Only now did the three Panzer divisions gain the units they still lacked — for example, the 3rd Panzer Division gained an engineer battalion only that spring — and preparations for establishing services to the rear were made everywhere. The so-called "Munich Accord" on the fate of the Sudetenland, signed by Great Britain, France, Italy and the German Reich on September 29, 1938, included the following sentence:

> ". . . The corresponding occupation of the predominantly
> German districts by German troops begins on October 1."

This area had been divided (from right to left) into five zones, which were to be occupied gradually. The troop units needed for this — including almost all the Panzer units — went directly from autumn maneuvers at the training camps to their mobilization areas on the border.

The General Command of the XVI. AK was in northern Bavaria and western Saxony with the 1st Panzer Division, and the 13th and 20th Infantry Divisions (mot.). The assignment of the divisions was the occupation of the area around Karlsbad and Eger. The 3rd Panzer Division — as the leftmost flank division of the army — marched into Zone 5 around Mährisch-Schönberg and Troppau, to name only two of the divisions involved. The occupation of the Sudetenland proceeded until October 10 in all zones, without notable problems.

The fast and almost friction-free occupation of Austria and the Sudetenland had shown that strong and fast troop units were fully suitable for such tasks. That was, among others, the reason that moved Hitler to order a strengthening of the Panzer troops in the autumn of 1938.

He created a new office in the OKH: "Chief of the Mobile Troops", to whom all former Panzer, motorized, antitank and cavalry units were subordinated.

Generalleutnant Guderian was promoted to General of the Panzer Troops and Chief of this office. Major i.G. Le Suirre became Chief of the General Staff, Hauptmann i. G. Röttiger (the subsequent first Inspector of the Federal Army) became First General Staff Officer.

On November 10, 1938 the following new units were formed:

4th Panzer Division in Würzburg,
5th Panzer Division in Oppeln,
4th Panzer Brigade in Stuttgart,
5th Panzer Brigade in Bamberg,
6th Panzer Brigade in Würzburg,
8th Panzer Brigade in Sagan.

The following new regiments were created: 23rd, at first only the 1st Unit, in Mannheim-Schwetzingen; 31st on Königsbrück and Gross-Born, later Jägerndorf; 35th in Bamberg; 36th in Schweinfurt; and the following independent units for

Chef der schnellen Truppen

Gen. d. Pz. Tr. **Guderian** (Kom. Gen. XVI. A. K.) 1.11.38 (1a)

Maj. **Röttiger** (Gen. St. 17. Div.) (Gen. St. d. H. [4. Abt] m. 1.12.38) (A. Gen. St.) 1. 1.36 (22)

Riebel (St. Gen. Kdo. XVI. A. K.) 1. 3.36 (91) Adj

Maj. **von Le Suire** (Gen. St. 2. Pz. Div. m. 1.12.38) (A. Gen. St.) 1.10.36 (76)

Hptm. (E) Dr. **Luther** 1. 4.34 (450)

Höherer Kavallerieoffizier

Oberst **Freiherr von Waldenfels** (Kdr. K. R. 5) 1. 4.36 (18)

Maj. **Tröger** (Jn 3 m. 30.11.38) [Jn 6] 1. 8.36 (43) Adj

Höherer Panzerabwehroffizier

Gen. Lt. **von Puttkamer** (Höh. Pz. Abw. Offz. 1), zugl. Höh. Pz. Abw. Offz. 1 Char. 1. 4.38

Hptm. **Engels** (b. Höh. Pz. Abw. Offz. 1), zugl. b. Höh. Pz. Abw. Offz. 1 1. 3.35 (35) Adj

(The staff of the Chief of the Mobile Troops — 3/1/39.)

light divisions were also formed: Pz.Abt.65 in Sennelager, later Iserlohn; 66th in Eisenach, later Gera; 67th in Gross-Glienicke, later Spremberg.

The establishment of the Panzer units, one of which was independently subordinated to each of the three light divisions, naturally did not take place at the same rate. For example, Pz.Abt. 67 was already formed in Gross-Glienicke, a suburb of Berlin, as of October 1, 1938. The cadre of the staff and the four companies equipped with P-I and P-II tanks came from the 8th Panzer Regiment. The I. Unit of this regiment, with men transferred from the 3rd Panzer Regiment (Mödling) and the 5th Panzer Regiment (Wünsdorf) and a unit of the Schleswig-Holstein State Police, formed Pz.Abt.67 of the 3rd Light Division.

The new year of 1939 arrived. The periodical previously called *Kraftfahrkampftruppen* was now retitled *Die Panzertruppe.* This illustrated magazine, issued by the staff of the Chief of the Mobile Troops and published by Mittler & Son Publishing in Berlin appeared monthly, cost 0.50 RM, and included information and news of Panzer units inside and outside Germany. The magazine existed until October of 1944.

On March 1, 1939 the German Panzer troops consisted of:

	Officers	Officials	Non-coms	Enlisted men
Field Army	961	174	5444	16988
Replacement Army	246	130	1608	9038

But before the spring maneuvers of the troops could begin, the order was given again: "March!"

On March 12, 1939 the OKH gave Army Group Commands 3 (Dresden) and 5 (Vienna) the order to march and occupy Czechoslovakia. In addition, the XVI. AK, now under the command of Generalleutnant Hoepner, was gathered around Reichenberg. The corps ((Leading Command of the Panzer Divisions) was commanded to reach Prague by the fastest route.

> "Bitter cold, stormy west wind and a wild snowfall do not allow a fast advance of the motorized columns on the ice-covered roads", as the history of the 3rd Panzer Division recorded.

The advance unit of this division reached the Czech capital at 8:20 A.M.. On account of the bad winter road conditions, the 6th Panzer Regiment arrived at Prague Castle only about 5:00 P.M. Two days later the first parade of German tanks took place at the Wenzelsplatz. The occupation of Czechoslovakia took place everywhere with almost no problems.

Parade of a Panzer unit at the Wenzelsplatz in Prague -1939.

The expansion of the German national territory by the absorption of Czechoslovakia naturally resulted in an expansion of the Panzer units. The OKH formed the staff of the 10th Panzer Division in Prague as early as April 1, 1939. The division's main task was to take over the job of occupation, and no actual units were subordinated to it. It received troops, when needed, from various units in the Reich. At first the 8th Panzer Regiment was subordinate to the division command.

At the same time, the expansion of the Panzer Lehr Unit at Wünstorf into a Panzer Lehr Regiment with three units took place in the Reich. This remained subordinate to the Panzer Troop School as before but was already equipped with the newest Type P-IV tanks.

Stoffgliederung 21	**Geheime Kommandosache!** Pz. Kpfw. IV (7,5 cm Kw.K. 40 L/48) (Sd. Kfz. 161/2)	Blatt G' 315 I

Dringl.-St.:

Technische Daten: (Ausf. H u. J) (Ausf. H zugleich Pz. Bef. Wg. IV)

Gesamtgewicht des Fahrzeuges (Gefechtsgewicht) 25 t

Motor Maybach HL 120 TRM 265 PS

Spez. Leistung 10,6 PS/t

Höchstgeschwindigkeit 38 km/Std.

Mitgeführte Kraftstoffmenge 430 / 680 l (einschl. Reservetank) Ausf. H / " J

Fahrbereich mit einer Kraftstoff-Füllung:

Straße ~210 / ~320 km; mittl. Gelände ~130 / ~210 km

Grabenüberschreitfähigkeit 2,2 m, Klettervermögen 0,6 m

Watfähigkeit 1,2 m; Steigvermögen aufw. 30°, abw. 40°

Besatzung wie Ausf. F1 u. G; Bodenfreiheit 0,4 m

spez. Bodendruck 0,89 Kg/cm²

Länge 7,015 m, Breite 2,88 m

Höhe mit Aufbau 2,68 m; 3,192 m. m. Ost Kette; 3,330 m m. Schürzen

Feuerhöhe 1,96 m

Bordmunition 87 Schuß 7,5 cm Kw.K., 3150 Schuß M.G., 192 Schuß MP.

Bestückung: 1 7,5 cm Kw.K 40 L/48, 1 M.G. i. Turm, 1 M.G. i. Kugelblende in Fahrerfront
1 M.P. lose (zeitweilig: 1 M.G. 34 f. Fliegerabwehr)

Abfeuerung Kw.K. 40 elektrisch, MG i. Turm d. Fußhebel, MG i. Kugelblende durch Handabzug

Optisches Gerät: a) Turmoptik TZF 5 f
b) Kugeloptik KZF 2
c) Fahreroptik KFT 2 (nur bei älteren Geräten)

Funkgerät (normale Ausstattung) 2 UKW-Emp., 1 UKW Sender (f. Pz Bef. Wg IV Sonderausstattung)

Panzerung: Front 80 mm; Seite 30 mm; Schürzen 5 mm
Turm 80 mm; Dach 15 mm
Bug 80 mm
(Pz-Schürzen an Fahrgestell u. Turm) teilweise aus Drahtgeflecht

Kette 99 Glieder, Kettengewicht 750 kg; Ostkette 1450 "

Rohstoffbedarf (ohne Waffe)	1 Eisen unleg. 20211,– kg; leg. 18752,– "; Eisen gesamt 38752,– "	dar. Grob u. Mi. Bl. 15841,–; Feinblech 852,–; Fertiggew. einschl. Waffe 23600, kg
Preis RM	Durchschn. Fertigungszeit Monate	Arbeitsstunden

Fertigungsfirmen:

Montage: / Fahrgestell: } Nibelungenwerk, St. Valentin

Panzerung: Gebr. Böhler + Co. Kapfenberg
Eisenwerke Oberdonau, Linz

The Panzer Troop School consisted in the summer of 1939 of the following:

Staff: Commander: Oberst Kühn
Staff Officer, Panzer: Oberstleutnant Theiss

Instructors for
Tactics: Major Fronhöfer
Technology: Oberstleutnant Spaeth
Gunnery: Oberstleutnant Kraeber

The greatest enrichment resulting from the occupation of Czechoslovakia, though, consisted of the addition of many Czech tanks. 300 of the P-35 (t) medium tank, built by the Skoda firm and armed with a 37mm gun and two machine guns, were taken over. These tanks, which stood out for their robustness and long life, were assigned to the 11th Panzer Regiment and Pz.Abt.65. Even more important was the P-38 (t) medium tank built by the Praga Works, and existing in several versions. This tank too was approximately comparable to the P-III in strength and utility, and continued to be built in the Czech factories until 1942. This tank formed the basis of the Panzer units of the subsequent 7th and 8th Panzer Divisions.

Reorganization, new formation and intensive training in the country were planned for the summer of 1939.

The structure of the Panzer units took on a uniform appearance only gradually — except for the supply troops.

The independent Panzer units serving with the light divisions were structured as follows:

Staff
3 light companies (P-I and P-II)
1 light unit
1 tank maintenance unit
1 tank column.

Since the small tanks used by these units were scarcely suitable for fast action, the companies were supplied with low-loader trucks. The 9-ton flatbed trucks could bring the light tanks quickly to the scene of action. But since these three-axle trucks were not built for cross-country use, that had been given up to some extent even before the Polish campaign.

The Panzer divisions gained their hitherto lacking supply units in late July and early August of 1939, with up to ten truck columns for fuel, ammunition, maintenance etc. A Panzer division at full strength now consisted of:

394 officers
115 officials
1962 non-commissioned officers
9321 enlisted men
561 passenger vehicles
1402 trucks
421 armored vehicles (tanks, scout cars, etc.)
1289 motorcycles, 711 of them with sidecars

The structure of a Panzer regiment was as follows:

Staff with intelligence and light engineer columns
Two Panzer units, each with staff, intelligence, reconnaissance and light engineer columns,
2 light tank companies (P-I and P-II)
1 medium tank company (P-III and P-IV)
1 tank column
1 workshop company.

The tanks and guns of the 2nd to 5th Panzer Divisions consisted of:

69 P-I and P-II tanks (20mm gun)
10 P-III tanks (37mm gun)
12 P-IV tanks (75mm gun),
plus 254 light machine guns (MG) and
168 machine pistols (MPi).

Panzerregiment 2

H. Gru. 4
XVI. A. K.
1. Pz. Div.
1. Pz. Brig.

Eisenach

Kommandeur: Obstlt. **Keltsch**	1. 8.36	(32)	
Obstlt. **Jesser** (Sch. R. 11)	1. 8.36	(78)	RSt
= **Voigt**	1. 1.38	(25)	II
Maj. **Graf Strachwitz von Groß-Zauche und Camminetz**	1. 4.37	(59)	I

Hptm. **Wenck** (Gen. St. XVI. A. K.)	1. 5.34	(36)	1
= (E) **Ulbricht**	1.10.36	(13)	RSt
= **Thiede**	1. 2.38	(40)	6
= (E) **Kleinert**	1. 4.38	(3)	St I
Oblt. **von Köckritz**	1.12.34	(45)	5
= **Carganico**	1.10.36	(43)	7
= **von Butler**	1.10.37	(22)	RAdj
= **Carl August Erbgroßherzog von Sachsen**	1.10.37	(143)	RSt
= **Otto**	1.10.37	(180)	3
= **Krajewski**	1. 8.38	(34)	4
= **von Kleist**	1. 8.38	(146)	8
= **von Grolman** (Pz. Abw. Abt. 28)	1. 8.38	(149)	2
Lt. **von Cramon**	1. 4.36	(244)	Adj I
= **Riedinger**	1. 4.36	(386)	St I
= **Graf von Harrach**	1. 4.36	(576)	Adj II
= **Baron Freytag von Loringhoven**	1. 4.37	(29)	RSt

Lt. **von Fritschen**	1. 4.37	(133)	St II
= **Freiherr von Fürstenberg**	1. 4.37	(319)	4
= **von Aulock**	1. 4.37	(392)	8
= **von Stünzner**	1. 4.37	(789)	St I
= **Brauer**	1. 4.37	(943)	1
= **Reichardt**	1. 4.37	(1175)	2
= **Freiherr von Meyendorff**	1. 4.37	(1234)	6
= **Fromme**	1. 4.37	(1521pp)	6
= **von Reinhard,** kdt. Aufkl. Fl. Schule Braunschweig	1. 4.37	(1566)	7
= **von Pogrell**	1. 4.37	(1596)	St II
= **Ohrloff**	1. 1.38	(3)	5
= **Bollert**	1. 1.38	(517)	8
= **Fähndrich**	1. 1.38	(895)	4
= **Müller**	1. 1.38	(1032)	3
= **Schwarz**	1. 1.38	(1396)	1
= **Stumme** Ern.	1. 9.38	(1243)	7
= **Scheidemann** Ern.	1. 9.38	(1402)	3
= **von Brauchitsch** Ern.	1. 9.38	(1737)	6

Kommandiert zur Dienstleistung:

Oblt. a. D. **Kirnbauer** 5

List of officers of the 2nd Panzer Regiment - 3/1/39

Only the 1st Panzer Division had a different structure. This division had 39 P-II, 56 P-III and 28 P-IV tanks.

During August of 1939 a further General Command for the Panzer troops was formed: the XIX. AK. The General Command — with the disguised name "Fortification Staff of Pomerania" — was assembled in Gross-Born. General of the Panzer Troops Guderian became its Commanding General; as of August he was in charge of the 3rd Panzer Division, 2nd and 20th ID (mot.), and the newest Panzer Lehr Unit and Armored Reconnaissance Unit, equipped with the newest vehicles, located in Pomerania.

The structure of the German Panzer troops in mid-August 1939 was as follows:

Division	Pz.Br.	Pz.Reg.	Pz.Abt.
1st Panzer Division	1st	1st, 2nd	
2nd Panzer Division	2nd	3rd, 4th	
3rd Panzer Division	3rd	5th, 6th	
4th Panzer Division	5th	35th, 36th	
5th Panzer Division	8th	15th, 31st	
10th Panzer Division		8th	
	4th	7th	
	6th	11th, 25th	
1st Lt.D			65th
2nd Lt.D			66th
3rd Lt.D			67th
4th Lt.D			33rd
Panzer Training School			

Then on August 17, 1939 the order came for the units "capable of moving out quickly" to prepare to march — these were all light and Panzer divisions. The troops moved to training camps near the eastern boundary of the Reich. A few days later — on August 25 — a camouflaged mobilization was ordered. This order was retracted the same night, but was renewed a few hours later. The regiments moved into the thick forests along the border. No movement was allowed during the day; the various regiments and units marched, drove or rolled forward only at night.

Shortly before midnight on August 31, 1939 the order to attack was given: the war was on!

Climax

The First War Years

1939-1943

At the beginning of the Polish campaign on September 1, 1939 two army groups of the German Army were ready for war; one group secured the western border. The Panzer units were divided among the focal points; for their first acid test was about to begin; would they know how to turn the words of their creator Guderian: "Clobber — don't slobber!" — into deeds?

Army Group South consisted of three armies — the 14th, 10th and 8th — of which the 10th Army, in the middle, was the spearhead. With the concerted power of two Panzer, three light, two motorized and five active infantry divisions, it was to tear the Polish front apart, overrun the enemies and force them to fight west of the Vistula.

Within this army group there were:

With the 14th Army:

2nd Panzer Division (Generalleutnant Veiel)

5th Panzer Division (Generalleutnant von Vietinghoff)

4th Light Division (Generalmajor Hubicki)

With the 10th Army:

1st Panzer Division (Generalleutnant Schmidt)

4th Panzer Division (Generalleutnant Reinhardt)

1st-3rd Light Divisions (Generalmajor von Loeper, Generalleutnant Stumme, Generalmajor Kuntzen)

With the 8th Army:

no Panzer unit.

Army Group North included two armies — the 3rd and 4th — , of which the 3rd Army (with only one Panzer division) was to advance from East Prussia across the Narev, while the 4th Army (likewise with just one Panzer division) had to cut off the so-called Polish Corridor from the rest of Poland and then attack Warsaw via Thorn.

The history of the 3rd Panzer Division (Generalleutnant Baron Geyr von Schweppenburg), which was subordinate to the 4th Army, described the action of its units on September 1, 1939:

> ". . . Early fog was still haunting the forests; it is already noticeably cold. But spooky restlessness prevails everywhere. The rattle of motors, the soft marching of columns. Whispers and curses, the soft clinking of weapons . . . The division is ready . . .
> Then: 4:45 A.M.! . . . Suddenly the tank motors begin to howl, chains rattle, motorcycles bark . . .
> The light tanks are the first vehicles to push through the barbed-wire obstacles broken by the engineers. . . ."

The Second World War began . . .

The German Panzer troops, with all their units, were in the battle from the first day on. A novelty was the Panzer unit formed in East Prussia under Generalmajor Kempf. It consisted of the staff of the 4th Panzer Brigade, the 4th Panzer Regiment, the SS Standarte *Deutschland*, an SS artillery regiment, an SS reconnaissance unit, and an antitank unit.

After the campaign the staff of the 10th Panzer Division (Generalmajor Schaal) took over the unit after being transferred from Prague, whereupon 7th Panzer Regiment was finally repositioned, so that the new Panzer division was now also composed of two regiments — 7th and 8th Panzer Regiments.

All 34 Panzer units of the Panzer troops took part in the Polish campaign. As of September 1, 1939 they possessed:

928 P-I tanks
1231 P-II tanks
202 P-35(t) tanks
98 P-38(t) tanks
148 P-III tanks
213 P-IV tanks
160 armored command cars

All of the tanks proved themselves well in the Polish campaign, especially through the use of ultra-short-wave radios. This allowed excellent communication within the Panzer units, and thus quick reactions.

The first week of the war in Poland showed clearly that the Wehrmacht, thanks to its modern weapons, which included the Luftwaffe, was far superior to the Polish Army. Even so, it was not possible to enclose the Polish Army west of the Vistula "according to plan." The beaten enemy forces were forced back to the Vistula, practically in the first week. Yet the XVI. AK, as part of the German 10th Army, advanced some 70 to 80 kilometers ahead of the front, and the 43th Panzer Division captured the bitterly defended suburbs of Warsaw on the eighth day of the war.

A P-II tank of the 35th Panzer Regiment opens the road into the suburbs of Warsaw for the riflemen. At this time the tanks still bore the white cross. Since it was visible from far away, it was replaced by the black Iron Cross after the campaign. The number R 05 indicates that this tank belongs to the regimental staff.

Two P-II tanks of the 4th Panzer Division support the infantry action in the capital of Poland.

Two battles in basins took place in the second week of the war, one of them on the right wing of the 10th Army in the Radom area, in which the 5th Panzer Division and the 1st to 3rd Light Divisions participated. The second battle took place on the Bzura and led to crises for the Germans, but these could be dealt with in ten days. Meanwhile the second phase of the campaign had been introduced by the 3rd and 10th Panzer Divisions, with the motorized forces of other divisions on the left wing of the army, advanced to attack in the direction of Brest on September 11 to cut off the Polish troops east of the Vistula. The report of the Wehrmacht High Command (OKW) reported on September 17, among other things:

"At Vlodava south of Brest, the foremost reconnaissance troops of the armies that advanced from East Prussia and from Upper Silesia and Slovakia shook hands."

With that, the Polish campaign was practically finished — and on the same day, units of the Red Army crossed the Russo-Polish border. In a communique of September 18, at 12:30 A.M., the OKH ordered the end of combat and the withdrawal of the German divisions behind a line along the Pissa, along the Narev to the Vistula, the Vistula to the mouth of the San, along the San to Przemysl and from Przemysl to the Uzsoker Pass.

On October 1, 1939 the battle for Poland ended.

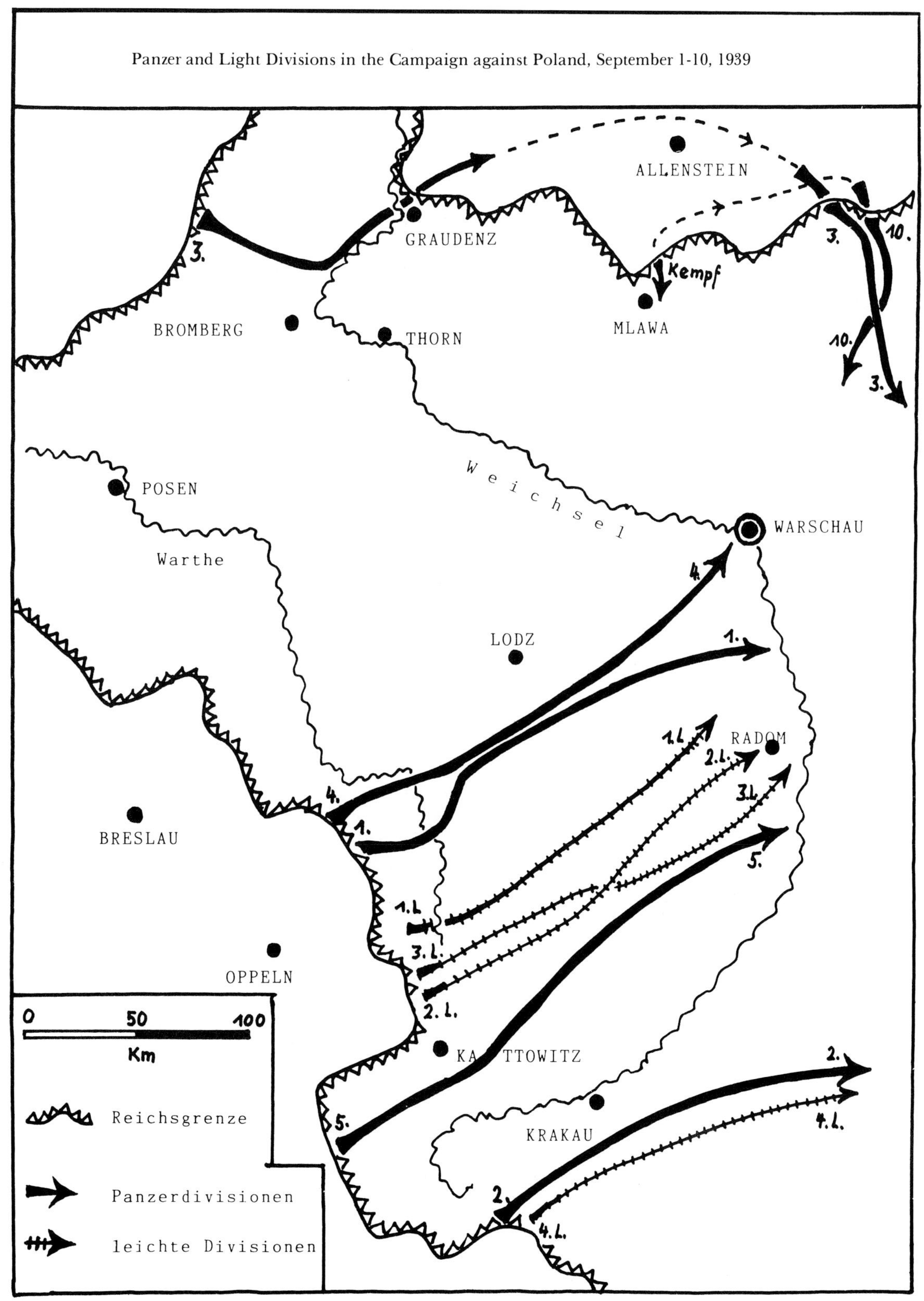

Panzer and Light Divisions in the Campaign against Poland, September 1-10, 1939

When the war began, a new command structure was introduced in the replacement forces as well. The former head of the *Schnellen Truppen* (Mobile Troops) staff was reorganized as the inspector of the *Schnellen Truppen*. The business of the staff was concerned with the weapons department In-6 of the General Army Office. The In-6 Department was called the *Panzertruppe, Kavallerie und Heeresmotorisierung* staff, and Generalleutnant Kühn became the Inspector.

While the Panzer regiments returned to their home garrisons to the jubilation of the people, the Panzer troops were expanded. New formations were:
6th Panzer Division with the 11th Panzer Regiment, of the
1st Lt.Div. and army troops,
7th Panzer Division with the 25th Panzer Regiment, of the
2nd Lt.Div. and army troops,
8th Panzer Division with the 10th Panzer Regiment, of the
3rd Lt.Div. and army troops,
9th Panzer Division with the 33rd Panzer Regiment, of the
4th Lt.Div. and army troops.

The four light divisions already in existence were taken over completely, along with the Panzer units formerly subordinated to them. On account of the lack of materials, the 6th, 7th and 8th Panzer Divisions were equipped with Czech Types P-35(t) and P-38(t) tanks.

Even before the war in Poland began, the replacement army had formed seven Panzer replacement units, with the cadre of each unit's staff made of officers from two Panzer regiments; for example:
Pz.Ers.Abt.1 (Erfurt) of 1. and 6./Panzer Regiment 1, 3. and
7./Panzer Regiment 2,
Pz.Ers.Abt.7 (Vaihingen) of 2. and 7./Panzer Regiment 7, 3.
and 6. Panzer Regiment 8.

At the beginning of 1940 two divisional staffs were formed in the replacement army to command the Panzer troops: 178th Division in Liegnitz (staying there till the war ended) and the 179th Division in Weimar (transferred to France in 1943).

The former In-6 unit of the General Mamy Office was divided at the same time into In-6 *Schnelle Truppen* (Mobile Troops) and In-11 "Army Motorization." Along with In-8 *Fahrtruppenabteilung* (Transport Troop Unit), they formed the new official group "Motor Vehicles and Motorization."

The experiences of the Polish campaign had already shown that the light tanks were scarcely suitable for front-line service; thus on September 27, 1939 the Army Weapons Office ordered the immediate continued and expanded construction of Types P-III and P-IV. Only now did large-series production, especially of the P-III, begin. The Altmark Chain Factory Inc. of Berlin-Spandau soon became the most important German tank manufacturer. Along with this firm, Daimler-Benz, Famo, Henschel, MAN and four smaller firms were engaged in producing this type. Large-series production of the P-IV began only in 1942, when it was already "too late."

The experiences of the Polish campaign also led to a new color scheme for the tanks. The former paint scheme, with shades of brown, had not proved practical; as of the autumn of 1939 all tanks were painted charcoal gray. The cross emblem, which could be seen in white on turrets and hulls during the campaign, now had to be replaced by a black cross with a white border. Tank construction from 1940 on

The Commander of the Army inaugurated, on December 20, 1939, along with the Infantry Assault Emblem, a Tank Combat Emblem.

This emblem could be awarded to members of Panzer units who, as of January 1, 1940, excelled as tank drivers, radiomen, gunners or leaders. The service is to have occurred in at least three actions on three different days.

The emblem had an oval form surrounded by an oak wreath, with an Army eagle attached to the upper part. The center of the emblem was formed by a heavy tank (Type P-III), which was moving from the left rear to the right foreground. The emblem was at first made in silver and intended for members of the Panzer regiments. An additional order of the Commander of the Army, dated June 1, 1940, extended the former guidelines to other units of the Panzer divisions and armored scout units. The color of the emblem for these units, though, was bronze.

Further directives from the Commander of the Army, dated December 31, 1942, January 31, 1943 and December 1, 1944, regulated new types and standards of awarding. Thereafter, for example, the silver version could be awarded to motorcycle messengers and maintenance troops that gave meritorious service at the foremost front. Likewise the silver emblems could be awarded to members of tank chaser and armored intelligence units.

In recognition of the many combat actions of the Panzer troops during the extended course of the war, an order of June 22, 1943 approved the introduction of higher stages. The tank combat emblem could then be awarded after 25, 50, 75 and 100 combat missions and included the appropriate number in the lower part of the oak-leaf wreath. The emblem for 100 missions had a somewhat different form, including a wider oak-leaf wreath and a more highly stylized tank. The number was in gold script on a black shield, which was in turn framed in gold.

The evaluation of missions took place only as of July 1, 1943. But for proven soldiers on eastern and African duty, an unbroken service of 15 months could be counted as up to 25 days of combat. Awards to badly wounded men could be made before the required number of days had been attained. The emblem was worn on the left.

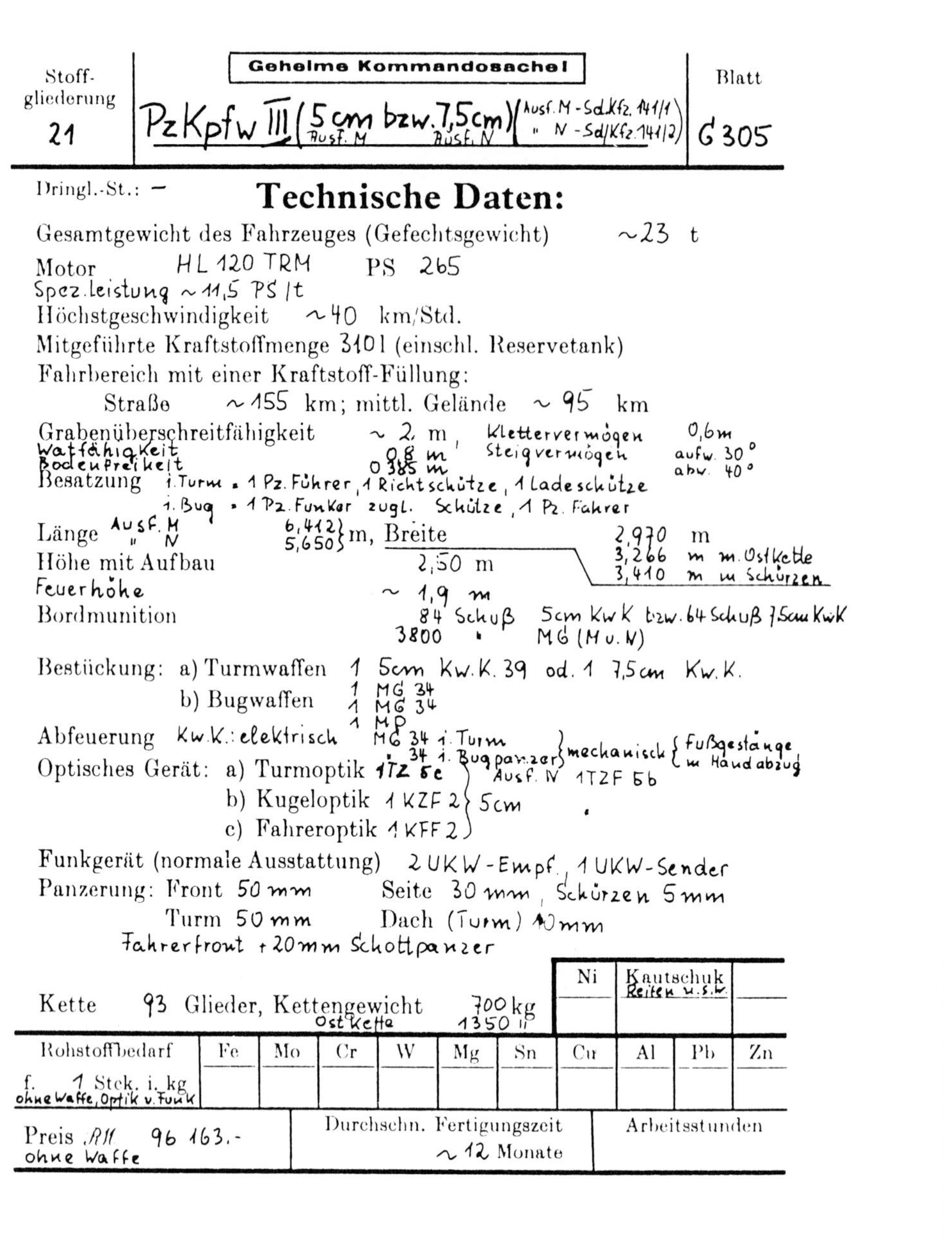

Stoff-gliederung 21 | **Geheime Kommandosache!** PzKpfw III (5 cm bzw. 7,5 cm) (Ausf. M - Sd.Kfz. 141/1; Ausf. N - Sd/Kfz. 141/2) | Blatt G 305

Dringl.-St.: –

Technische Daten:

Gesamtgewicht des Fahrzeuges (Gefechtsgewicht) ~23 t
Motor HL 120 TRM PS 265
Spez. leistung ~11,5 PS/t
Höchstgeschwindigkeit ~40 km/Std.
Mitgeführte Kraftstoffmenge 310 l (einschl. Reservetank)
Fahrbereich mit einer Kraftstoff-Füllung:
Straße ~155 km; mittl. Gelände ~95 km
Grabenüberschreitfähigkeit ~2 m, Klettervermögen 0,6 m
Watfähigkeit 0,8 m, Steigvermögen aufw. 30°
Bodenfreiheit 0,385 m abw. 40°
Besatzung 1. Turm • 1 Pz. Führer, 1 Richtschütze, 1 Ladeschütze
1. Bug • 1 Pz. Funker zugl. Schütze, 1 Pz. Fahrer
Länge Ausf. M 6,412 / Ausf. N 5,650 m, Breite 2,970 m; 3,266 m m. Ostkette; 3,410 m m. Schürzen
Höhe mit Aufbau 2,50 m
Feuerhöhe ~1,9 m
Bordmunition 84 Schuß 5 cm KwK bzw. 64 Schuß 7,5 cm KwK; 3800 Schuß MG (M u. N)

Bestückung: a) Turmwaffen 1 5 cm Kw.K. 39 od. 1 7,5 cm Kw.K.; 1 MG 34
b) Bugwaffen 1 MG 34; 1 MP
Abfeuerung Kw.K.: elektrisch; MG 34 i. Turm, 34 i. Bugpanzer – mechanisch – Fußgestänge u. Handabzug
Optisches Gerät: a) Turmoptik 1 TZF 5e (Ausf. N 1 TZF 5b)
b) Kugeloptik 1 KZF 2 } 5 cm
c) Fahreroptik 1 KFF 2
Funkgerät (normale Ausstattung) 2 UKW-Empf., 1 UKW-Sender
Panzerung: Front 50 mm Seite 30 mm, Schürzen 5 mm
Turm 50 mm Dach (Turm) 10 mm
Fahrerfront + 20 mm Schottpanzer

Kette 93 Glieder, Kettengewicht 700 kg (Ostkette 1350 kg) | Ni | Kautschuk Reifen u.s.w.

Rohstoffbedarf	Fe	Mo	Cr	W	Mg	Sn	Cu	Al	Pb	Zn
f. 1 Stck. i. kg ohne Waffe, Optik u. Funk										

Preis RM 96 163.- ohne Waffe	Durchschn. Fertigungszeit ~12 Monate	Arbeitsstunden

was to reach a monthly total of 600 tanks and assault vehicles, according to orders from the top. This goal was not actually attained until 1943!

The new war year of 1940 began without major military events. The German army prepared to take on the French and British armies. The General Staff in Berlin had drawn up numerous campaign plans, but they were only to become reality when the Chief of the General Staff of Army Group B, Generalleutnant von Manstein, presented his own plan, which went into war history under the name of "Sichelschnitt" (sickle cut).

Meanwhile, though, the theater of war had spread to the north. There in the Scandinavian area, German and British commercial interests clashed. The German war economy depended on the iron ore deposits of northern Sweden, and the British fleet depended on support points in Norway to blockade the German coasts.

Thus on April 6, 1940 British warships set out to mine the Norwegian coast — and two days later the German battle fleet, with almost all its warships and many transport ships, weighed anchor and headed north.

The occupation of Norway and Denmark took place, involving only one *Panzerabteilung* of the Panzer troops. This was Pz.Abt.40 (Oberstleutnant Volckheim, Tank Officer of World War I), assembled especially for this theater of war. The unit consisted of three companies with P-I and P-II tanks and three new-type tanks still available from the days of secret rearmament.

The unit had been formed in Dabendorf, near Berlin, in March of 1940, and consisted chiefly of two active companies of the 6th Panzer Regiment. The use of these light tanks in Norway was intended to support the infantry and to capture important objectives quickly.

A light tank protects passing infantry in southern Norway — April 25, 1940.

The light tanks of Pz.Abt.40 supported mountain *Jäger* troops in the last fighting in central Norway. (May 11, 1940).

Meanwhile, preparations for the western offensive were proceeding at full speed. The Panzer divisions had by now been brought to almost 100% of wartime completion in terms of personnel, weapons, equipment and vehicles. All the divisions had to make their vehicles recognizable by applying new markings ordered by the OKH, so that individual units could be contacted quickly on the battlefield or in blocked road transit. The markings of the Panzer troops had to be painted on in yellow.

The entire fleet of battle tanks in the German Army on May 10, 1940, when the western campaign began, added up to:

P-I	1026, 523 of them at the front
P-35(t)	143, 106 of them at the front
P-II	1079, 955 of them at the front
P-38(t)	228, all 228 at the front
P-III	349, all 349 at the front
P-IV	280, 278 of them at the front
Command Cars	243, 135 of them at the front

The German Panzer divisions were situated for the campaign against the western powers as follows, from left to right:

Panzer Division	w/Army	Destination
9th	18th	Moerdijk,, Amsterdam
3rd	6th	north of Brussels, Maubeuge
4th	6th	north of Brussels, Maubeuge
5th	4th	Dinant on the Maas
7th	4th	Dinant on the Maas
6th	12th	Maas south of Givet
8th	12th	Maas south of Givet
2nd	16th	Sedan
1st	16th	Sedan
10th	16th	Sedan

Thus early in the morning of May 10, 1940 all German Panzer regiments were at the foremost front. The focal point of the coming offensive was to be on the left wing of the two Army Groups B (right) and A (left). The third Army Group C had marched up from the border of Alsace-Lorraine and did not include any motorized troops in its ranks.

A special report on the German radio early that morning said:

> ". . . the German Western Army advanced over the western boundary of Germany at break of day to attack on the broadestfront."

Just three days later the first tank battle of World War II took place at the small Gette River between Orp-le-Grand and Hannut.

> "A tank-versus-tank battle developed", as a later report states. "The units and companies soon lost control, were

> thrown into a tangle, friend and foe sank their teeth in each other. Clouds of smoke and fire rolled over the land. The battle degenerated into single combat, which rolled back and forth. But finally the scene cleared up — after an hour. The Germans' rapid and disciplined fire decided the battle!"

The focal point of the first phase of this campaign was clearly the Sedan area. Here the four motorized army corps formed the nucleus of the German Army. General of the Cavalry von Kleist was the commander of this important group, which included in all more than 134,370 soldiers with 1250 tanks, 362 armored scout cars and 39,528 other motor vehicles.

While the first tank battle of the war was being fought north of this vital area, the Panzer divisions were taking up positions on the same day to cross the Maas near Sedan. By the time night fell, the crossing had been completed successfully. When six French divisions with an armored unit made a counterattack at dawn of the next day, they were not able to stop the German tanks.

The breakthrough on the French front had succeeded! The path for the battle tanks bearing the Iron Cross emblem was free, leading to the west, into northern and central France. The "sickle-cut plan" originated by Generalleutnant von Manstein, the subsequent field marshal, could be made a reality in the next ten days.

After the battle at Avesnes on May 24-25, 1940, German tanks — here a P-38(t) — roll farther west past destroyed French tanks.

The German tanks made their way unhampered through French, Belgian and later British troops to the Channel coast. St. Quentin, Maubeuge, Peronne, Cambrai, Valenciennes were passed through practically at a "quick march." Then on May 17 and 18 an incomprehensible command to stop came from the OKH and the army group command, before the move recommenced on May 19. 24 hours later the 1st Panzer Division reached Amiens and the 2nd Panzer Division passed through Abbeville to the mouth of the Somme.

German tanks were at the coast — the "sickle cut" had succeeded!

Four days later the battle of Dunkirk began. All the Panzer divisions took part in it. Three days later they pushed across the Belgian-French border together between Lens in the east and the coast in the west, and moved northeast toward Dunkirk. From right to left there were the 5th, 7th, 4th, 3rd, 8th, 6th, 1st and 2nd Panzer Divisions. This last tank attack in the first phase of the western campaign succeeded only after the lifting of the "order to stop", which Hitler had given a few days before in an attempt to rest the Panzer troops.

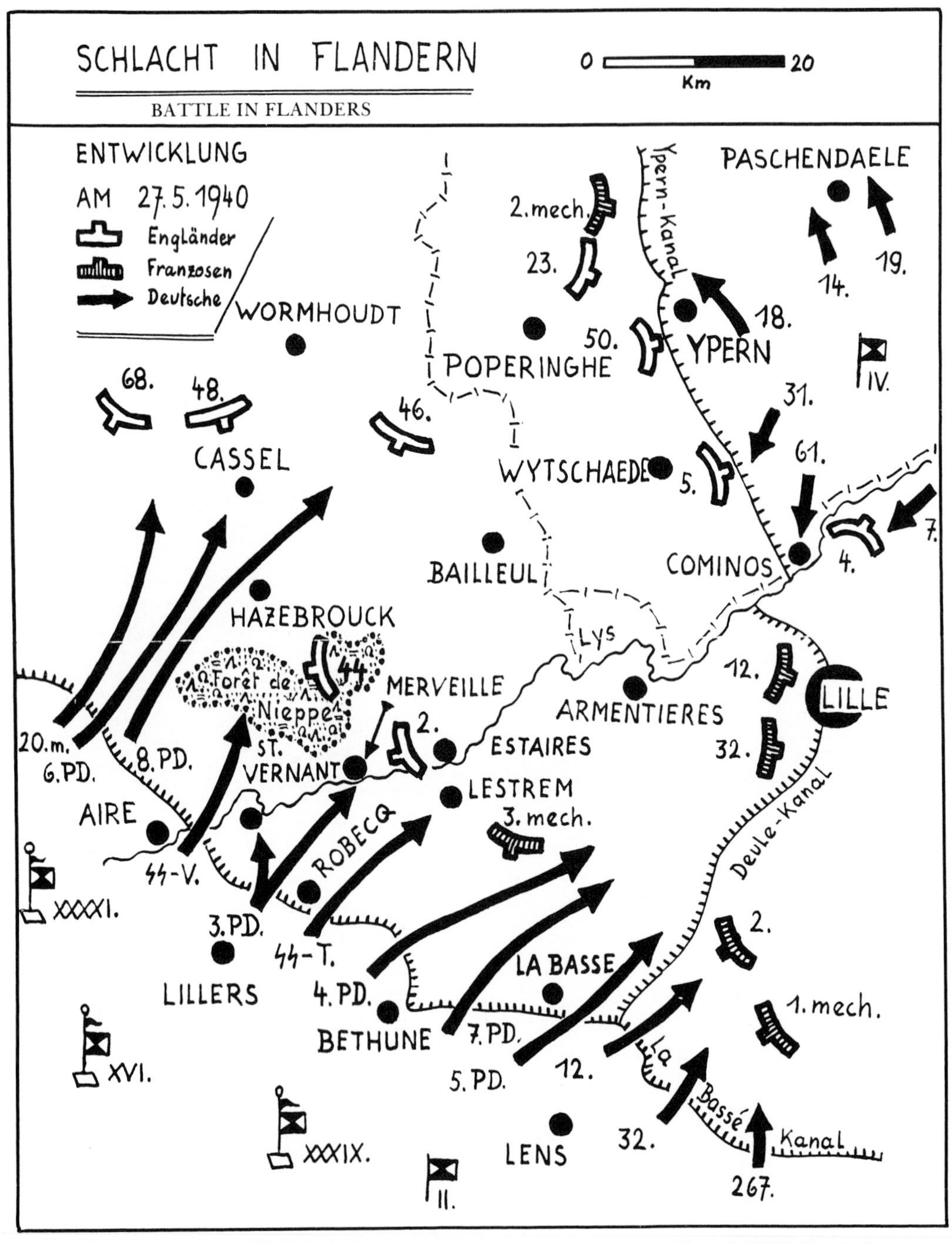

In the final battle around Dunkirk itself on and after May 30, only the 9th Panzer Division was involved, forming the left wing of the attacking forces.

But at this time the western army was already repositioning for an attack from the mouth of the Somme to the Swiss border. The Panzer divisions were gathered into two independent Panzer groups, commanded by General of the Cavalry von Kleist and General of the Panzer Troops Guderian. The positions of the Panzer groups on June 8, 1940 (three days after the new offensive began) were:

Panzer Group Kleist:
- XIV. AK mot. with 9th and 10th Panzer Divisions
- XVI. AK mot. with 3rd and 4th Panzer Divisions

Panzer Group Guderian:
- XXXIX. AK mot. with 1st and 2nd Panzer Divisions
- XXXXI. AK mot. with 6th and 8th Panzer Divisions

These eight divisions were at the heart of the new offensive, which began on June 5, 1940 under the code name "Fall Rot." The two divisions with the 4th Army — 5th and 7th Panzer Divisions — had the job of supporting the army in an attack on northwest France. These were the divisions that pushed the new offensive up to 50 kilometers deep in the enemy hinterland in the first two days. In the process, the 7th Panzer Division, led by Generalleutnant Rommel, was nicknamed the *Gespenster-division* (Ghost Division), as it moved faster than the retreating British and French troops and surrounded them at St. Valéry. The 5th Panzer Division rolled through the enemy center and reached the Atlantic harbor city of Brest on June 18.

A short break in the advance through northern France. A P-II in front of Rouen Cathedral.

A week after the second phase of the western campaign began, the situation changed as follows (situation on June 14, from right to left):
The 9th and 10th Panzer Divisions pushed over the Seine west of Romilly and headed southward; the 3rd and 4th Panzer Divisions were far to the west, close to Troyes; the 1st and 2nd Panzer Divisions reached the St. Dizier reached the St. Dizier area on the Marne (already behind the Maginot Line); the 8th and 6th Panzer Divisions marched toward Bar le Duc, far to the south of Verdun.

Three days later the Panzer Group Guderian was on the Swiss border at Pontarlier, and the 1st Panzer Division arrived in Belfort one day later; with that the French forces in Alsace were surrounded. The Panzer Group Kleist meanwhile headed for the French Alps and, with the 3rd and 4th Panzer Divisions, reached the beautiful mountain valley of the Isère near Grenoble. From here — the 9th and 10th Panzer Divisions were in Lyon — the Panzer Group Kleist moved toward the Atlantic coast and stormed through Royan and Bordeaux to the Spanish border.

After the battle in a destroyed town in central France, on June 29, 1940. A P-III tank waits for a delivery of ammunition.

In the days that followed, the OKW reports cited the highest officers of the Panzer troops (to regimental commanders) who had distinguished themselves particularly. They were Oberstleutnant Baron von Nolde (6th Panzer Regiment) on may 20, Oberleutnant von Jarowski (3rd Panzer Regiment) on May 27, Oberst Koll (11th Panzer Regiment) on June 1, and Oberleutnant Malguth (35th Panzer Regiment) on June 18.

On June 25, 1940, at 1:35 A.M., the bugle signal to halt rang out everywhere!
The western campaign had ended . . .

After this campaign, plans to land the German Wehrmacht in Great Britain were still being developed. According to them, four so-called *Tauchpanzer* (Diving Panzer) units were to be put ashore along with infantry and navy shock troops in the first phase. Military Zones III (Berlin), VIII (Breslau) and XVII (Vienna) were supposed to establish these units. The transferred officers, non-commissioned officers and enlisted men were retrained in amphibious tanks on the Baltic and North Sea coasts.

The kinds of tanks needed for this purpose were those of the P-III and P-IV types, which were prepared to operate in water up to 15 meters deep. The special equipment they needed consisted of floats with power sources and propellers, watertight fittings connecting the hull and turret, and snorkels and fresh air ducts. The tank — there were 210 of this type; every unit had 52 to 56 of them — attained a speed of 10 kph in seas of up to strength 4.

On July 24, 1940 the following Panzer units were formed for "Operation Sealion" (landing in Great Britain):

A of I./2nd Panzer Regiment staff and parts of the 1st and 2nd Panzer Regiments,

B of I./4th Panzer Regiment staff and parts of the 3rd and 4th Panzer Regiments,

C of I./5th Panzer Regiment staff and parts of the 5th and 6th Panzer Regiments,

D of I./15th Panzer Regiment staff and parts of the 15th and 31st Panzer Regiments.

After fulfilling their assignment of landing on the British Isles, Pz.Abt. A and B were to become the I. and II. units of the newly-formed Panzer Regiment 18; Pz.Abt. C and D would be the I. and II./ 28th Panzer Regiment. While the new 18th Panzer Regiment remained with the 18th Panzer Division, formed on December 6, 1940, the units of 28th Panzer Regiment were disbanded on February 27, 1941. The I./28th Panzer Regiment then became the III./6th Panzer Regiment (3rd Panzer Division), and the II./28th Panzer Regiment became the III./18th Panzer Regiment (18th Panzer Division).

In the late autumn, when the German leadership finally gave up the plans for "Operation Sealion", the Wehrmacht command planned to capture the fortress of Gibraltar with the help of Spanish troops. Here too, forces from each Panzer division were to be supplied, so that a (not yet formed) Panzer division would in the end handle "Operation Felix" (the capture of Gibraltar), while another (not yet formed) Panzer division would be used in Morocco. But when the Spanish chief of state declined to participate on December 7, 1940, "Operation Felix" was likewise filed away.

The experience gained in the western campaign led to changes in the structure and strength of the former Panzer divisions. Now every division was given a second infantry regiment but had to give up a Panzer regiment, which considerably weakened the striking force of the ten new divisions that were to be established. On the other hand, the tactics tested in the campaign were maintained, having shown great success in terms of building focal points. The instructional plan for tactical training in schools and among the troops was stated in the autumn of 1940:

> "Clear focal-point formation. Penetration at the places least expected by the enemy. Close cooperation with the Luftwaffe. Attack without regard for open flanks. Penetration and surrounding of the enemy."

Shortly after the campaign, the OKH gave the command to establish four new Panzer divisions; the command to form six more divisions ensued on July 22 and 28. The new units were:

Panzer Division	Reserve District	Month Founded	Ready for Service
11th	VIII	July	10/15/1940
12th	II	October	4/15/1941
13th	XI	August	10/10/1940
14th	IV	August	12/12/1940
15th	VII	October	3/15/1941
16th	VI	August	11/25/1940
17th	VII	October	3/15/1941
18th	IV	October	5/1/1941
19th	XI	October	3/15/1941
20th	IX	October	5/1/1941

To make up these few units, the 4th, 16th, 19th, 27th and 33rd Infantry Divisions, 2nd and 13th Infantry Divisions (motorized), the 11th Rifle Brigade and the disbanded 209th, 228th, 231st and 311th Infantry Divisions were utilized. The already active 2nd (1st Panzer Division), 4th (2nd Panzer Division), 5th (3rd Panzer Division), 36th (4th Panzer Division), 15th (5th Panzer Division) and 8th (10th Panzer Division) Panzer Regiments were transferred to the new divisions. The former staff of the 3rd Panzer Brigade (3rd Panzer Division) and the 5th Panzer Regiment became the new 5th Light Division, while the 3rd Panzer Division received a new Brigade Staff No.5. In addition, Brigade Staffs 8 (as of March 1, 1941 Panzer Brigade 100) and 18 (formerly amphibious tank units) were formed.

A further expansion of the Panzer command staffs followed on November 16, 1940. The OKH formed Panzer Group Commands 1 (formerly General Command XII. AK), 2 (formerly General Command XIX. AK) and 3 (formerly General Command XV. AK). A 4th Panzer Group Command was formed from the General Command of the XVI. AK on February 15, 1941, as a result of the preparations for the campaign against the Soviet Union.

The peace initiatives undertaken by the European powers in the autumn of 1940 - including the Soviet Foreign Minister's visit to Berlin — were nullified on October 28, 1940 when Italian troops attacked Greece from Albania. As a new theater of war came into being with the active participation of British naval and air forces three weeks later, the German Reich now feared that the vital Rumanian oil fields could be threatened. Thus in December of 1940 the OKH ordered the transfer of the 13th and 16th Panzer Divisions to Rumania and Bulgaria.

German troops move into Bulgaria on March 5, 1941. Medium tanks cross the Danube bridge built by German engineers.

These units were originally described as instructional troops for the Rumanian army. Thus the 13th Panzer Division was given the disguised name of "Instructional Staff Regiment" and the 16th Panzer Division was called "I. and II. Battalions of the Instructional Staff Regiment."

The experience gained in the western campaign had shown again that the German battle tanks were too lightly armed to be able to fight heavier tanks successfully.

At first, then, the P-III was equipped with a 50mm tank gun (KwK) 39 L/42 without a muzzle brake, later replaced by the improved 50mm KwK L/60. (A year later the P-III was to be given the 50mm KwK L/50, which attained a range of 7000 meters at a muzzle velocity of 785 meters per second.)

At the same time, the P-IV was improved as of the autumn of 1940 by fitting a 50mm KwK L/42.

During the autumn and winter of 1940-41, the OKH not only established new Panzer units for the 11th to 20th Panzer Divisions, but also increased the number of Panzer replacement units. A special unit came into being at the same time. This was Mine Removal Unit 1, which was founded on December 1, 1940. This unit was composed of two companies organized six months earlier (and known as the Glienicke Company), and operated with remote-control tanks (Type "Goliath"). Later this unit was designated Pz.Abt.300.

With the entry of Italy into the war in June of 1940, a theater of war never envisioned by the German leadership came into being: Libya.

After the Italian attack on the British border posts in Egypt collapsed and the Italian forces were driven back by the Greeks, the Italian government turned to the German Reich and asked for help in the form of weapons.

The OKH issued "Instruction No. 22" in mid-January 1941:

> "The Commander of the Army is to establish a blockading unit that is capable of providing worthwhile service to our allies in the defense of Tripolitania, particularly against the English tank divisions. . . ."

Since October of 1940 there were already units of the 3rd Panzer Division being prepared for war duty in North Africa through medical examination, development of tropical clothing, etc. But only in early February of 1941 did 20 Italian ships bring 8000 German soldiers and 1360 vehicles to Tripoli. On February 11, 1941 the first German soldiers, including their Commander, Generalleutnant Rommel, set foot on African soil.

Tanks were used by the staff of the 3rd Panzer Brigade and the 5th Panzer Regiment. This Regiment and the 3rd Reconnaissance Unit were the first German units to attack British positions, those of the 2nd British Armored Division, on March 31, 1941, after all the units of the blockading force — now renamed the 5th Light Division — had arrived.

The German troops advanced rapidly to the Libyan-Egyptian border. Only Tobruk remained in British hands behind the front. Here the first units of the 15th Panzer Division, which had arrived in April, went into action. The first member of this division in Africa was its Commander, Generalleutnant von Prittwitz und Gaffron — he was also the division's first man to fall before Tobruk.

With the arrival of the 15th Panzer Division, the General Command German *Afrika Korps* was formed, under the command of Generalleutnant Rommel (General of the Panzer Troops as of July 1, 1941). The former 5th Light Division was renamed the 21st Panzer Division in August of 1941. With the strengthening of the Panzer Group Command Afrika — so called as of August 15, 1941 — Rommel believed Tobruk could be taken by the end of November.

The first tanks (P-III of Panzer Regiment 5 have left Tripoli and are preparing to attack. (Photo taken on March 27, 1941.) The soldiers are still wearing field gray uniforms; tropical uniforms have not yet arrived.

The attack on Tobruk on June 27, 1941. Tanks secure the advance of German infantrymen and Italian troops in the open desert.

However, the British anticipated him. The British counterattack began on November 18, 1941 with one armored division, two tank brigades and two infantry divisions. The battle lasted four weeks. The German losses — including both division commanders — were too high. General of the Panzer Troops Rommel ordered a retreat of the *Afrika Korps* on December 15, 1941.

At this time two new theaters of war came into being: the Balkans and the Soviet Union.

After the failure of Italian forces in northern Greece and the withdrawal of Yugoslavia from the mutual defense pact it had signed with the German Reich, war developed in the Balkans.

The 2nd and 12th Armies of the German Army, plus the 1st Panzer Group, had set out to join the campaign against Greece and Yugoslavia in late March and early April of 1941. While the 2nd Army — including the 8th and 14th Panzer Divisions — was to attack Yugoslavia from Austria and Hungary, the 12th Army —including the 2nd, 5th, 9th and 11th Panzer Divisions — were to turn against Greece and southern Yugoslavia from Bulgaria and Rumania. The OKH also named the 4th, 12th and 19th Panzer Divisions as reserves, but they saw no action in the campaign.

The German attack began on April 6, 1941. On account of the cold, damp wintery weather, the roads were wet and soft, so that the Panzer columns could proceed only slowly. But the superior power and battle experience of the German officers, non-commissioned officers and enlisted men overwhelmed the strong Yugoslavian forces in the first ten days. As early as April 13, 1941 the OKH made a special announcement:

> "As of 5:30 A.M. today, Panzer troops of von Kleist's Army have moved into Belgrade!"

German tanks — P-III — move into Agram, greeted by the ethnic German population.

It was soldiers of the 8th Panzer Division and the 2nd SS-Panzer Division *Das Reich* who moved into the Yugoslavian capital at the same time. Now it could only last a few more days. The Panzer units had passed through Albania from the north, and one group of forces turned toward Ragusa. The History of the 8th Panzer Division, among others, described this course:

> "On narrow, steep mountain roads, past steep drops and high rock walls, the vehicles climbed to a 1400-meter pass first of all . . .
>
> The impenetrable mountain landscape makes the highest demands on drivers and vehicles. . . . The vegetation becomes more and more sparse and meager, the terrain more and more rough and rocky. The few inhabitants of the lonely mountain huts . . . have no idea of what is going on here. . . ."

It was difficult for the Panzer regiments to deal with the inhospitable mountain landscapes of Serbia and northern Greece.

With the ensuing occupation of the Adriatic coast around Ragusa and Catarro, the campaign in Yugoslavia was practically over. But a hard, bitter battle was still raging on Greek soil, against the Greeks and the recently landed British forces. The OKW report of April 27, 1941 said:

> "After ceaseless attack and pursuit fighting, the head of a German Panzer division, pursuing the fleeing English, made its way into Athens at 9:25 on Sunday morning."

It was the 5th Panzer Division, the only Panzer division that, along with the 6th *Gebirgs* (Mountain) Division, pushed through the pass at Thermopylae and advanced through Thebes in a bold attack on Athens. From here their course led past the straits of Corinth, attacked by the *Fallschirmjäger* (Paratroopers), to the Pelopennesus, where the tanks of the 31st Panzer Regiment rolled on to the south coast of the peninsula.

The 31st Panzer Regiment parades past Generalfeldmarschall List in Athens on May 7, 1941.

By the end of April 1941 the campaign in Greece was over. Twenty days later the attack on Crete began.

The Panzer troops did not participate in this battle. At the end of the battle, to be sure, a few light tanks of the 5./31st Panzer Regiment were shipped to the island, but were not used. After the battle for Crete ended, the company was renamed Pz.Abt. *Kreta*, and was officially designated the 1.Pz.Abt.212 in July of 1941.

The Panzer divisions prepared for the Balkan campaign by the OKH — with the exception of the 16th Panzer Division, which did not see action — were ordered back to Germany as soon as the fighting died down, in order to refresh and replace personnel, weapons, equipment and vehicles, for the campaign against the Soviet Union (of which the troops as yet knew nothing!) was about to begin! The following sites were planned for refreshment in May and June:

2nd Panzer Division - Munich, Upper Bavaria
5th Panzer Division - Berlin-Brandenburg
8th Panzer Division - Bohemia-Moravia
9th Panzer Division - Silesia and Upper Austria
11th Panzer Division - Vienna, Upper Austria
14th Panzer Division - Döberitz near Berlin
16th Panzer Division - Silesia

This refreshment was absolutely necessary, as the Balkan campaign had resulted in a great deal of damage to the tanks — losses had to be made up as well. For example, the 2nd Panzer Division lost most of their artillery during shipping from Patras to Tarento. The report of the 8th Panzer Division stated:

"In the 10th Panzer Regiment, the battle tanks of Czechoslovakian manufacture — 38(t) — stood the stress and strain of the steep mountains and passes best. Many of the tanks of Type P-II were put out of commission by suspension failure, and all the P-IV broke down. They had burned-out steering brakes, broken springs and loosened roller bands."

Yet all the Panzer divisions — with the exception of the 2nd and 5th Panzer Divisions — finished their refreshment and were able to be sent to the eastern boundaries of the Reich in early and mid-June 1941.

Preparation for "Operation Barbarossa" had been moving at full speed practically since December of 1940. In view of this coming campaign, the OKH demanded that the armaments industry produce up to 1250 tanks per month. The previous monthly production added up to only 230 tanks. This request, to be sure, was refused by the OKW and the Ministry of Weapons, since the Luftwaffe and the Navy had first priority as before.

Thus the planned establishment of additional Panzer divisions in the summer and autumn of 1940 had to be restructured to some extent. The formerly independent Pz.Abt.65, 66 and 67 were integrated into existing Panzer regiments and became the third units of the 5th, 7th and 8th Panzer Divisions respectively. Thus of the regiments of the 20 Panzer divisions existing in June of 1941, only the 6th Panzer Regiment (3rd Panzer Division), 11th Panzer Regiment (6th Panzer Division), 25th Panzer Regiment (7th Panzer Division), 10th Panzer Regiment (8th Panzer Division), 29th Panzer Regiment (12th Panzer Division), 39th Panzer Regiment (17th Panzer Division), 18th Panzer Regiment (18th Panzer Division), 27th Panzer Regiment (19th Panzer Division) and the 21st Panzer Regiment (20th Panzer Division) had three units.

The normal structure of a two-unit Panzer regiment was as follows:

Staff
with light tank, intelligence and music corps

(3 Pz.Bef.Wg. III, 5 P-II)
two Panzer units, each with
Staff
with Staff Company
(2 Pz.Bef.Wg. III, 5 P-II)
2 light Panzer companies
(each with 17 P-III and 5 P-II)
one medium company
14 P-IV and 5 P-II
plus one tank maintenance company

In the Panzer regiments with three units, the regiment had no maintenance company, but every unit had its own maintenance column.

The German Panzer corps had the following numbers of usable tanks as of June 22, 1941:

180 P-I
106 P-35(t)
746 P-II
772 P-38(t)
965 P-III
439 P-IV
230 Pz.Bef.Wg. (Armored Command Car) P-III

At this strength the German Army began the campaign against the Red Army. The Army was situated from right to left as follows for "Operation Barbarossa" - the attack on the Soviet Union:

Army Group South with 11th, 17th and 6th Armies and the 1st Panzer Group;
Army Group Center with Panzer Group 2, 4th and 9th Armies, and the 3rd Panzer Group;
Army Group North with the 4th Panzer Group, 16th and 18th Armies;
Army High Command Norway.

Most of the motorized and armored units were united under the command of the Panzer Group Command and situated at the focal points of the planned offensive. The division of the Panzer divisions among the individual armies on June 22, 1941 was, from right to left:

Panzer Group 1:
14th, 11th, 16th, 9th, 13th Panzer Divisions;
Panzer Group 2:
10th, 18th, 17th, 4th, 3rd Panzer Divisions;
Panzer Group 3:
7th, 20th, 12th, 19th Panzer Divisions;
Panzer Group 4:
8th, 6th, 1st Panzer Divisions.

The German ambassador in Moscow, Count von der Schulenburg (executed after July 20, 1944) gave the Soviet foreign minister a message on June 22, 1941:

> "... in view of the unbearable pressure of the Russian troops on the demarcation line that separates them from the German troops, the latter have received the command to march into the territory of the USSR!"

At this minute the war against the Soviet Union was already an hour old; for exactly at 3:15 A.M. on this day, Luftwaffe planes and German artillery had begun the hostilities. The Russian border patrols, which were taken completely by surprise, were quickly overrun and the bridges over the border rivers were captured at once. Then the tanks rolled in. . . .

. . . and all of a sudden it did not proceed as before; for an enemy suddenly faced them that the German General Staff officers had not included in their plans. The Panzer Group Guderian, at the focal point of Army Group Center, came to a stop.

> "There was the sand and there was the swamp. . . . The 3rd Panzer Division . . . was already hopelessly stuck in the moor at Stradecz, south of Brest-Litovsk. It . . . and the infantrymen had to literally fight their way through the morass, swamp and sand," as a report stated.

The Russian landscape became the prime enemy of the German tanks and was to remain so for a long, long time!

And when the landscape was not opposing them, the Russian soldiers did; by noon they had appeared and were waging a bitter battle everywhere. The 25th Panzer Regiment alone lost half of all its vehicles near Olita on this first day of the campaign.

Only on the second day were the tanks able to break through. At Kobryn in the middle sector, German tanks destroyed 107 Russian tanks, most of them "T-26", and two days later the companies of the 25th Panzer Regiment (7th Panzer Division) reached the superhighway to Moscow 20 kilometers northeast of Minsk.

This was the day on which the first great tank battle of the eastern campaign took place in the Army Group North sector.

The 2nd Soviet Tank Brigade attacked the advanced XXXXI AK (mot.) with Type "Kw-I" and "Kw-II" tanks and put the 1st and 6th Panzer Divisions in a bad spot. The battle lasted almost 48 hours, after which 186 Soviet tanks were left on the battlefield as burning or abandoned wrecks. On the very same day the 8th Panzer Division, with the 10th Panzer Regiment, advanced far ahead of all other units of the army group and captured the bridge over the wide river at Dünaburg!

But things did not move as fast as expected in the Army Group South either. To be sure, it was possible to capture the border territory quickly, where the 36th Panzer Regiment, for example, destroyed 156 Russian tanks west of Luzk and the 11th Panzer Division advanced as far as Dubno.

The first tank battle in this sector took place there when Soviet tank brigades attacked the 11th and 16th Panzer Divisions; Panzer Regiment 2 suffered considerable losses. In the end the tanks that bore the Iron Cross were victorious and the Soviets had lost 215 tanks.

The first great success came five days after the war had begun, when the tanks of the 12th and 20th Panzer Divisions moved in from the north and those of the 17th Panzer Division from the south simultaneously. For the first time, a large force of the Red Army was surrounded!

After the double battles of Bialystok and Minsk, the 2nd and 3rd Panzer Groups of Army Group Center continued to attack far to the east. In the south of that sector,

After putting down the first strong Russian opposition, the Panzer units were able to penetrate far into the country in July. Tanks of the 8th Panzer Division move toward Dünaburg in the northern sector of the eastern front.

The 4th Panzer Division moves into a village in central Russia on July 1, 1941, in the central sector of the front.

After the battle, the crews of this P-II (foreground) and P-III (background) stop to catch their breath at the edge of a Ukrainian village somewhere in the southern part of the front.

the 6th Panzer Regiment crossed the Drut and the 18th Panzer Regiment reached the Beresina. In the north the 7th and 20th Panzer Divisions pushed toward Smolensk, while the 19th Panzer Division took Polozk.

Then — it was July 3, 1941 — 600 (!) tanks of two Soviet corps attacked the 3rd Panzer Group west of Smolensk. This day became the hardest test ever for the German tanks. For among the ranks of the Russian tanks were those of the 1st Soviet Infantry Division, which were hitherto completely unknown: the "T-34" tanks.

26-Tonner Pz.Kpfw. **T 34**

Serienbez. T 34 A
T 34 B
T 34 B mit Gußturm

T 34

Gewicht: 26,3 t

Panzerung: T 34 A				**Panzerung: T 34 B**			
Wanne und Aufbau		**Turm**		**Wanne und Aufbau**		**Turm**	
Bug	45 mm	Blende	45+25 mm	Bug	45 mm	Blende	45+25 mm
Fahrerfront	45 mm	Front	45 mm	Fahrerfront	45+15 mm	Front	45+17 mm
Seite	40—45 mm	Seite	45 mm	Seite	45 mm	Seite	45+17 mm
Heck	40 mm	Heck	40—45 mm	Heck	45 mm	Heck	45 mm
Decke	18—22 mm	Decke	16 mm	Decke	18—22 mm	Decke	16 mm
Boden	14 mm			Boden	14 mm		

Bei der neuesten Ausführung soll die Fahrerfront auf 100 mm verstärkt werden.

Panzerung: T 34 B mit Gußturm

Wanne und Aufbau		**Turm**	
Bug	45 mm	Blende	45+25 mm
Fahrerfront	45+15 mm	Front	60—70 mm
Seite	45 mm	Seite	60—70 mm
Heck	45 mm	Heck	60—70 mm
Decke	18—22 mm	Decke	20 mm
Boden	14 mm		

Bewaffnung: 1 Kw.K. 7,62 cm, 2 MG
Besatzung: 4 Mann
Größenmaße: 5,90 m lang, 3,00 m breit, 2,45 m hoch
Geländegängigkeit: klettert 0,90 m, überschreitet 3,00 m, watet 1,10 m
Bodenfreiheit: 0,38 m
Fahrbereich: Straße 450 km, Gelände 260 km
Geschwindigkeit: 50 km/h

Auffallende Merkmale:

Flache Bauform, schräger Bug, Christie-Laufwerk (Laufräder). Führerfahrzeuge mit längerer Kw.K. 7,62 cm L/41,5, die übrigen Fahrzeuge mit kürzerer Kw.K. L/30,5 ausgerüstet.

Unterscheidungsmerkmale von dem äußerlich ähnlichen BT 7:

T 34

Bugplatte: rundkantig, obere Bugplatte einschl. Fahrerfront flach **(30° Neigungswinkel!)**
Panzerkasten: schräge Wände
Turmform: runde Kanten, abgeschrägte Form
Laufwerk: 5 Laufräder

BT 7

Bugplatte: scharfkantig, steil, gegen Fahrerfront abgesetzt
Panzerkasten: steile Wände
Turmform: steile Wände, scharfkantig
Laufwerk: 4 Laufräder

Im ganzen wirkt T 34 wuchtiger und abgerundeter (stromlinienförmig)

Verwendung:

Wichtigster Panzerkampfwagen für Panzerangriffe.

Beurteilung:

Weitaus der beste und brauchbarste sowjet-russische Panzerkampfwagen. Schnell, wendig, sehr stark bewaffnet und gepanzert. Infolge seiner günstigen Bauform (Neigungswinkel: Bugplatte 30°, Heckplatte 40° bis 45°, Panzerkastenseite 50°) ist er von allen sowjet-russischen Baumustern am schwersten zu bekämpfen.

Einzelheiten der Bekämpfung vgl. H. Dv. 469/3

The appearance of this tank was a real sensation — for all German tanks and antitank weapons were powerless against it; only the heavy 88mm anti-aircraft gun could score against it. The new Soviet tanks, which had been built under the strictest secrecy, remained almost invulnerable on account of its smooth form, its slanted side walls, its speed and maneuverability.

The appearance of the "T-34" made basic changes in the use of the tank in battle. To counteract it, the Germans needed their own heavy tanks with heavy guns!

German front officers wanted to simply copy the "T-34." But this request was in vain on account of the impossibility of producing the aluminum Diesel motor. The capacity of the German aluminum production and the lack of raw materials to make alloy steel were not sufficient to build.

Only in November 1941 did a commission of industrialists, manufacturers and officers of the Army Weapons Office decide to create a strong opposing weapon. Of course Hitler had already suggested in the spring 1941 that a stronger tank than the P-IV should be built; this plan was abandoned when the eastern campaign began, since the Soviets were not suspected of having such a weapon. According to the commission's decision, work was to begin immediately on a new tank weighing up to sixty tons (the later "Tiger") and another weighing up to 35 tons (the later "Panther").

The tank of the "Panther" type — also designated P-V — was developed by the firms of Henschel, MAN and Daimler, and Dr. Porsche designed an air-cooled Diesel motor. Reich Minister Speer decided on the apparently more maneuverable Henschel model. It was armed with a long (L/70) 75mm KwK. Production of the P-V began in May 1942.

Meanwhile the campaign proceeded without setbacks. In early and mid-August the 1st Panzer Group 1 was on the Dniepr on both sides of Dniepropetrovsk, the 2nd Panzer Group had reached the Dessna west of Briansk, 3rd Panzer Group was between Velikiye Kuki and east of Smolensk, the 4th Panzer Group was fighting on separate fronts. In the last sector the mistaken estimation of the OKH led to particularly serious problems. The 4th Panzer Group was torn apart. The 1st and 6th Panzer Divisions had to move against Leningrad and were stopped shortly before entering the city; the 8th Panzer Division fought its way laboriously along the Volkov, the most impassable district of northern Russia, where even horse-drawn wagons got stuck.

Nothing remained of the slogan "Clobber — don't slobber!"

But Generaloberst Guderian's slogan was no longer known in the overall planning of the further phases of the campaign either. The situation at the front in the central and southern sectors proved to be such that the Army Group Center was far to the east, while the Army Group South was some distance back. Then Hitler decided to call off the attack on Moscow and attack Kiev instead. The Panzer divisions were ordered into battle again.

When autumn came and brought rain, the Russian soil became a mud puddle. It was only possible to drive on hard-packed forest roads and paved highways. Here a P-III is stuck in the mud.

Tank Situation on the Eastern Front on 9/4/1941*)

	Pz.Verband	ein- satz- bereit	in Instand- setzung	Total- ver- luste	Summe
Panzergruppe 1	9. Pz.Div.	62	67	28	157
	13. Pz.Div.	96	30	21	147
	14. Pz.Div.	112	24	27	163
	16. Pz.Div.	61	26	70	157
	Summe Pz.Gr. 1	331	147	146	624
	(in %)	(53)	(24)	(23)	(100)
von Pz.Gr. 1 z. Zt. dem AOK 6 unterstellt:	11. Pz.Div.	60	75	40	175
Panzergruppe 2	3. Pz.Div.	41	157		198
	4. Pz.Div.	49	120		169
	17. Pz.Div.	38	142		180
	18. Pz.Div.	62	138		200
	Summe Pz.Gr. 2	190	557		747
	(in %)	(25)	(75)		(100)
von Pz.Gr. 2 z. Zt. dem AOK 4 unterstellt:	10. Pz.Div.	159	22	25	206
Panzergruppe 3	7. Pz.Div.	130	87	82	299
	19. Pz.Div.	102	47	90	239
	20. Pz.Div.	88	62	95	245
	Summe Pz.Gr. 3	320	196	267	783
	(in %)	(41)	(25)	(34)	(100)
Panzergruppe 4	1. Pz.Div.	97	24	33	154
	6. Pz.Div.	188	11	55	254
	8. Pz.Div.	155	33	35	223
	Summe Pz.Gr. 4	440	68	123	631
	(in %)	(70)	(11)	(19)	(100)
von Pz.Gr. 4 z. Zt. dem AOK 16 unterstellt:	12. Pz.Div.	96	34	101	231
Summe Ostfront (17 Panzerdivisionen):		1586	542	702	3397
			+ 557		
	(in %)	(47)	(ca. 23)	(ca. 30)	(100)

Note: The 2nd and 5th Panzer Divisions were still OKH reserves at that time. They are not included.

*) According to OKH Genstb.d.H./Org.Abt. No. 702/41, secret command information of 9/15/1941.

The Commander Gef.St. 9/23/41
of Panzer Group 2

Group Daily Order
Soldiers of Panzer Group 2!

On August 25 you moved southward to attack and defeat the enemy located on the Dniepr. In hard fighting, the enemy's front was penetrated, the waters of the Dyesna and the Sseym overcome and, on September 13, the ring around the enemy east of Kiev was completed by uniting with a Panzer group advancing from the south. All of the enemy's attempts to break out and get free were turned back. Captured at this time were:

86,000 prisoners,
220 tanks,
850 guns.

The Commander of the Russian 5th Army fell into our hands. The entire Russian south front is thereby shattered and the way opened to new, decisive moves.

In these weeks you have done your duty to the fullest again and taken all tasks upon yourselves, although you could not be granted any pause for rest since June 22.

With your often-proved fighting and attacking spirit, you have won yourselves new fame. I thank you for it.

Now it is time once again in this eventful war year to use all your powers to attain the goal of this campaign in one mighty effort. I know that I can depend on you and that we shall fulfill the commands of our Führer.

I take this opportunity, as I am about to depart from the group's area after three months of being your comrade-in-arms, to express my particular admiration and extend to you my very best wishes for your future.

Hail Germany and hail our Führer Adolf Hitler!

Guderian

Guderian

Panzer Group Guderian moved in from north to south with (from left to right) the 17th, 18th, 3rd and 4th Panzer Divisions, and Panzer Group 1 of Generaloberst von Kleist came toward them from the Krementshug bridgehead to the south with (from right to left) the 14th, 16th and 9th Panzer Divisions. On September 14, parts of the 6th Panzer Regiment from the north and the 16th Panzer Division from the south met near Lubny and closed the circle around the Soviet Southwest Front Army Group. The battle for Kiev ended as of September 20, 1941.

The Red Army's losses were enormous. But German tank losses since this campaign began were also higher than expected. The numbers of tanks in the individual Panzer groups at the end of the battle of Kiev were as follows:

Status at end of September	Replaced by mid-October
1st Panzer Group 53%	to 74%
2nd Panzer Group25%	to 50%
3rd Panzer Group 41%	to 73%
4th Panzer Group 70%	to 100%

The losses were modest in proportion to the success, since it had been possible to shatter the Soviet front and win free space to the east. Since there were practically no tanks in reserve when the campaign began, replacements for each Panzer regiment were limited to at most 15 tanks per month. Repairing damaged tanks caused great problems. The tanks that could not be repaired by the maintenance companies of the regiments themselves had to be towed back along the long and often scarcely passable roads by towing vehicles, which in turn cost time and caused new breakdowns. Despite that, 95% of the damage could be repaired at or behind the front, and only 5% had to be sent back to Germany for repairs. The total loss of German tanks from June 22 to November 30, 1941 added up to 2251 tanks; the new production during this time amounted to 1813 tanks.

When the battle around Kiev ended, the Panzer divisions were transferred from the front to be prepared for the attack on Moscow — "Operation Typhoon." Panzer Group Commands 1 to 3 were renamed Panzer *Armeeoberkommandos* on October 5, 1941. The renaming of Panzer Group Command 4 took place only on December 31, 1941. At the beginning of October the OKH ordered the establishment of the 22nd to 24th Panzer Divisions. The last division was formed from what had been the only cavalry division in the army, since closed cavalry units were of no further use in the eastern theater of war.

Panzer Group 1 (Generaloberst von Kleist) remained in the southern sector of the front and advanced from the Dniepr into the vast Ukrainian plains to the industrial area around Donetz and to Rostov before the winter began. Panzer Group 2 (Generaloberst Guderian) had made a 180-degree turn from the battlefield at Kiev and stood ready east of the Dessna and west of Ssevsk. In mid-September its divisions still had 347 tanks. Panzer Group 3 (Generaloberst Hoth) moved northeast from Smolensk to its point of departure with 320 tanks. Panzer Group Command 4 (Generaloberst Hoepner) had left the northern sector and was sent to the front between the 2nd and 4th Armies.

Panzer Group 4 was supposed to form the focal point of the offensive against Moscow and included the 1st, 6th, 19th and 20th Panzer Divisions as well as the 5th Panzer Division that had been transferred from the Balkans, though it really was supposed to have been sent to the North African theater of war and appeared for

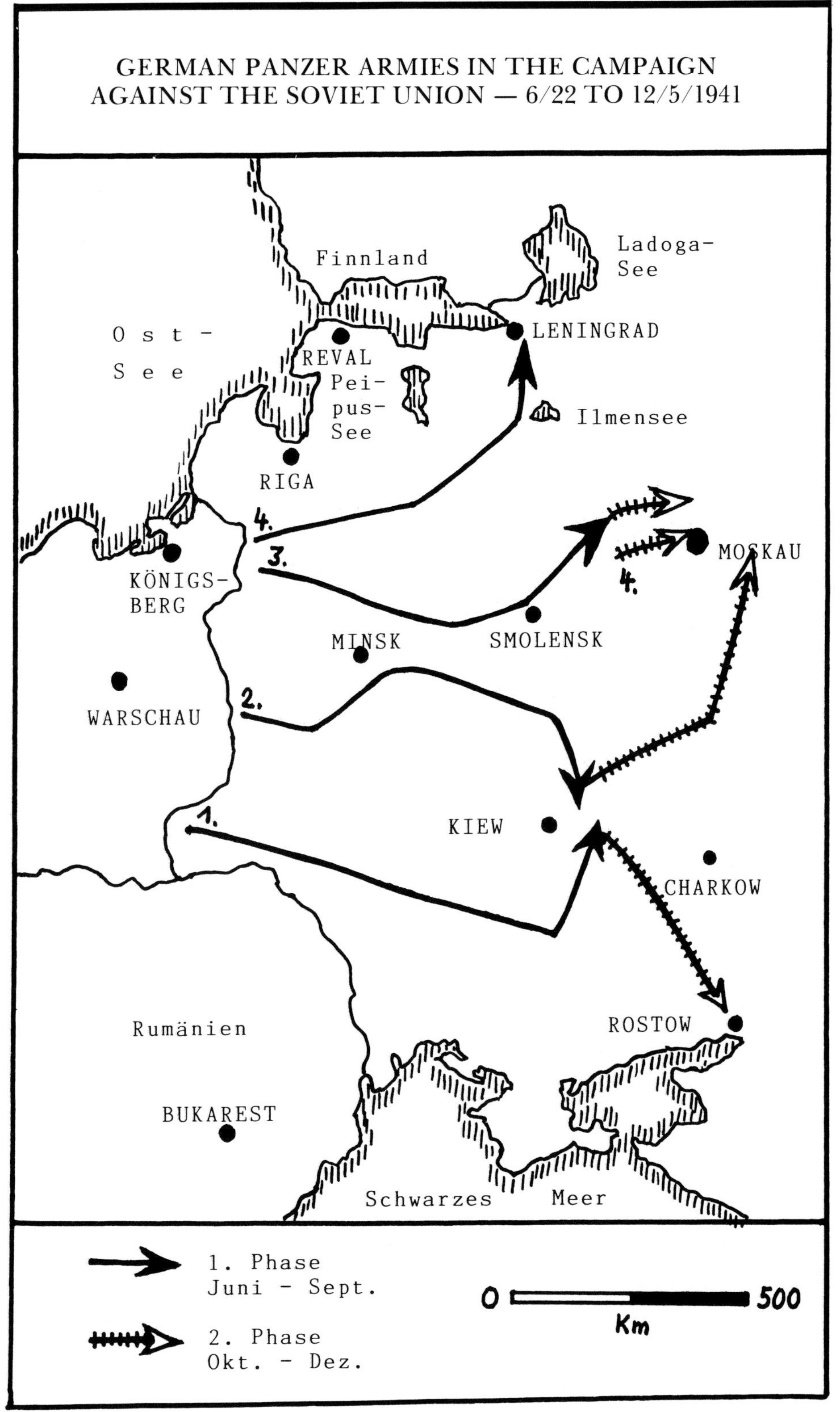
GERMAN PANZER ARMIES IN THE CAMPAIGN
AGAINST THE SOVIET UNION — 6/22 TO 12/5/1941
Finnland
Ladoga-
See
Ost-
See
LENINGRAD
REVAL
Pei-
pus-
See
Ilmensee
RIGA
4.
3.
4.
MOSKAU
KÖNIGS-
BERG
MINSK
SMOLENSK
WARSCHAU
2.
1.
KIEW
CHARKOW
Rumänien
ROSTOW
BUKAREST
Schwarzes Meer
1. Phase
Juni - Sept.
2. Phase
Okt. - Dez.
0
500
Km

Russian winter action in tropical (yellow) camouflage. The 8th and 12th Panzer Divisions of the Panzer Group were left in the northern sector and later had to withstand the storming of Tichvin in the cold of winter, under unbelievable weather and transit conditions.

"Operation Typhoon" began for the 2nd Panzer Army on September 30 and for the other attacking troops on October 2, 1941. To be sure, the Panzer troops were able to encircle the Soviet troops at Vyasma and Briansk by October 8, but as they continued to advance on Moscow, a new enemy entered the field: mud.

It was the night of October 8 when the rain set in. A report on the fighting near Moscow stated:

> "The vehicles of the Panzer divisions tried to move forward through the deep mud of the suddenly disappeared roads.
>
> But what the sticky ground had once seized, it did not release. Tanks and trucks, motorcycles and wagons and even people sank into the mud. . . . Every movement led no longer forward, but only deeper into the dirt and mud."

Only when, just four weeks later, the winter finally set in with temperatures well below zero and the ground became as hard as stone, could progress be made. In three days the temperature sank to 18 degrees below zero, and to 24 below in another three days. The motors of the vehicles and the moving parts of the guns froze.

The Command of Army Group Center ordered the last attack on Moscow on October 30. The Chief of the General Staff in the OKH wrote in his diary on that day:

> "The attack is a better solution that wintering in the wilderness. . . ."

Once again the hungry, dirty, vermin-infested and freezing German soldiers attacked. The 6th Panzer Division formed a bridgehead over the Lama, the 2nd Panzer Division turned toward Volkolamsk, the 5th Panzer Division was south of Novopetrovskoya, and to the south of them the last tanks of the 18th Panzer Division moved against Yefremov and those of the 3rd and 4th Panzer Divisions against Tula.

Only with difficulty could the German Panzer regiments fight their way through deep snow toward Moscow in the biting cold.

The 2nd Panzer Division had advanced farther than any other Panzer division; in the last week of November it was only 50 kilometers from Moscow, where it met new Soviet tank regiments which had been established recently and equipped with British "Mark III" tanks. At the same time — at thirty below zero — the 5th and 10th Panzer Divisions stormed past the Istra Reservoir. The 25th Panzer Regiment (7th Panzer Division) seized the Moscow electric works at Yakroma. A few days later the two units of the 3rd Panzer Regiment (2nd Panzer Division) won Babaika and Katyuski, the terminal stations of the Moscow city railway — just 27 kilometers from the Kremlin!

Five days later the great attack of the Red Army on the Army Group Central began. Generaloberst Guderian wrote:

"Our attack on Moscow was broken. All sacrifices and all
efforts of the brave troops were in vain. . . ."

Then on December 5, 1941, in bitter cold and drifting snow, the Soviet counteroffensive began. Shortly before that, the commanders of the 2nd and 4th Panzer Groups (Generaloberste Guderian and Hoepner) had given their troops the command to retreat, and were promptly relieved of their positions by Hitler. The ensuing retreat from Moscow cost the German eastern army tremendous losses of men and materials. The situation settled down only after four weeks. Now the main German battle line ran (from right to left) more or less from east of Kursk in the south past Mzensk on the east, then curved far to the west around Suchinitski, then formed a semicircular arc back to the east and north, stopped just short of Rshev, and south of Lake Sselig the connections with the nearby Army Group North were broken.

The loss of tanks from the beginning of the eastern campaign to December 31, 1941 added up to:

P-I 428
P-II 424
P-38(t) 796
P-III 660
P-IV 348
Pz.Bef.Wg. 79
Pz.Fu.Wg. 18

Of these, those lost in the last week of December alone were:
16 P-II, 21 P-III and 4 Pz.Bef.Wagen.

The heavy losses led to another regrouping of the Panzer troops, as the OKW had already begun to prepare for the 1942 summer offensive. After the winter and the ensuing spring mud were gone, the 6th, 10th and 11th Panzer Divisions were transferred to France as of April 1942, where they were to be refreshed. These divisions left all their tanks, heavy guns and equipment behind, as it was urgently needed by the Panzer divisions remaining at the front.

The Panzer regiments of the divisions at the front could thus be restored in part to three units, whose composition now consisted of two light companies and one medium. In addition, the formation of army Panzer units was continued; they were given numbers beginning with 100 and equipped with heavy tanks, including as of 1943 the first P-V ("Panther") tanks. The Panzer unit *Grossdeutschland* was also founded by renaming the 1./Panzer Regiment 100; this unit, only at company

The Course of a Panzer Division in the Eastern Campaign
(Center and South Sectors)

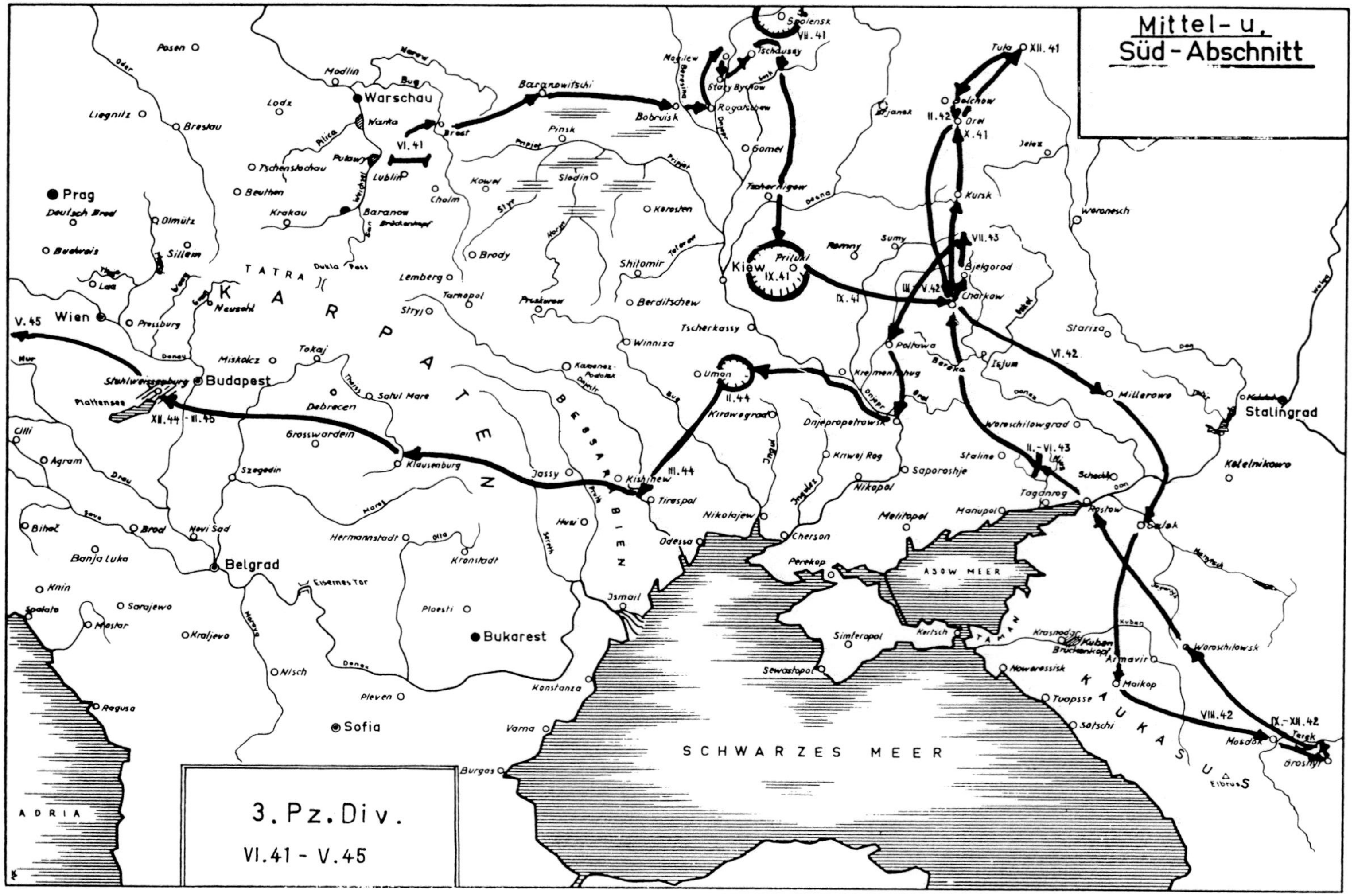

Mittel- u. Süd-Abschnitt

3. Pz. Div.
VI.41 - V.45

strength, was expanded to three companies on March 1, 1943 and called the I./Panzer Regiment *Grossdeutschland.*

In February the OKH also ordered the formation of a 25th Panzer Division in southern Norway, originally formed of the formerly independent Pz.Abt.40 plus replacement troops and only having one tank unit.

In the summer of 1942 the German leadership decided to unite all available tanks for a major offensive in the southern sector under the jurisdiction of the Army Group Center. The goal of the new offensive was to destroy the enemy between the Donets and the Don and then, after securing their rear and flanks along the Don, to capture the oil fields in the Caucasian area and the routes through the Caucasus. To prepare for this major offensive, the German 11th Army, with the 22nd Panzer Division as its only Panzer division, mopped up the tense situation in the Crimea, which only ended with the capture of Sevastopol in early July.

Two P-III tanks of the 22nd Panzer Division have taken up a position at the harbor of Sevastopol on July 4, 1942.

In addition, the deep Soviet breakthrough near Kharkov had to be smashed. On May 17, in blistering hot weather, the 6th and 17th Armies and 1st Panzer Army advanced for this purpose. The 3rd, 14th, 16th and 23rd Panzer Divisions, the last just arrived at the front, took part splendidly in this battle, which ended in a total victory for the German tanks.

The summer offensive — "Operation Blue" — was carried out by the two newly-formed Army Groups A and B, to which the 1st and 4th Panzer Armies were subordinated for the purpose.

The German attack began on June 28, 1942 from the Kursk area in the direction of Voronesh. The 9th Panzer Division (left) and 24th Panzer Division (right) of the 4th Panzer Army were present; two days later the 6th Army, with the 3rd and 23rd Panzer Divisions, followed from the Voltshansk area. Voronesh and Rossosh were reached on the 3rd and 6th of July respectively — but the Soviets had escaped over the Don.

Both photos were taken on June 1, 1942 and show P-III tanks advancing toward the Don.

Then Hitler decided to turn the 4th Panzer Army to the south and have it attack the Caucasus along with the 1st Panzer Army and the 17th Army. At first the 3rd, 13th and 23rd Panzer Divisions were present. The 3rd Panzer Division reached the Mayntsh on July 29, and after the river was crossed, German tanks were on Asian soil! Just a few days later the 4th Panzer Army (Generaloberst Hoth) had to turn around and move against Stalingrad from the south. When the 24th Panzer Division (from the south) and the 16th Panzer Division (from the north) met at Kalatsh on August 8, Russian forces were surrounded. The advance groups, including tanks of the 2nd Panzer Regiment, were in Rynok on the highlands of the Volga on August 23 — and to their right the men saw the skyline of Stalingrad.

The 1st Panzer Army (Generaloberst von Kleist) had meanwhile pushed forward across the Mayntsh and the Kuma. The tanks stormed southward until they ran out of fuel. The old Czarist spas of Piatigorsk and Mineralny Vody were behind them — and they went on farther.

The 5./6th Panzer Regiment advancing to the Caucasus. It is July 10, 1942. The turret of the P-IV with the short gun is easy to recognize.

The lead tank of an advance unit of the 13th Panzer Division reaches the Laba, a tributary of the Kuban, not far from Maikop on August 15, 1942.

The P-IV tanks of the 3rd Panzer Division roll toward the Caucasus. Midsummer heat prevailed in August of 1942.

> "The II./6th Panzer Regiment is moving across country with its tanks, through the fruitful country with the rolling fields and green meadows." Thus it is written in the history of the 3rd Panzer Division. "There are scarcely any paths or roads going off from our course, so that we navigate only by the compass. The German soldiers can see the snow-capped mountains of the Causasus on the horizon already, far in the distance."

As early as August 8, 5633-meter Mount Elbrus, the highest mountain of the Caucasus, could be seen. The 13th Panzer Division was advancing southward via Maikop, while the 3rd and 23rd Panzer Divisions turned off to Terek. Here the advance came to a stop at the beginning of September.
The homeland was 3000 kilometers away!

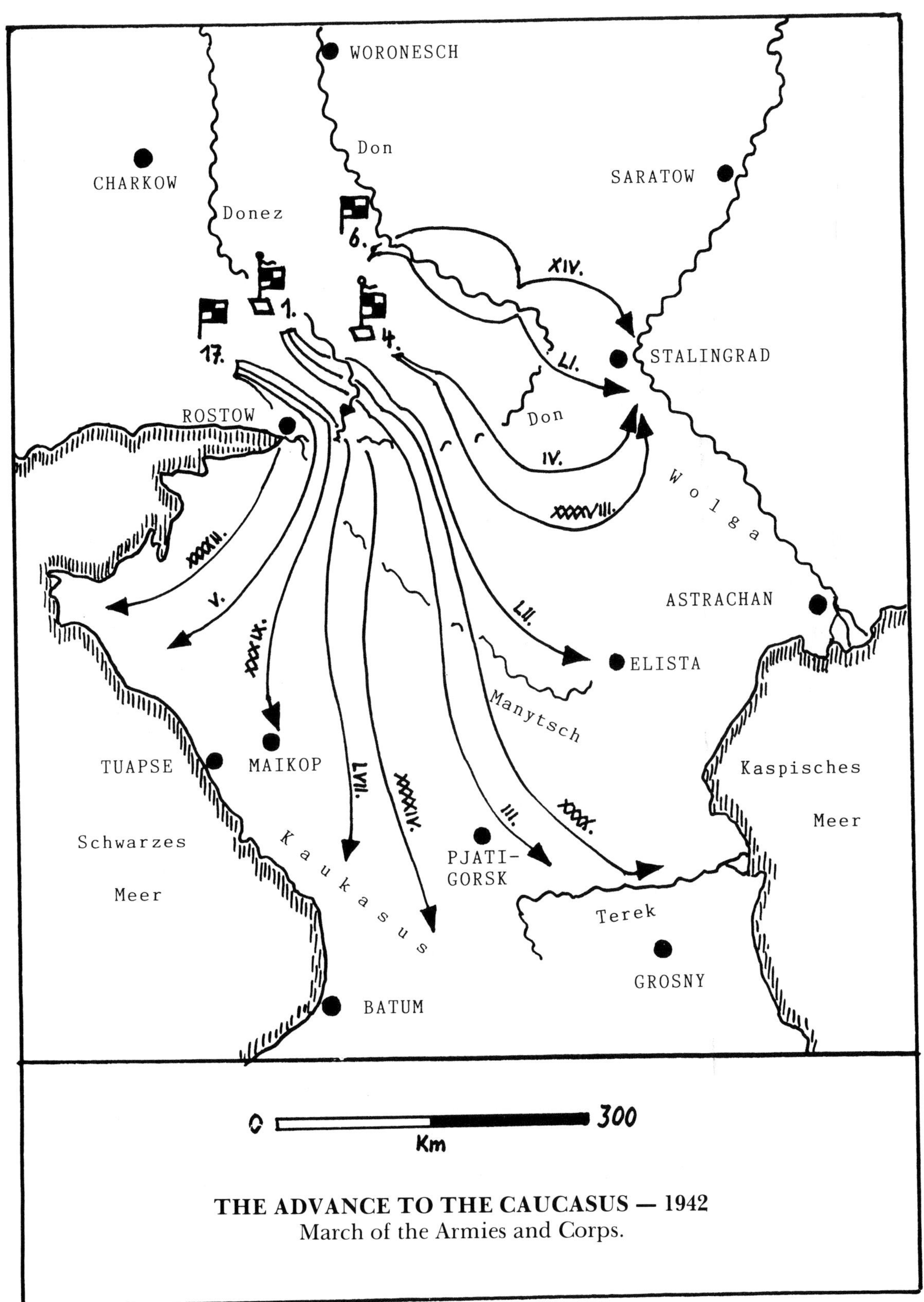

THE ADVANCE TO THE CAUCASUS — 1942
March of the Armies and Corps.

Meanwhile the battle raged in and around Stalingrad. The tanks of the 14th Panzer Division saw action at the "Dsershinski" industrial works, among other places, the tanks of the 24th Panzer Division fought at the main railway station, and the men of the 16th Panzer Division were at the north edge of town until . . . yes, until November 19, when the Soviet major attack on both sides of Stalingrad began.

On this day the following tanks were present at Stalingrad:

Panzer Division	with P-IIP-III	P-IV tank types
14th	3	2
16th	17	11
24th	36	17
3rd ID (mot.)	22	7
60th ID (mot.)5	17	5

Pz.Abt.103 was with the 3rd ID (mot.), Pz.Abt.160 with the 60th ID (mot.).

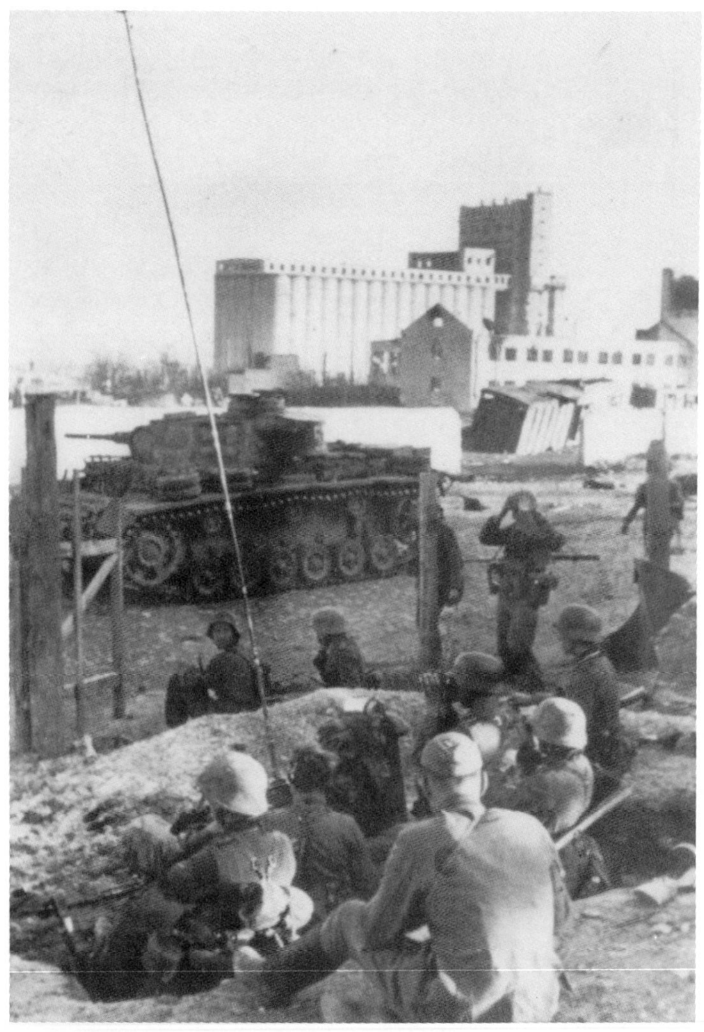

Panzer-grenadiers and P-III tanks take up positions in the industrial area of Stalingrad on October 5, 1942.

In mid-November ten Soviet tank brigades, eleven independent tank regiments and one independent tank unit attacked the weakened German troops.

The 4th Panzer Army was ordered to move toward Stalingrad from the south to free the surrounded 6th Army. The 6th, 17th and 23rd Panzer Divisions were present and pushed forward to the north as far as Vassiliyevka under the worst conditions — driving show, cold, lack of fuel — and never reached Stalingrad!

The battle of Stalingrad ended early in February of 1943. The history of the 14th Panzer Division stated, among other things:

> "Here too, in the very last pocket, which only measured 100 meters across, . . . the Russian thrust could no longer be stopped. To be sure, the forces that were still at the front consisted of the burned-out remains of the division. There were absolutely no veteran infantrymen left. The equipment consisted only of rifles and machine guns; in some positions there were antitank guns — but without ammunition. . . ."

The German tank development also suffered in 1942 from the irrational concepts of the highest military and economic officials. As early as the spring of 1942, Hitler refused to increase tank production. Only in July did he suddenly insist on the production of 1450 tanks, assault guns and self-propelled guns per month.

The new "Tigers" wait for transport to the front. The tanks are painted in camouflage colors, and the muzzle brakes on the barrels are still "packed up."

Nummer 82 | FRONTZEITUNG EINER PANZERGRUPPE | Sonntag, 19. Oktober 1941

Sowjets dem Untergang geweiht

Einleitungsschlacht von Moskau verloren - Nur noch fragwür...
quellen - England will Sowjetunion vom F...

Die Blicke der Welt richten sich ... gegenwärtig auf das ... Moskau ...

Der Sieg der Rumänen

Von Hauptmann Werner Stephan

Die Einnahme von Od... Sieg der ...

... teren Widerstand dort in keiner Weise vom unablässigen Vorderingen nach Osten hin abhalten liess, da versuchten die Bolschewisten mit Ausfällen aus ihren Feldbefestigungen eine Aenderung der deutschen Taktik herbeizuführen. Aber alles blieb vergeblich. Trotzdem noch am 10. Oktober der englische Nachrichtendienst „Exchange Telegraph" behauptete, der Erfolg der sowjetischen Angriffe auf die Rumänen scheine festzustehen, wurde die Lage in der Stadt immer schwieriger.

In diesen zwei Monaten den eisernen ...ing um Odessa geschmiedet und so ...en deutschen Vormarsch zum Asow...hen Meer ermöglicht zu haben, ist ...s unvergängliche Verdienst der ru...nischen Armee unter der Führung ...es verdienten Marschalls Antonescu. ...r hat sie gezeigt, dass sie auch ...ksten Sowjetverbänden als über...ner Gegner entgegenzutreten ver... War schon die Befreiung der Bu...na und Bessarabiens ein Erfolg, ... in erster Linie den tapferen ru...schen Soldaten zuzuschreiben ist, ...haben unsere Verbündeten ...m ...fe um den grössten und wichtig... Schwarzmeerhafen bewiesen, was

Nummer 17 | Sonnabend, 19. Juli 1941

PANZERFAUST

Feldzeitung für die Soldaten einer Panzergruppe – Herausgegeben von der Feldeinheit 10792

Gewaltige Kampfhandlungen zu unseren Gunsten

Krisenzeichen in Sowjetrussland: Die Armee wurde erneut dem Terror der GPU. ausgeliefert

Das Eichenlaub für Generaloberst Hoth

Aus dem Führerhauptquartier, 17. Juli.

Der Führer und Oberste Befehlshaber der Wehrmacht verlieh heute für ihren heldenmütigen Einsatz im Ostfeldzug folgenden Offizieren des Heeres und der Luftwaffe das Eichenlaub zum Ritterkreuz des Eisernen Kreuzes:

dem Befehlshaber einer Panzergruppe, Generaloberst G u d e r i a n,

dem Befehlshaber einer Panzergruppe, Generaloberst H o t h,

dem Kommandierenden General eines Fliegerkorps, General der Flieger Freiherr v o n R i c h t h o f e n.

Die tapferen Befehlshaber erhielten die Mitteilung über die erfolgte Verleihung durch ein persönliches Telegramm auf ihre Gefechtsstände.

Verzweiflungsschritt des Obersten Sowjets

Berlin, 17. Juli.

Der Zusammenbruch der sowjetischen Angriffspläne zwingt Stalin zu einer Verzweiflungsmassnahme. Durch ein vom Obersten Rat ... Sowjetunion beschlossenes De... wird die Institution der Kriegsk... missare wieder eingeführt und ... gesamte Wehrmacht damit dem ... rorregime der GPU ausgeliefert ...

Stalin versucht durch diese ... richtung alle Verantwortung f... Niederlagen der bolschewisti... Heereshaufen auf die Tr... führung abzuwälzen. Er ste... Sachlage so hin, als sei es de... zieren nicht gelungen, Diszipl... Einsatzfreudigkeit aufrechtz...

... alle Regiments-, Divisions-, Verwaltungs- und Behördenbefehle von dem Kommandeur und dem Kriegskommissar gemeinsam zu unterzeichnen sind. ... jedem

Der ertappte Churchill

Churchill bei einem Essen in Aldwych Club am 11. 4. 1919.

Wir können mit den Bolschewisten keine Verträge schliessen. Wir haben zu unterscheiden zwischen Recht und Unrecht, zwischen Ehre und Verrat, zwischen Fortschritt und Anarchie. (*Daily Chronicle 12. 4. 1910*).

... Churchill im Unterhaus am 30. 5.

Nr. 18 | Nachrichtenblatt einer rhein.-westf. Panzer-Division | November 1944

Im Trommelfeuer

Die Kämpfe in der Narewschleife vom 5. bis 22. Oktober

Am 5. Oktober um 10 Uhr, fünf Wochen nach den ersten Kämpfen bei Napiorki, beginnt der zweite Großangriff der S...ts. Fünfviertelstunden Trommelfeuer aus Hunderten von Rohren und Salvengeschützen, laufende Schlachtfliegerangriffe auf die vordere Linie, die Sehnenstellung und die Stellungen der schweren Waffen leiten ihn ein. Das Trommelfeuer wühlt die Gräben um. Zwischen den Einschlägen springen die Bolschewisten vor, werden von dem Feuer ihrer eigenen Salvengeschütze erfaßt, haben große Ausfälle, brechen aber überraschend ein.

Beim Feindeinbruch in Napiorki fällt H a u p t m a n n R i c h t e r. Er war

bis zum letzten Atemzug das Vorbild seiner Männer

Unter dem Schutze zahlreicher Baum-... Wäldchen zurück. Auch er bleibt vor dem Feinde. Oberleutnant G u t t e r m a n n, kriegsbeschädigt, mit steifem Bein, bringt hoch zu Roß die Reserven nach vorn, bleibt wegen seines Beines auch bei den Einschlägen der ... versucht, die beiderseits der Einbruchsstelle stehenden Bataillone III./Stahl und II./Quentin einzudrücken. Am frühen Nachmittag greift ein Infanterie-Rgt. von Westen und die Panther-Abteilung von Wietersheim von Norden nochmal Napiorki an. Das Infanterie-Regiment dringt in der Nacht in Napiorki ein, muß aber einem starken feindlichen Gegenangriff wieder weichen. Napiorki bleibt gegen übermächtigen Feind verloren. Wir setzen uns in der neuen Linie fest, graben uns ein, verminen das Gelände und erwarten den Gegner. Den ganzen Tag über trommeln Granatwerfer, Artillerie und Salvengeschütze, hämmern ungezählte feindliche Schlachtflieger; aber der Feind kommt nicht mehr voran.

Am 10. Oktober um 10 Uhr beginnt ein eineinhalbstundenlanges Trommelfeuer auf die ganze Divisionsfront.

Field Newspapers of German Panzer Units

In the whole production year of 1942, a total of 9300 tanks were manufactured, most of them P-IV, which were delivered to the troops as of April with long gun barrels. The production of P-IV tanks since 1942 took place chiefly at the Steyr works in St. Valentin, Vomag in Prague and the Bohemian-Moravian Machine Factory (formerly Praga) in Prague. At the same time, production of the new P-VI ("Tiger") proceeded.

The manufacture of such a tank had been urged as early as May of 1941, and German industry was able to present two prototypes by Porsche and Henschel on April 20, 1942. Hitler insisted on producing both types, although the Porsche tank showed considerable weaknesses when it was introduced. The Henschel firm turned out the first "Tigers" in August of 1942 and had already built 83 of the tanks by the end of the year.

The first use of the "Tiger" at the front took place in September of 1942 in a sector of the front near Leningrad. The *Panzerabteilungen* 500 to 510, newly formed in 1942, were equipped with the P-VI ("Tiger"). Pz.Abt.502 and 503 moved southeastward from Leningrad to their first service at the front. The heavy tanks sank into the mud and morass and stayed there.

The first "Tiger" lost to enemy fire was lost in January of 1943 at Rabochii-Posselok 5, outside Leningrad.

The "Tiger I" featured boxed running gear without return rollers, had vertical walls and a cylindrical turret. It was a heavily armored vehicle with an 88mm KwK 36 L/56 gun and a machine gun. Its disadvantages were its impractical shape, the technical weaknesses of its drive system and its limited mobility, especially in limited-visibility and swampy terrain.

In the autumn of 1942 the OKH established heavy tank units that were equipped with the "Tiger." These units remained army troops and were not subordinated to any division. They were:

s.Pz.Abt.500-504	from Military District VI (Münster)
s.Pz.Abt.505	from the 5th Panzer Division
s.Pz.Abt.506	from the III./33rd Panzer Regiment
s.Pz.Abt.507	from the I./4th Panzer Regiment
s.Pz.Abt.508	from the III./4th Panzer Regiment
s.Pz.Abt.509	from 36th Panzer Regiment
s.Pz.Abt.510	from what remained of the 14th Panzer Division

The "Tiger" units 501 and 504 were immediately sent to Tunis, where they could take part in only the last battles of the Army Group Africa. The others all went to the eastern front and remained independent units; only Pz.Abt.509 was subordinated to the *Führer-Begleit-Division* at the end of 1944.

From a textbook for officers' orderlies.

School for Fhj. of the Panzer Troops
Abt. Ia

Only for official use
within the school

Guidelines for Cooperation Between Tanks and Panzer-grenadiers

STRUCTURE:

A. General
1. Relation of the weapons to each other
2. Training and education
3. Strengths and weaknesses of the sister weapons

B. Tank combat with disembarked armored grenadiers
1. Attack
   a) wrong — right
   b) Means of communication
   c) Unified action against known pockets of resistance
   d) Tanks to the fore
   e) Armored grenadiers to the fore
   f) United action of tanks and armored grenadiers
2. Defense
3. Combat under special conditions

C. Unified combat of tanks and SPW.
1. Attack
2. Pursuit
3. Grenadiers on unarmored vehicles
4. Questions of leadership

A. General:

1. The Panzer division is a closed combat entity. Its main task is to attack with low-level aim against the enemy's weak points, thus not an ordinary attack on an enemy ready to defend itself, but an operative, battle-deciding attack on the enemy's flanks and rear. The breakthrough of Panzer units through an enemy position can precede the aforementioned task.

The OKH established a 27th Panzer Division at the end of 1942, when the Stalingrad debacle became clear. It was composed of the former 22nd Panzer Division, which was disbanded, and army troops.

The heavy Panzer units that were shipped to Tunisia arrived just in time to take part in the final battle in North Africa. Here the Panzer Armee Oberkommando *Afrika*, as it had been renamed on January 22, 1942, was doing battle with the 1942 spring offensive with the 15th and 21st Panzer Divisions and the 90th Light Division and advance to the Egyptian border again in July.

The *Afrika Korps* launched a second offensive in Cyrenaica in January of 1942. The P-III tanks of the 15th Panzer Division are opening the battle.

The columns of the 21st Panzer Division on the march toward the Egyptian border. The first two tanks are Type P-III, the next two P-II.

Tobruk is reached. While the infantry digs itself in, the tanks roll forward — toward the fortress.

But in September of 1942 the Allies struck back. The Panzer Armee *Afrika*, now strengthened by the 164th ID and the Ramcke Paratroop Brigade, had to fight its way back to Cyrenaica, sustaining heavy losses. After US troops landed in Morocco and advanced to Tunis, the OKH transferred the 10th Panzer Division to Tunisia. The German command was renamed the Oberkommando of the 5th Panzer Armee on December 8, 1942. But the war in North Africa ended early in May of 1943 — the 10th, 15th and 21st Panzer Divisions no longer existed!

FIELD POST NUMBERS
of the two Panzer regiments of the 21st Panzer Division in North Africa.

Einheiten	FPN	+ = ab − = bis
Pz.Rgt.5		
Rgts.Stab	17 960	− 5.43
Stab I	28 770	− 4.43
1.Kp.	01 793	− 8.43
2.Kp.	13 237	− 8.43
3.Kp.	18 786	− 5.43
4.Kp.	19 233	− 5.43
Stab II	**15 815**	**− 8.43**
5.Kp.	02 292	− 8.43
6.Kp.	17 853	− 5.43
7.Kp.	19 158	− 5.43
8.Kp.	02 365	− 9.43
Werkst.Kp.	24 734	− 8.43
Pz.Rgt.100		
Rgts.Stab	17 697	+ 3.42
	13 301	12.42-2.43
Stab I	17 687	+5.42
Stabs Kp.I	17 687S	+5.42
Fla.Zug	17 687F	+7.44
1.Kp.	02 741	
2.Kp.	05 078	
3.Kp.	18 346	−8.43
	56 592	−11.43
Stab II	03 386	+ 9.42
Stabs Kp.II	03 386S	
5.Kp.	36 634	−11.43
	56 592	+11.43
6.Kp.	07 696	+ 7.42
7.Kp.	15 103	11.42- 2.44
	58 366	
8.Kp.	15 103	
Werkst.Kp.	06 111	+ 7.42

New formations were made in the autumn for the Panzer regiments lost in Tunisia. Some examples:

Pz.Abt.5	in place of the former 5th Panzer Regiment (21st Panzer Division), formed at Neuruppin in September 1943 with three companies and subordinate to the 25th Panzer-Grenadier Division. Lost in the central sector of the eastern front in July 1944.
Pz.Abt.7	in place of the former 7th Panzer Regiment (10th Panzer Division), formed in France in October 1943 with three companies and subordinate to the 10th Panzer-Grenadier Division. Lost in Bessarabia in August 1944.
Pz.Abt.8	in place of the former 8th Panzer Regiment (15th Panzer Division), founded in France in October 1943 with three companies and subordinate to the 20th Panzer-Grenadier Division. Lost in Silesia in April-May 1945.

After the defeats in Stalingrad and Tunisia, the Panzer corps were regrouped. Generaloberst Guderian, who was removed by Hitler after the battle of Moscow, was commanded on February 20, 1943 to report to the Führer's headquarters at Vinniza, in the Ukraine. Here Hitler appointed him, effective February 28, to be Inspector General of the Panzer Troops. Thus he not only received extensive powers but was now independent to make decisions, answerable only to Hitler. The staff to be appointed represented the following departments: Organization, training, personnel, development, and the higher officers for motor vehicles, armored artillery and antitank gunnery.
The Inspector General's staff was composed of:

Chief of Staff:	Oberst i.G. Thomale
Staff Officers:	Oberstleutnant i.G. Freyer, Major i.G. Kauffmann, Major i.G. Baron von Wöllwarth
Adjutant:	Oberstleutnant Prince of Waldeck
School Commander:	Generalmajor von Hauenschild

With the establishment of an Inspector General of the Panzer Troops the units formerly classified as *Schnelle Truppen* (mobile troops) were now designated *Panzertruppen*. The mounted and motorcycle units formerly included among them were now transferred to the infantry.

Effective April 1, 1943 the office of the General of the *Schnelle Truppen* in the OKH was abolished. In its place there was now a "Panzer Officer to the Chief of the General Staff." This office was abolished after July 20, 1944. The responsible officer's job was to provide the departments of the General Staff with necessary documentation and information on tanks. At the same time, the Inspector of the Mobile Troops in the Replacement Army was given the new title of Inspector of the Panzer Troops. He was no longer subordinate to the Commander of the Replacement Army, but directly to the Inspector General of the Panzer troops.

Generaloberst Guderian, Inspector General of the Panzer Troops, creator of this type of weapon.

PANZERLIED

1) Ob's stürmt – oder schneit – ob die
Sonne uns lacht, der Tag glühend heiß –
oder stürmisch die Nacht, bestaubt sind
die Gesichter – doch froh ist unser Sinn –
ja unser Sinn – es braust unser Panzer im
Sturmwind dahin –
bestaubt . . .

2) Mit donnerndem Motor so schnell wie der
Blitz – dem Feinde entgegen im
Panzergeschütz – Voraus den Kameraden
im Kampfe ganz allein – ja ganz allein –
so stoßen wir tief in die feindlichen
Reihen –
Voraus . . .

3) Mit Sperren und Pak's hält der Gegner
uns auf – wir lachen darüber und fahren
nicht drauf – und schüttelt er auch
grimmig und wütend seine Hand – ja
seine Hand – wir suchen uns Wege die
keiner sonst fand.
Und . . .

4) Wenn vor uns ein feindlicher Panzer
erscheint – dann Vollgas gegeben und
rann an den Feind – Was nützt unser
Leben für unseres Volkes Wehr – ja
Volkes Wehr – für's Vaterland zu sterben
ist unsere höchste Ehr.
Was . . .

5) Und läßt uns im Stich einst das treulose
Glück – und kehren wir nie mehr zur
Heimat zurück – trifft uns die Todeskugel
ruft uns das Schicksal ab – ja Schicksal
ab – dann wird unser Panzer ein ehernes
Grab.
Trifft . . .

THE PANZER SONG

In storm or in snow, or when the sun shines,
the day glowing hot, or stormy the night,
our faces are dusty, but our spirits are high, our spirits
high, then our tanks are rolling into the storm;
our faces are dusty . . .

With thundering motors, they move lightning-fast,
we roll toward the enemy, as tank guns fire;
ahead of our comrades, in the battle alone, yes, all alone,
we penetrate deep in the enemy lines;
ahead of our comrades . . .

With tank traps and guns, the enemy hinders us,
we laugh at it all and don't drive into traps;
and even if he grimly, furiously shakes his fist, and shakes
his fist, we find ourselves routes that nobody else found;
and even if . . .

When an enemy tank appears before us,
then we step on the gas and run straight at the foe,
what matters our life in our people's defense, people's
defense, to die for our homeland is our highest honor;
what matters . . .

And if fickle fortune leaves us in the lurch,
and we never return to our homeland again,
if the fatal shot hits us and fate calls our name, yes, calls
our name, then our tank becomes a grave made of iron;
if the fatal shot . . .

Among the home guard units too, the office of "Commander of the Panzer Troops" was established, with the military zone number added. The following three offices are examples of the whole system:

Commander of the Panzer Troops I (Insterburg). Subordinate:
10th Panzer Replacement & Training Unit (Zintern)
413th Grenadier Replacement & Training Battalion (mot) (Insterburg)
24th Armored Reconnaissance Replacement and Training Unit(Insterburg)
1st Panzerjäger Replacement & Training Unit (Allenstein)
Panzerzug Replacement Unit Warsaw (Rembertow);

Commander of the Panzer Troops IV (Dresden). Subordinate:
18th Panzer Replacement & Training Unit (Kamenz)
14th Panzer-Grenadier Replacement & Training Regiment (Laisnig)
14th Panzerjäger Replacement & Training Regiment (Borna);

Commander of the Panzer Troops X (Hamburg). Subordinate:
76th Panzer-Grenadier Replacement & Training Unit (Rahlstedt)
90th MPanzer-Grenadier Replacement & Training Unit (Wandsbeck)
20th Panzerjäger Replacement & Training Unit (Harburg).

The divisions that ceased to exist in the defeat at Stalingrad — the 14th, 16th and 24th in the basin and the 22nd and 27th outside it — had to be replaced, as did those lost at Tunis. The 6th and 7th Panzer Divisions having been refreshed in France were already transferred to the eastern front in January of 1943. The 23rd Panzer Division, also being refreshed there, had to form a new 26th Panzer Division out of its ranks. The Reserve Divisions 155 in Ulm and 233 (motorized) in Frankfurt an der Oder were turned into Reserve Panzer Divisions, and the 233rd Reserve Panzer Division was transferred to Denmark.

Four of the divisions stationed in Germany for reorganization or refreshment were sent to the front during the summer on account of the changed war situation. Thus the newly formed 16th and 26th Panzer Divisions were sent to Italy in July, and the 24th Panzer Division followed in August, while the 1st Panzer Division went to the Balkans.

Loading of tanks for shipment to the front.

The development of the tank situation at the eastern front in the first half of 1943 was as follows:

Day	Tanks Ready	Being Repaired	In Transit
2/28	902	784	135
4/10	953	711	226
5/10	1536	372	347
5/31	1846	363	216
6/30	2287	297	261

On the same day, the following numbers of tanks were in action or in repair shops at the fronts in the European theaters of war:

Front	P-III & P-IV (long gun)	P-II & P-III (short gun)
Eastern	2269	556
Western	351	107
Norwegian	59	47
Balkan	118	15
Italian	345	16

The Italian islands and mainland had become a theater of war on July 9, 1943, for on that day 280 Allied warships, 320 transports and 2125 landing craft had landed the 7th U.S. and 8th British Armies. The Italians had 300,000 troops on the island of Sicily, but most of them left their posts and fled without fighting. Only a few German forces, including the Fallschirm-Panzer Division *Hermann Göring* fought hard in defense, but could not prevent the loss of Sicily on August 17. After the Italian forces capitulated, German troops occupied the most important cities and transit lines all over Italy. The 24th Panzer Division was among them, in Verona. The other two Panzer divisions in Italy — the 16th Panzer Division on the Riviera and the 26th Panzer Division in northern Calabria — had been alerted in July and prepared for the Allied invasion of the mainland.

A P-IV rolls through a central Italian city to the front. (Photo taken 11/9/1943.)

The landing took place on September 3, 1943. The 26th Panzer Division was the first to face the enemy; shortly thereafter the 16th Panzer Division took part in the battle near Salerno. From then on the 16th, 24th and 26th Panzer Divisions were in the Italian campaign to the end. The line of battle and march of the 16th Panzer Division — to mention just one division — went from the Bari area to Salerno, then along the coast via Naples to just short of Gaeta, then across Italy to the Adriatic coast near Termoli and northward along the coast via Ancona and Pesaro and to Rimini from July to November 1943.

The reverses suffered by the German Army in all theaters of war during the winter of 1942-43 had not depressed the German high command. On the contrary: As of March 1943, Hitler ordered a great offensive to start on the eastern front, intended to restore freedom of mobility. Operational Order No.6 of April 15, 1943 said:

"I have decided to conduct the "Citadel" attack as soon as the weather conditions allow, as the first of this year's attacking strikes!"

Operationsbefehl Nr. 6 (Zitadelle) vom 15. 4. 1943

Der Führer
OKH, GenStdH, Op.Abt.(I)
Nr. 430246/43 g.Kdos.Chefs.

F.H.Qu., den 15. April 1943

Geheime Kommandosache
Chefsache!
Nur durch Offizier!

13 Ausfertigungen
4. Ausfertigung

AOK 2 Ia 591/43 g.Kdos.Chefsache
Eing. 17. 4. 43 (2 Anlagen) Do.

Operationsbefehl Nr. 6

Ich habe mich entschlossen, sobald die Wetterlage es zuläßt, als ersten der diesjährigen Angriffsschläge den Angriff „Zitadelle" zu führen.

Diesem Angriff kommt daher ausschlaggebende Bedeutung zu. Er muß schnell und durchschlagend gelingen. Er *muß* uns die Initiative für dieses Frühjahr und Sommer in die Hand geben. Deshalb sind alle Vorbereitungen mit größter Umsicht und Tatkraft durchzuführen. Die besten Verbände, die besten Waffen, die besten Führer, große Munitionsmengen sind an den Schwerpunkten einzusetzen. Jeder Führer, jeder Mann muß von der entscheidenden Bedeutung dieses Angriffs durchdrungen sein. Der Sieg von Kursk muß für die Welt wie ein Fanal wirken.

Hierzu befehle ich:

1.) *Ziel des Angriffs ist,* durch scharf zusammengefaßten, rücksichtslos und schnell durchgeführten Vorstoß je einer Angriffsarmee aus dem Gebiet Belgorod und südlich Orel die im Gebiet Kursk befindlichen Feindkräfte einzukesseln und durch konzentrischen Angriff zu vernichten.

   Im Zuge dieses Angriffs ist eine verkürzte kräftesparende neue Front zu gewinnen in der Linie: Neshega — Korotscha-Abschnitt — Skorodnoje — Tim — ostw. Schtschigry — Ssossna-Abschnitt.

2.) *Es kommt darauf an*
   a) *das Überraschungsmoment* weitgehend zu wahren und den Gegner vor allem über den Zeitpunkt des Angriffs im Unklaren zu lassen,
   b) die *Angriffskräfte auf schmaler Breite schärfstens zusammenzufassen,* um mit örtlich überwältigender Überlegenheit *aller* Angriffsmittel (Panzer, Sturmgeschütze, Artillerie, Nebelwerfer usw.) in *einem Zuge* bis zur Vereinigung der beiden Angriffsarmeen im Feind durchzuschlagen und damit den Kessel zu schließen,
   c) den Angriffssturmkeilen so schnell wie möglich *aus der Tiefe* Kräfte zum Abdecken der Flanken nachzuführen, damit die Sturmkeile selbst nur *vorwärts* zu stoßen brauchen.
   d) durch frühzeitiges *Hineinstoßen* von allen Seiten *in den Kessel* dem Feind keine Ruhe zu lassen und seine Vernichtung zu beschleunigen,
   e) *so schnell* den Angriff durchzuführen, daß der Feind sich weder aus der Umklammerung absetzen, noch starke Reserven von anderen Fronten heranziehen kann,
   f) durch raschen *Aufbau der neuen Front* frühzeitig Kräfte, insbesondere schnelle Verbände, für weitere Aufgaben freizubekommen.

Supply of Tanks (Pzkpfw.) and Assault Guns (Stug.) to the Troops Participating in Operation "Citadel"

(Situation according to reports of 6/30/1943)

1. Heeresgruppe Süd

Verband	einsatzbereite Pzkpfw.		Stug.	in Instandsetzung Pzkpfw.		Stug.	in Zuführung Pzkpfw.		Stug.	Summe Pzkpfw.		Stug
Pz.Gren.Div.:												
G-D	113	(11)	34	16	(1)	1	34	(0)	0	163	(12)	35
SS-LAH	100	(7)	34	8	(0)	1	16	(0)	0	126	(7)	35
SS-R	113	(0)	34	15	(1)	0	0	(0)	0	128	(1)	34
SS-T	104	(5)	27	27	(3)	8	9	(0)	0	140	(8)	35
SS-W	31	(15)	6	0	(0)	0	0	(0)	0	31	(15)	6
Panzerdiv.:												
3.	56	(32)	2	2	(2)	0	5	(5)	0	63	(39)	2
6.	78	(29)	0	8	(2)	0	0	(0)	0	86	(31)	0
7.	81	(22)	0	6	(3)	0	0	(0)	0	87	(25)	0
11.	74	(15)	0	23	(5)	0	1	(0)	0	98	(20)	0
19.	62	(19)	0	3	(1)	0	5	(1)	0	70	(21)	0
23.	55	(11)	0	2	(0)	0	4	(0)	0	61	(11)	0
Panzerbrig.:												
10	244	(0)	0	5	(0)	0	3	(0)	0	252	(0)	0
Stug. Abteilungen			94			3			9			106
Summe:	1111	(166)	231	115	(18)	13	77	(6)	9	1303	(190)	253

2. Heeresgruppe Mitte

Verband	einsatzbereite Pzkpfw.		Stug.	in Instandsetzung Pzkpfw.		Stug.	in Zuführung Pzkpfw.		Stug.	Summe Pzkpfw.		Stug
Panzerdiv.:												
2.	84	(29)		5	(9)		9	(0)		98	(38)	
4.	88	(15)		6	(1)		0	(0)		94	(16)	
9.	66	(6)		4	(11)		26	(0)		96	(17)	
12.	51	(28)		4	(0)		0	(3)		55	(31)	
18.	30	(33)		2	(9)		0	(1)		32	(43)	
20.	57	(21)		4	(4)		0	(0)		61	(25)	
Panzerbrig.:												
21	76	(8)		7	(0)		28	(0)		111	(8)	
Pz.Jäg.Regt.:												
656	5	(15)		0	(0)		0	(0)		5	(15)	
78. Stu.Div.	0	(1)		0	(0)		0	(0)		0	(1)	
Stug. Abteilungen			274			6			0			280
Summe:	457	(156)	274	32	(34)	6	63	(4)	0	552	(194)	280

The commanders of the armies in this sector of the front did not agree at all to an early attacking date. Generaloberst Model, Commander of the 9th Army, categorically demanded: "More tanks!" Generaloberst Guderian wanted to postpone the operation until 1944, since the new heavy tanks were "not yet ready for the front." But Hitler remained firm. The OKH commanded in his name on June 14 that the "Operation Citadel" attack — which would lead to, among other things, the greatest tank battle in military history — should begin on July 5.
The following German Panzer divisions participated:

Army Group Center: 2nd, 4th, 9th, 12th, 18th and 20th Panzer Divisions;
Army Group South: 3rd, 6th, 7th, 11th, 19th and 23rd Panzer Divisions.

The new "Panther" and "Tiger" heavy tanks were deployed here in large numbers for the first time. The Army set up the 10th and 24th Panzer Brigades as "Tiger" brigades. The 10th Panzer Brigade and the independent Panzer Units 51, 52 and 503, with 45 "Tigers" in all, were with Army Group South; the 21st Panzer Brigade and Panzer Units 216 and 505, also with 45 "Tigers", were with Army Group Center. The "Tigers" in Army Group South formed a focal point with the three Panzer divisions of the Waffen-SS and Panzer-Grenadier Division *Grossdeutschland.*

The Panzer divisions with Army Group South went into battle on July 5 with the following numbers of tanks:

3rd Panzer Division: 56
6th Panzer Division: 78
7th Panzer Division: 81
10th Panzer Brigade: 45
11th Panzer Division: 74
19th Panzer Division: 62
23rd Panzer Division: 55

A P-III tank with a long gun ready for action south of Belgorod on July 13, 1943.

A P-IV with "Panzer skirts" attached to the turret and the sides of the hull (for protection against hollow charges) rolls past an infantry post. The crew "enjoys" the sunny June day in 1943.

The German troops were able to penetrate the first Soviet positions, but as they attacked the second Russian line, the tanks were stopped by the fire of the enemy artillery and their air attacks. While the Panzer divisions of Army Group Center laboriously fought their way through the enemy positions into the open, the Red Army's counterattack against the leading German tank units of Army Group South began on the night of July 10.

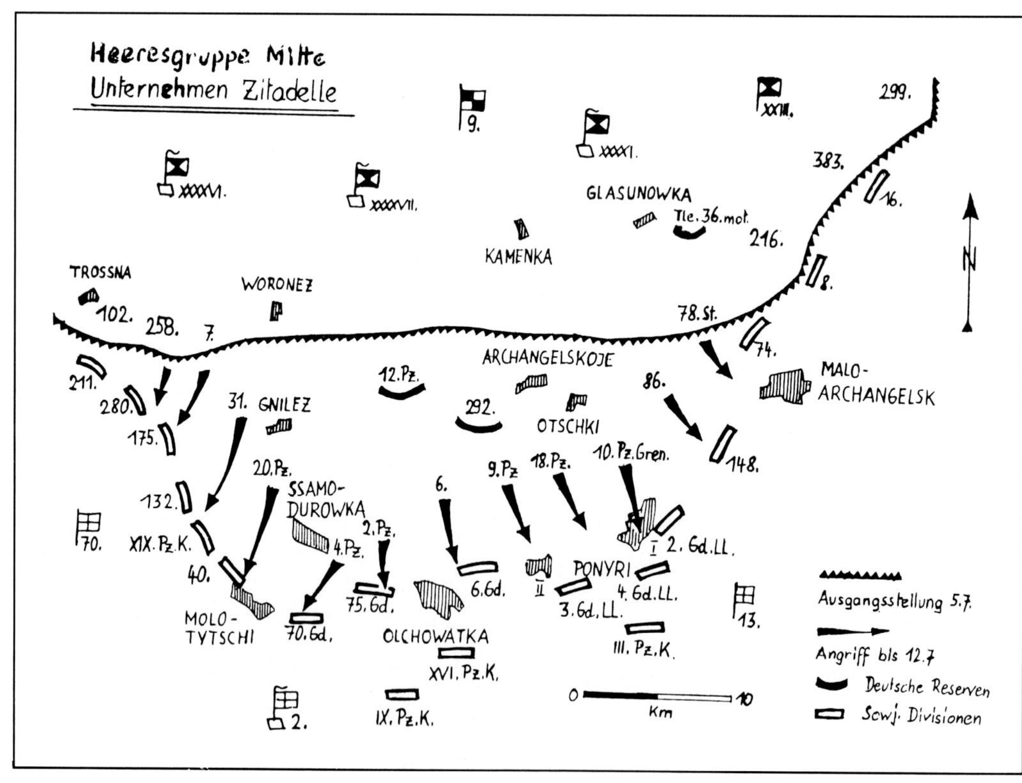

The greatest tank battle of World War II took place in the Prochochovka area when 10,000 (!) Soviet tanks of five armies advanced. What good did it do when the tanks bearing the Iron Cross destroyed 400 tanks with the red star on the first day of the battle? The enemy's superiority was too great. . . .

. . . and the superior forces facing Army Group Center were also too great. Here the 2nd and 4th Panzer Divisions reached the area west of Olchovatka, 20 kilometers from their starting position, by July 12. That night they were ordered to stop — for the Soviet Army Group "Central Front" attacked the position of the 2nd Panzer Army beyond Orel and Briansk with three armies, including 3000 tanks.

Generaloberst Model broke off the battle around Kursk and turned the 5th, 18th and 20th Panzer Divisions around that night for a counterattack. In the Army Group South area the attack continued for three more days. Here the units of the 4th Panzer Army were able to push forward to a distance of 30 kilometers before they came to a halt. Their losses were too great: 1500 German tanks were left behind on the battlefield, wrecked. The Soviets, to be sure, lost twice as many tanks, but they had plenty.

After the Allied landing in Italy succeeded, the Commander of the Wehrmacht ordered the battle around Kursk broken off.

The two new German tanks — P-V "Panther" and P-VI "Tiger" — had had their baptism of fire. To be sure, "teething troubles" still needed to be eliminated. It turned out that the "Tiger" had too little speed and radius of action.

A "Tiger" standing ready at Orel on September 3, 1943 is admired by curious infantrymen.

Stoffgliederung 21	**Geheime Kommandosache!** Panther I (VK 3002) Ausf. D A u G	Blatt G325

Dringl.-St.: SS AH Pogr. Bo Stck. I DF

Technische Daten:

(zugleich auch Pz Bef Wg Panther)

Gesamtgewicht des Fahrzeuges (Gefechtsgewicht) ~ 44,8 t

Motor HL 230. 600ˣ⁾ – 700ˣˣ⁾ PS ˣ) bei 2500 U/Min ˣˣ) bei 3000 U/Min

Spez. Leistung 13,4ˣ⁾ – 15,6ˣˣ⁾ PS/to

Höchstgeschwindigkeit 45,7ˣ⁾ – 55ˣ⁾ km/Std.

Mitgeführte Kraftstoffmenge 730 l (einschl. Reservetank)

Fahrbereich mit einer Kraftstoff-Füllung:

Straße ~ 200 km; mittl. Gelände ~ 100 km

Grabenüberschreitfähigkeit ~ 2,45 m Kletterfähigkeit 0,9 m

Watfähigkeit 1,9 m Steigvermögen 35°

Besatzung 5 Mann Spez. Bodendruck 0,87 kg/cm²

Bodenfreiheit 0,56 m

Länge ~ 8,860 m, Breite ~ 3,27 m

Höhe mit Aufbau ~ 2,995 m 3,420 m m. Schürzen

Feuerhöhe 2,30 m

Bordmunition 79 Schuß Kw K, 4200 Schuß MG, 192 Schuß MP

ab Ausf. G = 82 " "

Pz. Bef. Wg. – 64 " "

Bestückung: = 1 7,5 cm Kw. K. 42 (L/70)

2 MG. 34 (1. i. Turm, 1 i. Kugelblende); 1 MP

Abfeuerung Kw K elektr., MG mech. Fußhebel u. Bandérzug (i. Turm)

MG f. Kugelblende durch Handabzug

Optisches Gerät: a) Turmoptik TZF 12 (binocular), später TZF 12 a (monocular)

b) Kugeloptik KZF 2

c) Fahreroptik Prismeneinsätze

d) i. Pz. Führerkuppel Primenspiegel

Funkgerät (normale Ausstattung) Fu 5 + Fu 2 (für Pz. Bef. Wg. Panther Sonderausstattung)

Panzerung: Front 80 mm Seite 40 mm Schürzen 5 mm

Bug 60 mm Dach 16 mm

Turm 100 mm (Front), 100 mm, Gußstahl

45 mm (Seite) Walzstahl

Kette 86 Glieder, Kettengewicht 2050 kg

Rohstoffbedarf: (o. Waffe) f. Stck. i. kg	Eisen unleg. 33409,– kg	dav. Grob u. Mi Bleche 30735,– kg
	leg. 44060,– "	Feinbleche 1888,– "
	Eisen gesamt 77469,– "	Fertiggew. (einschl. Waffe) 43400,– kg

Preis RM 117100.–	Durchschn. Fertigungszeit ~ 14 Monate	Arbeitsstunden

Fertigungsfirmen:

Montage und Fahrgestelle: MAN, Augsburg-Nürnberg; Daimler-Benz, Bln.-Marienfelde; MNH, Hannover

Panzerung: Dortm.-Hoerd.-Hütt. Verein – Dortmund, Eisenw. Oberdonau, Linz; Ruhrstahl-Hattingen, Böhler-Kapfenberg, Bismarckhütte O/S;

The P-V "Panther", which first saw service in 1943, had an overall length of 6.90 meters without and 8.65 meters with its gun barrel. This KwK was a 75mm Type 42 L/70. Two machine guns were also installed. The tank's height was 3.00 meters, its weight 42 to 45 tons. With a 750-HP motor it could attain a speed of 46 kph. The armor plate on the front was 80 to 120mm thick; that of the side walls 46 to 60mm.

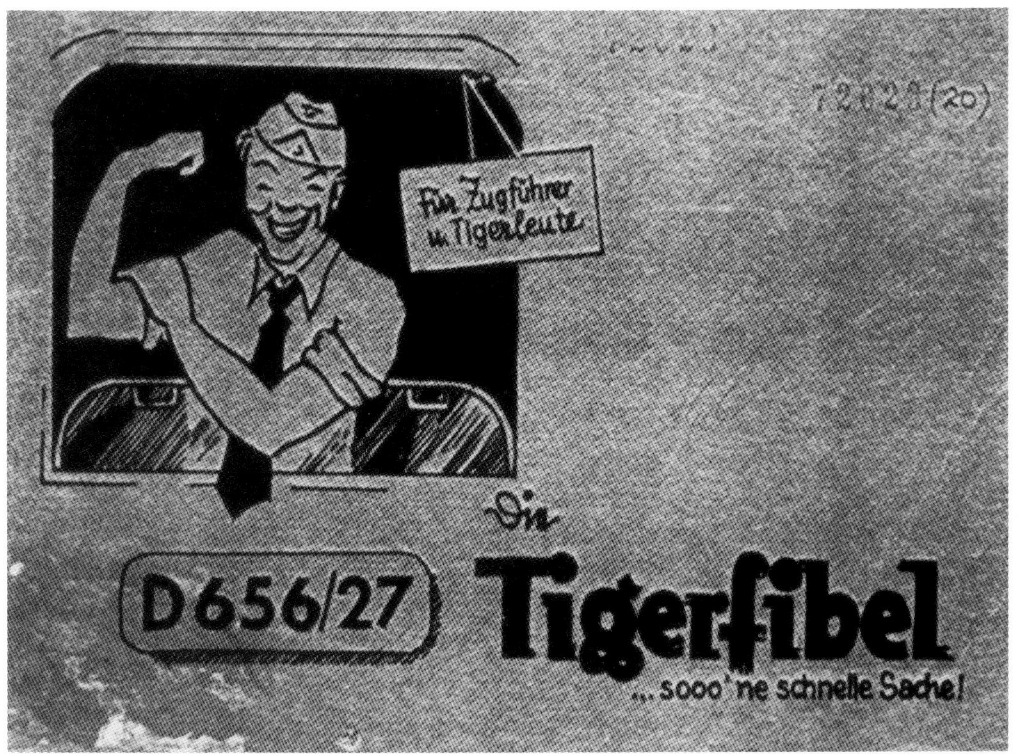

The P-VI "Tiger", already tested in combat since September of 1942, had a length of 6.20 meters without and 8.25 meters with its gun barrel. Its weight was 62 to 72 tons. The 650-HP motor gave a top speed of 40 kph. The armament consisted of an 88mm KwK 36 L/56 without a muzzle brake, plus two machine guns. The front armor was 102 to 110mm thick, the side armor 60 to 82mm. Production of this tank was speeded up in 1943 to the extent that up to 25 a month were produced.

The tank production figures ordered by Hitler in 1942 — the P-I and P-II were no longer being made — was reached only in the spring of 1943 with 600 tanks. From then on, production ran at full speed, so that, for example, in September 1943 a thousand tanks were produced; the number grew to 1450 tanks in May of 1944!

A "Tiger" damaged in battle is repaired by the workshop company.
Left: the heavy turret is put in place; right: the motor is replaced.

In the autumn of 1943 there were at the front:

Type	Armament	Spl. Vehicle #
P-38(t)	37mm	140
P-III	50mm L/42	141
	50mm 39 L/60	141/1
P-IV	75mm L/24	161
	75mm L/43	161/1
	75mm L/48	161/2
P-V	75mm 42 L/70	171
P-VI	88mm 36 L/56	181
	88mm 43 L/71	182

There were also armored command vehicles of the P-III, P-V and P-VI types.

The repair work of the maintenance and workshop companies on duty at the front (in army groups) prepared the following numbers of damaged tanks for service: October: 973, November: 911, December: 1294 and January: 2190. In the same period, 250 tanks were repaired for service at facilities in Germany.

The road wheels of a P-38(t) are cleaned.

An enemy antitank shell damaged the tracks of a P-III. The tank has to be jacked up.

After a P-IV with a short barrel has been repaired, it is prepared to return to action.

After the loss of the battles at Kursk ("Operation Citadel") and Orel, the Panzer corps were reorganized. The 18th Panzer Division became the 18th Artillery Division; in April of 1944 it was finally disbanded. The Panzer corps consisted in October of a total of 22 Panzer divisions with a strength of 288,486 men, of whom 22,264 men belonged to Panzer regiments and independent units. The Panzer troops made up, in all, 10.7% of the German field army.

The structure of the Panzer troops in October of 1943 consisted of four Panzer Army Commands (1 to 4) and twelve general commands of Panzer corps (III, XIV, XXIV, XXXIX, XXXX, XXXXI, XXXXVI, XXXXVII, LVI, LXXVI), and 22 Panzer divisions.

Pz.Div.	Pz. Reg.	Notes on the Units
1st	1	2 units of 4 companies with P-IV
2nd	3	I: army troop ("Panther"), II: 4 companies with P-V
3rd	6	I: 4 companies with P-V II: 4 companies with P-IV
4th	(none)	I/35: 3 companies, P-III, 1 co. P-IV, III/15 rearmed with P-V
5th	31	I: rearmed with P-V II: 4 companies with P-IV
6th	11	(same as 31st Panzer Regiment)
7th	25	I: rearmed with P-V II: 2 companies with P-III, 1 company, P-IV
8th	(none)	I./70 (as II./25)
9th	33	I: (as II./25), II became Army Pz.Abt.51, III became Army Pz.Abt. 506
11th	15	I: 4 companies, P-IV, II: rearmed w/P-V
12th	29	(same as 3rd Panzer Regiment)
13th	4	I became Army Pz.Abt. 507, II: 4 cos., P-IV, III rearmed with P-V
14th	36	I: 4 companies, P-IV, II: 2 cos., P-IV, 2 companies with assault guns
16th	2	I & II: 4 companies each, P-IV, III: 4 companies, assault guns
17th	(none)	II./39: 3 companies, P-III, 1 co., P-IV
19th	27	I: rearmed with P-V, II: 2 cos., P-III, 2 companies, P-IV
20th	(none)	III./21 (as II./39)
21st	100	I & II newly formed with P-III
23rd	23	I: 4 companies, P-IV, II: 4 cos., P-V, 1 company with assault guns
24th	24	(same as 36th Panzer Regiment)
25th	9	II: 4 companies, P-IV
26th	26	(as 31st Panzer Regiment), I with 25th Panzer Division at times
Norwegen	(none)	I: 3 companies, P-III.

6.Pz.Div.: Pz.Gren.Rgt.4, 114; Pz.Rgt.11; Pz.A.R.76; Nr.57; (W.K.VI)

Pz.Rgt.11 nur mit Stab und II. (4 Kp.Pz.IV), I.zur Umrüstung auf "Panther" in der Heimat; Pz.Gren.Rgt.ohne Fla.Kp.; II./Pz. Gren.Rgt.114 (SPW); Pz.Aufkl.Abt.6 mit Stab, 1 s.Pz.Spähzug, 1 le.Pz.Späh Kp., 1 Aufkl.Kp. (SPW), 2 Kradschtz.Kp., 1 s.Kp., Kol.; Pz.Jäg.Abt.41 mit Stab, 1 Kp.(sf), 1 Kp.(mot.Z.); Pz.Art. Rgt.76 wie Pz.Art.Rgt.75, zusätzl. Pz.Beob.Bttr.76; H.-Flakabt. 298 wie H.-Flakabt.288 bei 5.Pz.Div.; Pz.Pion.Btl.57 in Normalgliederung; Pz.Nachr.Abt.82; Felders.Btl.57 mit 4 Kp.; bei Nachschubtruppen Kraftf.Kp. u.Betr.Stoff Kol.wie bei 3.Pz.Div.; Ersatzteilstaffel fehlt

7.Pz.Div.: Pz.Gren.Rgt.6, 7; Pz.Rgt.25; Pz.A.R.78; Nr.58;(W.K.IX)

Pz.Rgt.25 mit Stab und II.mit 2 Kp.Pz.III u. 1 Kp.Pz.IV - Um - rüstung auf 4 Kp. Pz.IV vorgesehen-, I./Pz.Rgt.25 in der Heimat zur Umrüstung auf "Panther"; Pz.Gren.Rgt.ohne Fla.Kp.; II./Pz. Gren.Rgt. 6 (SPW); Pz.Aufkl.Abt.7 wie Pz.Aufkl.Abt.6; Pz.Jäg.Abt. 42 wie Pz.Jäg.Abt.41 b.6.Pz.Div.; Pz.Art.Rgt.78 in Sollgliederung jedoch ohne III.Abt.; Pz.Beob.Bttr.78; H.-Flakabt.296 wie H.-Flakabt.288 b. 5.Pz.Div.; Pion.Btl.58 und Pz.Nachr.Abt.83 in Sollgliederung; Felders.Btl.58 mit 5 Kp.; bei Nachschubtruppen 6 Kraftf.Kp. (90 t); Ersatzteilstaffel fehlt; zusätzlich von Heerestruppen Werkst.Kp.2./127 als 4.Kp.der Div.; sonst in Normgliederung

8.Pz.Div.: Pz.Gren.Rgt.8, 28; I./10; Pz.A.R.80; Nr.59; (W.K.III)

I./Pz.Rgt. 10 mit 3 Kp. Pz.III und 1 Kp.Pz.IV-Ausstattung aller Kp.mit Pz.IV vorgesehen; Pz.Gren.Rgt.ohne Fla.Kp.; 1 Kp.bei Pz. Gren.Rgt.28 auf SPW; Pz.Aufkl.Abt.8 wie Pz.Aufkl.Abt.3; Pz.Jäg. Abt.43 mit Stab, 2 Kp. (sf); Pz.Art.Rgt.80 wie Pz.Art.Rgt.76 bei 6.Pz.Div.; Pz.Beob.Bttr.80; H.-Flakabt.286 wie H.-Flakabt.288 bei 5.Pz.Div.; Pz.Pion.Btl.59 u.Pz.Nachr.Abt.84 in Normgliederung Felders.Btl.fehlt; bei Nachschubtruppen Kraftf.Kp.und Betr.Stoff Kol.wie bei 3.Pz.Div.; zusätzl.Ost Kp.59; sonst in Normgliederung

9.Pz.Div.: Pz.Gren.Rgt.10, 11; Pz.Rgt.33; Pz.A.R.102; Nr.60; (W.K.XVII)

Pz.Rgt.33 nur mit Stab und I.mit 3 Kp.Pz.III und 1 Kp.Pz.IV-Ausstattung aller Kp.mit Pz.IV vorgesehen; II./Pz.Rgt.33 unter Umrüstung auf "Panther" als Pz.Abt.51 zu den Heerestruppen; III./Pz.Rgt.33 unter Umrüstung auf "Tiger" als Pz.Abt.506 zu den Heerestruppen; I./Pz.Gren.Rgt.11 (SPW); Pz.Aufkl.Abt.9 wie Pz. Aufkl.Abt.1 (1.Kp.mit "Luchs"); Pz.Jäg.Abt.50 wie Pz.Jäg.Abt.43 bei 8.Pz.Div.;Pz.Art.Rgt.102 wie Pz.Art.Rgt.103 bei 4.Pz.Div. ohne le.Art.Kol.; Pz.Beob.Bttr.102; H.-Flakabt.287 wie H.-Flakabt.288 bei 5.Pz.Div.; Pz.Pion.Btl.86 und Pz.Nachr.Abt.85 in Normgliederung; Felders.Btl.fehlt; bei Nachschubtruppen Kraftf. Kp.wie 4.Pz.Div., jedoch keine Betr.Stoff Kol.; zusätzl.1 Kraftf. Kp. (60 t); sonst wie Normgliederung

11.Pz.Div.: Pz.Gren.Rgt.110,111; Pz.Rgt.15; Pz.A.R.119; Nr.61; (W.K.VIII)

Pz.Rgt.15 mit Stab und I.Abt., diese z.Zt.wie II./Pz.Rgt.25 bei 7.Pz.Div.-Umrüstung auf 4 Kp.Pz.IV vorgesehen; II./Pz.Rgt.15 in der Heimat zur Umrüstung auf "Panther"; I./Pz.Gren.Rgt.110 (SPW); Pz.Aufkl.Abt.11 mit Stab, 1 le.Pz.Späh Kp., 2 Kradschtz.Kp., 1 s. Kp., 1 Kol.; Pz.Jäg.Abt.61 wie Pz.Jäg.Abt.543 bei 3.Pz.Div.; Pz. Art.Rgt.119 wie Pz.Art.Rgt.74 bei 2.Pz.Div.; Pz.Beob.Bttr.119; H.- Flakabt.277 wie H.-Flakabt.288 bei 5.Pz.Div.; Pz.Pion.Btl. 209 und Pz.Nachr.Abt.89 in Normgliederung; Felders.Btl.61 mit 5 Kp.; bei Nachschubtruppen Kraftf.Kp. wie bei 7.Pz.Div., zusätzl. 1 Kolonne; sonst Normgliederung

12.Pz.Div.: Pz.Gren.Rgt.5, 25; Pz.Rgt.29; Pz.A.R.2; Nr.2; (W.K.II)

Pz.Rgt.29 mit Stab und II.Abt., diese z.Zt.wie II./Pz.Rgt.25 bei 7.Pz.Div.; Umrüstung auf 4 Kp.Pz.IV vorgesehen; I.Abt.z.Zt.in der Heimat zur Umrüstung auf "Panther"; Pz.Gren.Rgt.ohne Fla.Kp., 1 Kp./Pz.Gren.Rgt.25 (SPW); Pz.Aufkl.Abt.12 mit Stab, 1 le.Pz. Späh Kp., 3 Kradschtz.Kp., 1 s.Kp., 1 Kol.; Pz.Jäg.Abt.2 wie Pz. Jäg.Abt.543 bei 3.Pz.Div.; Pz.Art.Rgt.2 wie Pz.Art.Rgt.76 bei 6. Pz.Div.; Pz.Beob.Bttr.2; H.-Flakabt.303 wie H.-Flakabt.288 bei 5.Pz.Div.; Pz.Pion.Btl.32 und Pz.Nachr.Abt.2 in Normgliederung; Felders.Btl.2 mit 4 Kp.; bei Nachschubtruppen Kraftf.Kp.wie bei 2.Pz.Div.; sonst in Normgliederung

13.Pz.Div.: Pz.Gren.Rgt.66, 93; Pz.Rgt.4; Pz.A.R.13; Nr.13; (W.K.XI)

Pz.Rgt.4 mit Stab und II.Abt.mit 4 Kp.Pz.IV; III./Pz.Rgt.4 z.Zt. in der Heimat zur Umrüstung auf "Panther"; I./Pz.Rgt.4 unter Umrüstung auf "Tiger" als Pz.Abt.507 zu den Heerestruppen; I./Pz. Gren.Rgt.66 (SPW); Aufkl.Abt.13 mit Stab, 1 le.Pz.Späh Kp., 1 Kp. (Sd.Kfz.251),1 Kradschtz.Kp., 1 mot.Schtz.Kp., 1 s.Kp., 1 Kol.; zusätzl.Stu.Gesch.Abt.259 von den Heerestruppen; Pz.Jäg.Abt.13 wie Pz.Jäg.Abt.37 bei 1.Pz.Div.; Pz.Art.Rgt.13 in Normgliederung; Pz.Beob.Bttr.13; H.-Flakabt.271 wie H.-Flakabt.298 bei 5.Pz.Div.; Pz.Pion.Btl.4 und Pz.Nachr.Abt.13 in Normgliederung; Felders.Btl. mit 3 Kp.; bei Nachschubtruppen 3 Kraftf.Kp. (90 t), keine Ersatzteilstaffel

14.Pz.Div.: Pz.Gren.Rgt.103,108; Pz.Rgt.36; Pz.A.R.4; Nr.4; (W.K.IV)

Pz.Rgt.mit Stab, Stabskp., I.Abt.mit 4 Kp.Pz.IV, II.Abt.mit 2 Kp. Pz.IV und 2 Kp.Stug.G.; I./Pz.Gren.Rgt.103 (SPW); Pz.Aufkl.Abt. 14 wie Pz.Aufkl.Abt.1; Pz.Jäg.Abt.fehlt z.Zt.; Pz.Art.Rgt.4 in Normgliederung; Pz.Beob.Bttr.4; H.-Flakabt.276 wie H.-Flakabt. 299 bei 1.Pz.Div.; Pz.Pion.Btl.13 wie Normgliederung; Pz.Nachr. Abt.4; bei Nachschubtruppen 8 Kraftf.Kp. (120 t); Ersatzteilstaffel fehlt; sonst in Normgliederung; Felders.Btl.fehlt

Listing of Panzer divisions and their units, summer 1943.

The normal composition of a Panzer regiment in October of 1943 was, as specified by OKH I/4500 g. Kdos of 10/4/1943:

Staff with staff company, I. Unit with staff, staff company, three to four companies with 17 tanks each; II. Unit with staff, staff company, four companies with 17 to 22 tanks, sometimes a flame-throwing tank column; one workshop company. The rearming of individual companies (see above) with P-V "Panther" tanks sometimes took place in Germany; the rearming of individual units as independent Panzer units of the army troops with P-VI "Tiger" tanks likewise took place back home.

The numbers of tanks in individual Panzer divisions on, for example, November 20, 1943 was as follows (tanks ready for service in parentheses):

1st Panzer Division 140 (46)
6th Panzer Division 38 (25)
7th Panzer Division 47 (16)
8th Panzer Division 66 (7)
9th Panzer Division 30 (6)
13th Panzer Division 32 (15)
14th Panzer Division 52 (37)
23rd Panzer Division 27 (16)
24th Panzer Division 57 (34)
25th Panzer Division 63 (31)

Finale

The Last War Years

1944-1945

The year 1943 brought setbacks for the German forces on all fronts. The supreme command of the Reich was still willing to continue the war in Europe. But the Allies too were determined, on the basis of their agreements, to force Germany to surrender unconditionally.

The Red Army, which, thanks to a total mobilization of its manpower and industrial pents, had grown so strong that it could carry on its offensives over the entire eastern front despite its manpower losses, attacked from the Baltic to the Black Sea in January of 1944!

The Soviet Army Group "1st Ukrainian Front" advanced in the direction of Vinniza in January, penetrated the front of the 4th Panzer Army and reached the Odessa-Lemberg railway line. The counterattack by units of the 1st Panzer Army won back some ground, but ultimately led to the encirclement of eight divisions in the Tcherkassy area and to the battle of Kirovgrad. In these battles the 1st, 3rd, 11th, 14th, 16th and 17th Panzer Divisions stood out. But just two months later the whole 1st Panzer Army (Generaloberst Hube) was surrounded near Kamenez-Podolsk. This army — including the 1st, 3rd, 6th, 11th, 16th, 17th and 19th Panzer Divisions —was able all the same to break loose, suffering heavy losses, and make contact with German troops in eastern Galicia.

But as the front moved closer to Germany in the south, the Crimea was evacuated; thus the divisions of Army Group Center were also fighting hard as they withdrew. As early as January of 1944, the battle raged on the outermost left wing around Vitebsk. The 20th Panzer Division was involved here. The second focal point developed in the Pripyet marshes. Here the city of Kovel was enclosed. The 4th and 5th Panzer Divisions took part in the liberation, during which the I./35th Panzer Regiment were in the vanguard and reached the city first. At the end of April 1944 the situation in the central sector became more quiet.

Army Group North was hit hardest at the beginning of January. 200,000 shells of all calibers tore up the German front before Leningrad and at the Oranienbaum bridgehead on January 15. The German troops — with no Panzer units among them — were pushed back. Only in February did the 12th Panzer Division arrive. The Army Group North drew back to the "Panther position" on both sides of Pleskau. At Narva Pz.Abt.502 stood firm in a storm of Soviet troops. As the spring mud season set in, the enemy attacks came to a stop here too.

The Red Army meanwhile prepared for its last strike against the German eastern army. Along with its own tank manufacturing, which attained much higher production than did Germany's, there were, as of April 1944, 3734 tanks shipped from the USA 4292 from Great Britain. This Allied support added up to a total of 13,000 tanks bearing the red star by April of 1945.

It was just after midnight on June 22, 1944 — just three years after the campaign began — when the Red Army, with four guard armies, sixteen armies and two tank armies including 166 divisions in all, attacked the Army Group Center (four armies

Die Panzertruppe

Verlag von E. S. Mittler & Sohn in Berlin SW 68, Kochstraße 68—71 / Erscheinungsweise: Monatlich ein Heft / Bezugspreis für das Vierteljahr RM. 1.50, für das Ausland RM. 3.— / Abbestellungen können nur bis spätestens 4 Wochen vor Beginn eines neuen Vierteljahres angenommen werden.

6. Jahrgang — Januar 1944 — 1. Heft

Inhaltsverzeichnis.

(Die Aufsätze geben nur die persönlichen Ansichten der Verfasser wieder. Durch gegensätzliche Anschauungen sollen zeitgemäße Fragen geklärt werden.)

Seite

Soldaten der Panzertruppen! 1
Hohe Auszeichnungen bei den Schnellen Truppen 2
Auf dem Schlachtfeld haben sich durch besondere Tapferkeit hervorgetan 4
Im Großdeutschen Freiheitskampf opferten ihr Leben 5
Wer hat den Panzerkampfwagen erfunden? . . . 5
Deutsche Eisenbahn-Panzerzüge 7
Schulung der Marschzucht bei mot. Einheiten . . 9
Interessante Zusammenhänge von Zündung und Vergaser 12
25 Jahre Panzerabwehr 13
Kampftag auf Stützpunkt „U". 17
Fahrer 18
Der Panzergrenadier, ein Meister der Aushilfe . . 19
Buchbesprechungen 19

Umschlagbild: „Tiger im Angriff". PK.-Aufnahme Kriegsberichter Henisch (PBZ.).

Soldaten der Panzertruppen!

Wieder liegt ein Jahr härtester Kämpfe hinter uns. Mit beispielhafter Tapferkeit habt Ihr gegen eine vielfache Übermacht gekämpft und dem Gegner schwerste Verluste zugefügt. Den feindlichen Materialmassen habt Ihr Euren harten Willen entgegengestellt und alle, oft unlösbar erscheinenden Aufgaben mit starker Hand gemeistert.

Wie die Panzertruppen in den vergangenen Jahren als Stoßkeile an llen Fronten vorwärts stürmten, so sind sie jetzt als stärkste Waffe der Wehrmacht das Rückgrat der Abwehr geworden. Mit gleicher Hingabe und Verantwortungsfreudigkeit haben alle Soldaten der Panzertruppen des Ersatzheeres ihre Aufgabe auf dem Gebiet der Ausbildung und Organisation unter oft schwierigen Voraussetzungen gelöst und die Front gestärkt.

Unser aller Dank gilt dem deutschen Arbeiter, der mit unerhörtem Fleiß und Zähigkeit trotz Luftterrors unsere starken Waffen geschmiedet hat, die gut zu führen für uns Soldaten Verpflichtung ist.

Soldaten der Panzertruppen!

Dieser größte und härteste aller Kriege nähert sich seinem Höhepunkt. Einig im Vertrauen auf den Führer und im Glauben an den Endsieg wollen wir in der Stunde der Entscheidung uns der Größe unserer Zeit und unserer eigenen Vergangenheit würdig erweisen.

Es lebe der Führer!

H.Qu., den 1. Januar 1944. — Guderian.

with 29 infantry, four armored grenadier, one assault and two Luftwaffe field divisions — there were no Panzer divisions at the front). When the 5th Panzer Division and Pz.Abt.505 were sent to close the gap between the 3rd Panzer Army and the 4th Army on June 28, it was already too late. The German front was broken everywhere.

Field Marshal Model, the new Commander of the Army Group, moved the 4th, 5th and 7th Panzer Divisions up to Moledechno, bringing the Soviet advance to a stop for the first time since the beginning of July. Later the 12th Panzer Division reinforced the defensive front at Vilna. The front of Army Group Center came to a standstill. In the first week of August the German tanks scored their first victory in a long time when the 4th and 19th Panzer Divisions surrounded the III. Russian Tank Corps at Wolimin, north of Warsaw.

A "Tiger" tank passes an infantry combat troop in the Moledechno area on July 28, 1944.

The eastern front was stabilized at the end of September and beginning of October 1944. In the north it reached the East Prussian border — after the Army Group North, later Courland, had been separated from the rest of the front north of Memel. A Soviet breakthrough north of the Rominten Heath was stopped by the 5th Panzer Division. The other Panzer divisions of Army Group Center were situated (from left to right): 6th Panzer Division east of Zichenau, the 17th and 16th Panzer Divisions east of Kielce, and 24th Panzer Division east of Krakow.

In East Prussia several units, called "firemen" by the soldiers, stayed behind the main battle line as a combat reserve: the 20th Panzer Division at Tilsit, 5th and 7th Panzer Divisions between Lötzen and Ortelsburg, 3rd and 6th Panzer Divisions in the Proszkovo area.

When the Army Group North was cut off from the rest of the front by Russian armored forces between Memel and Libau, the 12th and 14th Panzer Divisions

One of the last combat-ready double-fuselage short-range reconnaissance planes drops a message to a P-IV tank of the 5th Panzer Division on September 15, 1944.

stayed in the Courland sector until the 1945 armistice. The 4th Panzer Division, also located there, was shipped out of Courland and saw service in West Prussia in January of 1945.

The war situation had changed rapidly on all fronts by the end of the year, to the disadvantage of the German Wehrmacht. One bit of harm was done the upper leadership by the attempted assassination at the Führer's "Wolf's Den" headquarters on July 20, 1944. The Inspector General of the Panzer Troops, Generaloberst Guderian, was called to be Chief of the General Staff of the OKH the very next day. His successor was the General of the Panzer Troops, Baron Geyr von Schweppenburg, who was then recovering from a wound sustained in the west, and who, like Guderian, had been a pioneer in the organization of the Panzer troops in the early Thirties.

In the summer of 1944 the establishment of independent Panzer brigades took place, but what with the war situation, they were gradually integrated into existing divisions. Thus the Panzer Brigades 101 to 113 came into being. They were utilized wherever needed. Later Pz.Brig.105 joined the 9th Panzer Division, Pz.Brig.111 the 11th Panzer Division, Pz.Brig.112 the 25th Panzer-Grenadier Division, to give just a few examples.

The structure of a Panzer brigade was as follows:

Staff with staff company,
Panzer unit with staff and 4 companies, each with 17 P-IV or P-V tanks,
A Panzer grenadier battalion with staff, 4 companies,
A Panzer engineer company, a workshop column, and a motor vehicle column.

A directive of the OKH in the summer of 1944 established the following personnel structure of a normal Panzer regiment:

Unit	Officers	Officials	Noncoms	Enlisted Men
Staff with staff company	8		63	105
Per company	3-5	2	51-59	123-211
Workshop co.	3	3	39	185

A Panzer company was thus supposed to have at full strength: 59 officers, 7 officials, 750 non-commissioned officers, 1190 enlisted men and 72 helpers (*Hilfswillige*, or "*Hiwis*", Russian volunteers). The numbers of tanks amounted to 86 P-IV, 73 P-V, 99 P-IV and P-V armored command vehicles, and two P-III recovery tractors.

The total number of tanks in the German Army was, for example: 3452 on July 1, 1943, 5013 on March 1, 1944 and 5481 on June 1, 1944.

The previous total production of tanks added up to 2055 in 1941, 4093 in 1942, 5255 in 1943 and 6656 in 1944. Production in various months of 1944 was:

January - 657	April - 638	October - 462
February - 590	May - 706	November - 650
March - 804	June - 740	December - 696

Despite continual Allied air attacks on the factories in 1944 and 1945, manufacturing reached its highest totals. Only as of February 1945 were several important factories destroyed by bombs. After that the manufacture of tanks was cut back in favor of assault guns, self-propelled antitank guns and other self-propelled guns, which were quicker and easier to build, and which were gradually added to the Panzer divisions.

The highest production of the P-V "Panther" tank occurred in July of 1944, when 380 of them could be shipped to the troops. The firms of MAN, Daimler-Benz and Henschel were engaged in producing them.

For the sake of simplifying production of tanks and spare parts, the "Tiger II", also known as the "King Tiger", was designed and put into production by Henschel at the beginning of 1944. The "King Tiger" was similar to the P-V but much heavier. The increased weight, plus the use of the new 88mm KwK 43, required a different type of running gear as well as a new turret design. Thus the first fifty tanks were equipped with the smaller turret of the P-VI (I); as of the 51st example, the so-called cylindrical turret developed by Krupp was installed.

The "King Tiger" had a length of 7.30 meters without and 8.20 meters with the barrel of the 88mm KwK 43 L/41 with muzzle brake. The width was 3.75 meters, the height 3.10 meters. The weight was 68 tons. A 700 HP motor gave a speed of 40 kph. The armor was 150mm thick at the front, 80mm on the sides. The tank had rounded, sloping surfaces, had a five-wheel running gear and showed good cross-country performance.

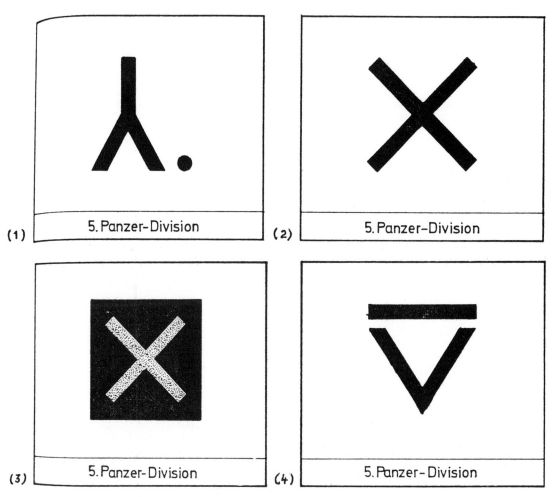

(1) 5. Panzer-Division

(2) 5. Panzer-Division

(3) 5. Panzer-Division

(4) 5. Panzer-Division

Various troop emblems of a Panzer division during the course of the war. (1) French campaign, 1940. (2) and (3) Eastern campaign, 1941-45. (4) Disguise emblem during "Operation Citadel."

Panzer regiments also bore disguise emblems during particular operations. Left: battle of Kharkov, 1942; right: "Operation Citadel, 1943."

Large-series production of the "Panther" went on in the summer of 1944. This picture shows an assembly hall of the MAN firm on September 1, 1944.

A "Panther" transport train is loaded for the trip to the front on August 18, 1944.

The "King Tiger" — P-VI/II — the best version of the German tank, entered the war too late. (Photo taken January 13, 1945.)

The first combat service of the "King Tiger" units took place not long afterward. This time France had again become a theater of war. The German leadership had, of course, awaited the so-called "second front" of the Allies in the west for a long time, but the OKW believed an enemy landing would take place on the Channel coast and located the focal point of the defense there; the other stretches of the coast were to be protected by the structures of the "Atlantic Wall."

Panzer troops were stationed there in France and Belgium only to be refreshed or reconstituted. Only in the spring of 1944 were Panzer units assigned their own fixed locations in the occupied western territory.

The number of tanks in occupied France in 1944, for example, was:

Day	P-III	P-IV	P-V	P-VI
1/31	98	410	180	64
2/29	99	587	290	45
3/31	99	527	323	45
4/30	114	674	514	101
6/10	39	748	663	102

Stoff-gliederung 21	Geheime Kommandosache! **Tiger II (VK 4503) Ausf. B** 8,8 cm 43 L/71 (Sd.Kfz. 182) (als Gerät 51 auch Pz Bef Wg. Tiger Ausf B)	Blatt G 331

Dringl.-St.: DE

Technische Daten:

Gesamtgewicht des Fahrzeuges (Gefechtsgewicht) 68 t

Motor HL 230 P30 600+)-700++) PS bei 2500+) bezw. 3000++) U/min

Höchstgeschwindigkeit 34,6+)/41,5++) km/Std. +) bei 2500 U/min, ++) bei 3000 U/min

Mitgeführte Kraftstoffmenge 860 l (einschl. Reservetank)

Fahrbereich mit einer Kraftstoff-Füllung:

Straße ~170 km; mittl. Gelände ~ 120 km

Grabenüberschreitfähigkeit ~ 2,5 m, Steigvermögen +35° - 35°

Watfähigkeit 1,75 m, Kletterfähigkeit 0,85

Besatzung 5 Mann, Spez. Bodendruck 1,03 kg/cm², Bodenfreiheit 0,485 m

Länge 10286 mm, Breite 3625 mm, 3755 " m. Schürzen

Höhe mit Aufbau 3075 mm

Bordmunition ~ 72 Schuß KwK; 5850 Schuß MG; 192 Schuß MP

Bestückung: a) Turmwaffen = 8,8 cm KwK 43 L/71 + 1 MG 34

b) Bugwaffen 1 MG 34 i. Kugelblende

c) 1 MP

Abfeuerung KwK elktr. MG i. Turm (mech.); MG i. Kugelblende (Handabzug)

Optisches Gerät: a) Turmoptik TZF 9 b/1 (binocular); später monocular TZF 9 d

b) Kugeloptik KZF 2

c) Fahreroptik Prismeneinsätze

d) Pz. Führerkuppel Prismenspiegel (auch bei Ladeschützen)

Funkgerät (normale Ausstattung) Fu 5 + Fu 2; (f. Pz. Bef. Wg. Tiger B Sonderausstattung)

Panzerung: Front 150 mm, Bug 100 ", Seite 80 mm

Turm 180 " (Front), 80 " (Seite), Dach 40 mm

Kette 46+46 Glieder, Kettengewicht 3350 kg

Rohstoffbedarf: (o. Waffe)	Eisen unleg. 44009,– kg	dav. Grob u. Mi. Bl. 62976,– kg
	leg. 75789,– "	Feinblech 2248,– "
	Eisen gesamt 119.798,– "	Fertiggew. (einschl. Waffe) 68000,– kg

Preis RM	Durchschn. Fertigungszeit Monate	Arbeitsstunden

Fertigungsfirmen:

Montage: Henschel, Kassel; Wegmann, Kassel

Fahrgestell: Henschel, Kassel

Panzerung: Skoda, Pilsen; Dortm. Hoerd-Hütt-Verein, Dortmund; Krupp, Essen

The increase took place because there were now four Panzer divisions in the country — the 2nd, 9th, 11th and 21st — and two new divisions were founded. These were the Panzer Lehr Divisions, which were formed in the Nancy-Verdun area and whose staff was taken from the command staff of the School for Mobile Troops (Krampnitz). The 113th Panzer Lehr Regiment, which was subordinate to it, consisted ofa staff and the I./Pz.Lehr-Reg. plus a newly organized "Tiger" unit. The division was, in fact, transferred to Hungary in April, but returned to Paris in May and took up a position as OKW reserve.

The heavy tanks (Tiger I) of the 130th Panzer Lehr Regiment on the march in the Nancy area.

The second newly formed Panzer Division was the 166th Panzer Division, formed of what remained of the 16th Panzer-grenadier Division, which had been smashed in Russia, and parts of the 179th Reserve Panzer Division (Hamburg Military Zone). The Panzer Regiment 16, subordinate to it, consisted of the staff of the 68th Panzer-grenadier Regiment, the 116th Panzer Unit and the 1st Reserve Panzer Unit. The restructuring of the division was still in process when the invasion began.

In addition, the independent Panzer Brigades 105, 106, 111, 112 and 113 were formed in Belgium and France in the spring of 1944. Of these Panzer troops, only the 21st Panzer Division was in Normandy when the Allied landing began on June 6, 1944.

These troop units were subordinate to the Commander of Panzer Group West. (From this staff the Command of the 5th Panzer Army was formed on July 27, 1944.) The outlook of the Commander of Panzer Group West, General of the Panzer Troops Baron Geyr von Schweppenburg, clashed greatly with those of the Commander of Army Group B (the highest command position in northwestern

France), Field Marshal Rommel. While Rommel wanted to have the Panzer units placed right along the coast — he feared the Allied air superiority in the hinterlands — the Commander wanted to set up his troops in the hinterlands to be able to have them make a counterattack at any threatened location.

The Allies left them no time to think it over. They landed in Normandy in the early hours of June 6, 1944 under the fire of heavy ships and constant air attacks. Despite the desperate counterattacks of the defenders, the Allies were on the Continent by evening. A counterattack by the 22nd Panzer Regiment (21st Panzer Division) pushed through to the Channel coast and separated the landed enemy forces, but by evening all its force had been lost.

The Panzer Lehr Division, alerted early in the morning, lost 1/3 of its tanks to air attacks on its way to the coast. Near Bayeux it was brought to a stop by the enemy, despite the brave combat of the II./130th Panzer Regiment. On the third day of the battle, the 2nd Panzer Division arrived, having come from the Somme, and opposed the advancing enemy forces near Villers-Bocage.

Tiger I tanks on the training grounds.

The newest German Panzer division — the Panzer Lehr Division — had to find out the hard way how tough the fighting was. The division had already lost 123 tanks by June 19, and on July 6 it had absolutely none left!

The first "King Tiger" unit, Panzer Brigade 503 *Feldherrnhalle,* arrived in the battle zone (as the first of these units) on June 17, and by early August it had already lost all its heavy tanks. On account of the heavy losses, the OKW transferred the 9th Panzer Division from the Nimes area to Alençon at the end of July.

Now the 11th Panzer Division was alone in southern France. It was the only motorized division that remained to oppose the French and American armored units that had landed in southern France and later during the retreat in the Rhone valley.

The Panzer divisions serving in the north were surrounded in the basin of Falaise after the Allied breakthrough near Avranches, along with the entire German 7th Army. When the combat groups broke out of the basin, the three divisions formed the rear guard. The 2nd Panzer Division, and particularly the 3rd Panzer Regiment, held the escape route near Chambois open by itself for 24 hours. The Allied advance to the east continued. In the defense of Paris itself, the 9th Panzer Division prevented the Americans from crossing the Marne in the Meaux area for days. In Paris a Panzer company equipped with captured and training tanks and named *Paris* took part in the fighting in the western suburbs.

At the end of August 1944 the Allies were at the western border of the German Reich. The 11th Panzer Division blocked the roads to Lyon in the foothills of the Alps - and early in September the first major combat took place in the Aachen area. Here the 116th Panzer Division and 165th Panzer Brigade stood out particularly. Then when American and British paratroopers landed behind the defenders around Arnheim, battle groups of the 116th Panzer Division, 108th Panzer Brigade and the newly arrived "King Tiger" Unit 506 took part in a counterattack.

A "Panther" in Normandy.

A "Tiger I" on its way to the front in a central French city.

In the course of the ensuing combat, the 166th Panzer Division drew back into the Hürtgenwald. The 9th Panzer Division fought near Geilenkirchen and the 11th Panzer Division was on the border north of Trier.

After enemy units coming from the Channel coast had united with those from the Mediterranean coast, the battle raged in Alsace-Lorraine. In mid-September there were, from left to right: the 11th Panzer Division and Pz.Brig.113 south of Belfort, 21st Panzer Division west of Epinal, Pz.Brig.112 north of Epinal, Pz.Brig.111 advancing toward Epinal, and Pz.Brig.106 south of St. Avold.

In the next two months the front began to stabilize, and the OKW was already planning a counterattack, which later went down in history as the "Ardennes Offensive." Thus all the armored and motorized forces were withdrawn from the front to be refreshed and restocked with personnel, weapons and equipment in the hinterlands. Only (from right to left) the 116th, 9th, 21st, 11th Panzer Divisions, the Panzer Lehr Division and Panzer Brigade 106 remained on the front until November.

The OKH had formed a new Panzer Army Command 6 on September 6, 1944; it was to lead the offensive at the focal point. Here it was a command office of the Waffen-SS, whose leadership Generaloberst Sepp Dietrich, a Feldwebel of the tank troops in World War I, assumed.

The Ardennes Offensive

Development to December 24

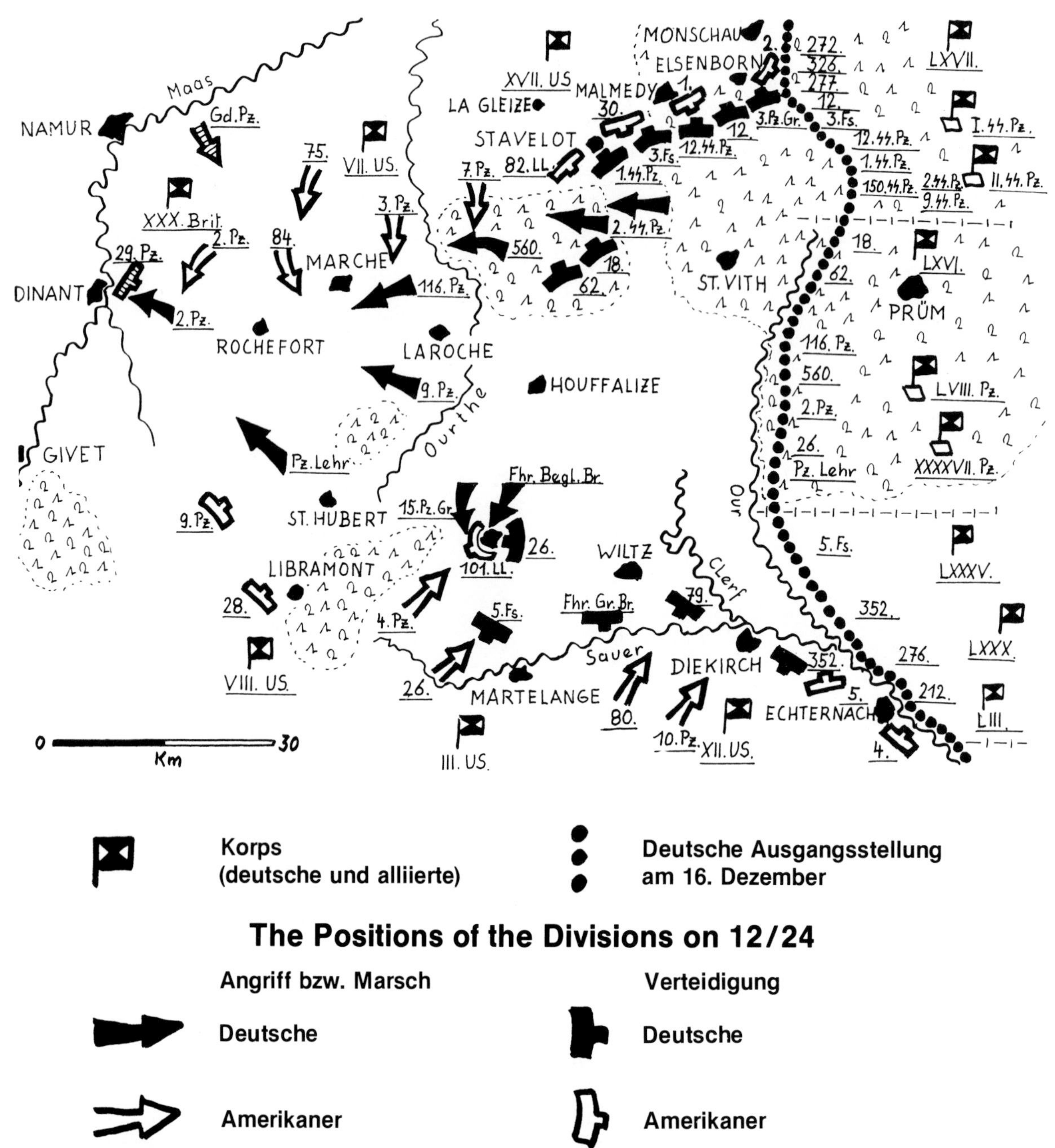

The German leadership had set a large-scale goal for the planned offensive. The troops of three armies were to break through the Allied front in the Eifel Mountains in a surprise attack and press forward across the Meuse to Antwerp in a bold stroke. The goal was the separation of the American and Canadian-British forces and the halting of any supplies moving toward the Continent of Europe. The new command of the 6th Panzer Army led two SS Panzer corps with four well-equipped SS-Panzer divisions in the right focal point. The 5th Panzer Corps had likewise moved up with two Panzer corps of the Army — the XXXXVII and LVIII — and three Panzer divisions (Panzer Lehr, 2nd and 116th Panzer Divisions), while the 7th Army had the job of securing the flank with only five infantry divisions.

The attack, which began on December 16, 1944, developed only laboriously after the successful initial attacks, once the Allied air forces had been able to bring the German troops to a standstill through mass attacks. The Panzer divisions — to whom the 9th Panzer Division was added — were able to cross the Ourthe.

P-V tanks of the 2nd Panzer Division roll toward Dinant, December 23, 1944.

Just as it had before Moscow in 1941, the 2nd Panzer Division advanced the farthest and was just five kilometers from Dinant on Christmas Eve 1944, but then the Allies struck back.

This move opened the Allies' way to the Rhein and Ruhr region!

The year of 1944 had once again brought changes in the structure of the Panzer troops. Among others, the former Panzer Company *Rhodos* had become the Panzer Unit *Rhodos*, with a staff and three companies, that stayed on the island of Rhodes until the war ended. The Panzer Unit *Nord*, founded in Munich in February of 1944 and intended to be transferred to the Army Group North, had a short history, being disbanded after only four weeks. The former Panzer Division *Norwegen* provided the cadre for the newly formed 25th Panzer Division, which was organized at the Wildflecken training camp in the Rhön Mountains in August. This division was immediately transferred to the eastern front and saw service near Warsaw. In its place a new Panzer Unit *Norwegen* came into being in Norway, subordinate to the Panzer Brigade *Norwegen*, which was founded on July 13, 1944 (with only one Pz.Abt. and one Panzer-grenadier Battalion).

25. Panzer-Division*

Aufstellung Anfang 1942

aus Besatzungstruppen in Norwegen

1943	
	West
September	Auffüllung in Nordfrankreich (Somme-Mündung)
Oktober	Verlegung zum Südabschnitt der Ostfront
	Ost
	1. Einsatz:
Oktober—Dezember	Verlustreiche Kämpfe im Raum Kiew-Fastow-Shitomir
	Abwehrkämpfe im Raum Bjelaja Zerkow
Dezember bis	
1944	
März	Rückzugskämpfe über Pawolotsch, Rushin bis Kalinowka
	Verlustreiche Abwehrkämpfe im Raum Berditschew-Kalinowka-Winniza
	Auflösung der dezimierten Division
	Reste auf andere Einheiten verteilt
	West
August	Neuaufstellung auf dem Tr.Üb.Pl. Wildflecken/Rhön
	(Stammpersonal aus Dänemark und Norwegen)
	Verlegung an die Weichselfront
	Ost
	2. Einsatz:
September	Einsatz in Warschau
Oktober	Verlustreiche Kämpfe am Narew-Brückenkopf, Raum Serock-Nasielsk, Ciechanow-Rozan
November—Dezember	E-Transport in den Raum Radom
	Verlustreiche Kämpfe am Warka-Brückenkopf südlich Warschau (Weichselbogen)
1945	
Januar	Ausbruch aus dem Kessel über Radom-Bialobrzegi, die Pilica, Nowe Miasto in den Raum Lodz
Februar—März	E-Transport nach Pommern
	Einsatz im Raum Stettin
April—Mai	E-Transport nach Wien
	Abwehrkämpfe bei Poysdorf und Laa an der Thaja
	Panzerschlacht bei Mistelbach-Zistersdorf
	Kapitulation
	Amerikanische Gefangenschaft
	Teilweise Übergabe an die Russen im Raum Budweis, teilweise Entlassung in die Heimat

Additional large units came into being in September and October of 1944. One of them, Panzer Brigade 101, was transferred to the Army Group North. In October it was sent to rebuild the 20th Panzer Division, which had been shattered in Rumania, and renamed Panzer Regiment 21. A further division came about in August 1944, formed of replacement army troops: Panzer Division *Tatra*. This was a Panzer division in name only, as it included only one Panzer company (made of Panzer Lehr and the 4th Replacement Unit). When this division was redesignated the 232nd Panzer Division of the field army in February, it was not given any additional tank companies. The division came to grief on the Raab in March of 1945.

In September and November the OKH founded two new general commands of the Panzer troops: the *Grossdeutschland* and *Feldherrnhalle* Panzer Corps. These general commands each received one heavy tank unit along with their corps troops (Pz.Abt. *GD* and *FHH*). Both corps saw service on the eastern front. Another newly formed unit, the Panzer-grenadier Division *Brandenburg*, made out of the special troops of the German home guard, was given its own Panzer Regiment *Brandenburg* under its command.

Manual of tank shot tables

Anlage zu
H. Dv. 469/3 b

Nur für den Dienstgebrauch!

Nicht in Feindeshand fallen lassen!

Do not let it fall into enemy hands!

Panzer-
Beschußtafel

(Abwehr schwer zu bekämpfender Panzerfahrzeuge)

8,8 cm KwK 36

Stand: 15. 2. 43

B 7

The former Panzer brigades and independent Panzer units were now integrated into various divisions, since they — often on their own — had not gained the anticipated success. Thus in 1944 the independent Panzer units were first made into Panzer brigades, for example:

Pz.Abt.2101 became Pz.Brig.101
Pz.Abt.2102 became Pz.Brig.102
Pz.Abt.2103 became Pz.Brig.103, etc., to Pz.Abt.2113.

Then (beginning inPz.Brig.108 to the 116th Panzer Division,

Pz.Brig.116 to the 16th Panzer-Grenadier Division,
Pz.Brig.125 to the 25th Panzer-Grenadier Division,
Pz.Brig.190 to the 90th Panzer-Grenadier Division, etc.

The 109th Panzer Brigade was used to establish the Panzer Division *FHH* and the 110th Panzer Brigade to rebuild the 13th Panzer Division.

In addition, new Panzer regiments bearing names were founded:

Panzer Regiment *Brandenburg* for Pz.Gren.Div. *Brandenburg*,
Panzer Regiment *Führer Begleit Div.* for the division of the same name,
Panzer Regiment *Führer-Grenadier Div.* for the division of the same name,
Panzer Regiment *Grossdeutschland* for the division of the same name,
Panzer Regiment *Kurmark* for the division of the same name.

The heavy units founded in the spring of 1944 and equipped with the new "King Tiger" tank were sent to the front as soon as they were assembled; there they sometimes fought independently. Only Pz.Abt.503 was utilized to form the first Pz. Abt. *FHH*.

The action seen by these units can be summed up briefly:

Pz.Abt.501:	Service in Poland as of August 1944, renamed Pz.Abt.424 in December ("Tiger I"). Smashed in January of 1945.
Pz.Abt.503:	Service at Caen early in July 1944, lost all tanks in retreat; later new *FHH*.
Pz.Abt.505:	Service on the Narev as of September 1944, later in East Prussia until the war ended.
Pz.Abt.506:	Service at Arnheim as of September 1944, later at Aachen and in the Eifel, smashed in March of 1945.
Pz.Abt.509:	Service in attack on Budapest in January 1945, retreat via St. Pölten to the Moldau, surrendered there in May 1945.

Tests of remote-control tanks were carried out since 1943. These were the smallest tanklike vehicles (called "Goliath"), which carried mines and were guided toward their targets from command tanks. The first units formed for them were numbered 301, 302, 305 and 311 to 317.

The Command of the Panzer Troops under the Commander of the Reserve Army regularized the organization of the former Panzer Replacement and Training Units in 1944. As of August 10, 1944 there were:

Pz.Ers. Unit Ausb. Abt.	Garrison City	Commander of the Panzer Troops
1	Erfurt	IX Erfurt
4	Vienna	XVII Vienna
5	Neuruppin	III Küstrin
7	Böblingen	V Stuttgart
10	Zinten	I Insterburg
11	Bielefeld	VI Coesfeld
15	Sagan	VIII Liegnitz
18	Kamenz	IV Leisnig
33	St. Pölten	XVII Vienna
35	Bamberg	XIII Bamberg
204	Schewtzingen	XII Landau

The action of the Panzer troops in the war year of 1944 was often noted in OKW reports. The 106th Panzer Brigade was cited three times in these reports, the 5th, 7th and 13th Panzer Divisions twice each.

And now the war had come to Germany. Now not only the *Volkssturm* was called on to defend the homeland, but so were what remained of the shattered front units; from them and the units of the Replacement Army all soldiers who were in any way usable were assembled into quickly improvised battle units, generally without appropriate equipment. Even within the Panzer troops regiments, units and companies came into being, often bearing a name that was certainly not matched by appropriate equipment in terms of vehicles, weapons and supplies. The following are only a few of the units thus formed:

1/26/1945	Panzer Regiment *Coburg*,
1/31/1945	Panzer Regiment *Kurmark*,
2/1/1945	Pz.Abt. *Stahnsdorf*,
2/10/1945	Panzer Division *Holstein* with Pz.Abt.44,
2/20/1945	Panzer Division *Schlesien* with Pz.Abt.303,
2/20/1945	Panzer Division *Jüterbog* with Pz.Abt. *Küterbog*,
2/20/1945	Pz.Verband *Stegemann*,
3/8/1945	Panzer Division *Müncheberg* w/Pz.Abt. *Kummersdorf*,
3/20/1945	Panzer Division *Feldherrnhalle 2* with the 4th Panzer Reg.,
3/28/1945	Pz.Ausb.Verb. *Thüringen*,
3/28/1945	Pz.Ausb.Verb. *Böhmen*,
3/28/1945	Pz.Ausb.Verb. *Franken*,
3/28/1945	Pz.Ausb.Verb. *Ostsee*,
3/28/1945	Pz.Ausb.Verb. *Westfalen*,
3/28/1945	Pz.Ausb.Verb. *Donau*,
3/28/1945	Pz.Auffr.Verb. *Krampnitz*,
3/28/1945	*Führer-Panzer Regiment 1* and Führer Panzer Regiment 2,
4/6/1945	Panzer Division *Clausewitz*,
4/6/1945	233rd Panzer Division in Denmark.

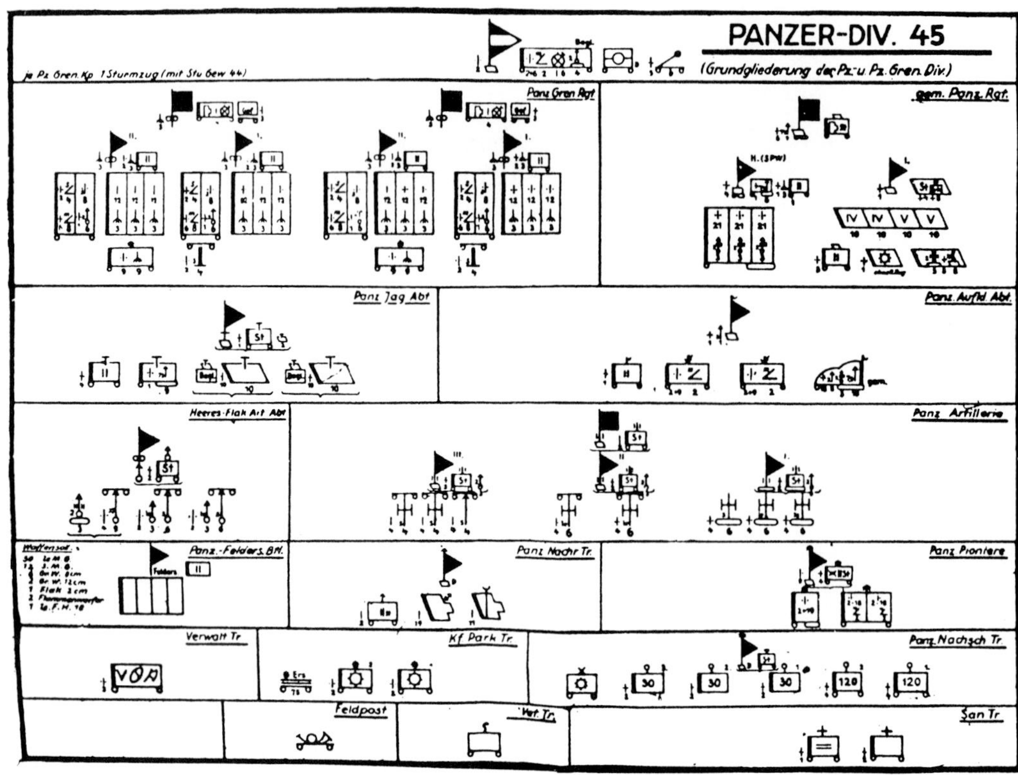

Pattern for the structure of a Panzer division, 1945.
The Panzer regiment consists of one tank unit (four companies) and one Panzer-grenadier battalion.

The structure of these units could no longer be compared with the corresponding structure and combat strength of the previous war years. According to a directive of the OKH, a 1945 Panzer regiment consisted of 1361 officers, non-commissioned officers and enlisted men in total, with 129 trucks, 121 other motor vehicles, 54 tanks and 39 SPW (armored gun cars). The structure was arranged as follows:

Staff with staff company
(6 MG, 2 P-III with 7.5 cm KwK)
I. Panzer unit:
Staff with staff company (13 MG)
2 Panzer companies with ten P-IV each
2 Panzer companies with ten P-V each
Anti-aircraft company with two columns
(8 37mm Flak 43, 3 20mm quadruple guns, 8 MG)
Workshop company (1 MG)
Supply company (3 MG)

II. SPW battalion:
Staff (4 MG)
3 Panzer-grenadier companies, each with
3 20mm triple Flak, 21 MG
1 heavy tank column with six P-IV
Supply company (1 MG, 3 heavy antitank guns)

The Panzer supply companies had been established in 1944 to lift some burdens from the combat companies. Their most important task was bringing needed fuel and ammunition to the combat companies on the battlefield, so as to avoid any need to move backward. The former Panzer, anti-aircraft and armored engineer columns were integrated into the staff companies.

Despite setbacks on all fronts and constant heavy air attacks on armaments factories, the production of tanks went on, even though the number made grew steadily smaller. In January 1945 473 tanks were still produced at the factories; in February the number dropped to 378.

The misfortunes on all fronts did not inspire Hitler to draw military or political conclusions; instead he "exchanged" personnel again. Generaloberst Guderian — the creator of the German tank weapon — was relieved of his position as Chief of the General Staff of the OKH. At the same time the ever-critical Inspector General, General of the Panzer Troops Baron Geyr von Schweppenburg, had to go. The last Inspector General was Generalleutnant Thomale, Guderian's longtime confidant and close collaborator.

In January of 1945 Germany had finally become a war zone. While hundreds of thousands were fleeing from the eastern territories to central and western Germany and the cities of western Germany were being burned and destroyed by Allied bomb attacks, there were still soldiers along the borders, fighting against the superior forces of the enemy.

The fighting west of the Rhine was practically over by mid-March of 1945 when Canadian, British, American and French forces occupied the west bank and units of the U.S. 1st Army crossed the river at Remagen. The positions of the Panzer divisions at the beginning of the month was as follows, from north to south: With Army Group H in Holland were Pz.Brig.106 and the 116th Panzer Division, with Army Group B on the middle Rhine were the Panzer Lehr Division, the 2nd, 9th and 11th Panzer Divisions, and with Army Group G in Baden there was not one Panzer unit capable of fighting.

Until mid-March the 11th Panzer Division fought bitterly in the Reichswald area near Kleve, while the 9th Panzer Division's remaining men held fast in Cologne until they went down.

Early in April the Allied armies crossed the Rhine all along the front. Army Group B under Feldmarschall Model was surrounded and defeated in the so-called "Ruhr Basin." The 116th Panzer Division met its end at Iserlohn, the Panzer Lehr Division went down fighting with its last tanks in the Lüdenscheid area. Only the 2nd and 11th Panzer Divisions were able to fight their way eastward in the southern part of the front. Almost without tanks, they reached Thuringia and the Vogtland, where they laid down their arms on the day of surrender. Shortly before that, the Panzer Division *Clausewitz* — which was part of the 12th Army that had just been established in April — went down fighting in the Harz Mountains, along with other named divisions of the infantry.

A P-IV company of the 11th Panzer Division on the march through a village on the lower Rhine in March of 1945.

A "Panther" with a load of grenadiers prepares to fight back at the edge of a village in the Hürtgenwald.

The *Clausewitz* Division had been formed of troops from the Panzer Gunnery School at Putlos, the Panzer Replacement Brigade *Grossdeutschland*, the 233rd Reserve Panzer Division, the Panzer-Grenadier Division *Feldherrnhalle* and various schools from Military Districts III (Berlin) and IV (Dresden).

At the beginning of 1945, the OKH had not given up the war on the eastern front either. When the Ardennes Offensive ended in a fiasco, Hitler wanted to force a decision in the east. The Panzer Army Command 6 was transferred to Hungary with the most capable Waffen-SS divisions and, along with the Panzer divisions of the army, was to liberate Budapest, which had been surrounded by the Red Army.

A "King Tiger" on the march through Budapest in 1944.

The 13th Panzer Division, along with various army and Waffen-SS units, had been cut off from the rest of the front in the Hungarian capital. In the fighting that followed, it was defeated along with all the other units. The attack, in which the 1st, 3rd, 23rd and 232nd Panzer Divisions took part, started well on January 18, 1945.

> "A tank raid begins as our soldiers have not experienced it since the Caucasus days," the history of the 3rd Panzer Divisionreported. "The tanks, armored gun vehicles and self-propelled guns storm through the midst of the enemy troops without hesitation. The Russians flee across country, head over heels. . . ."

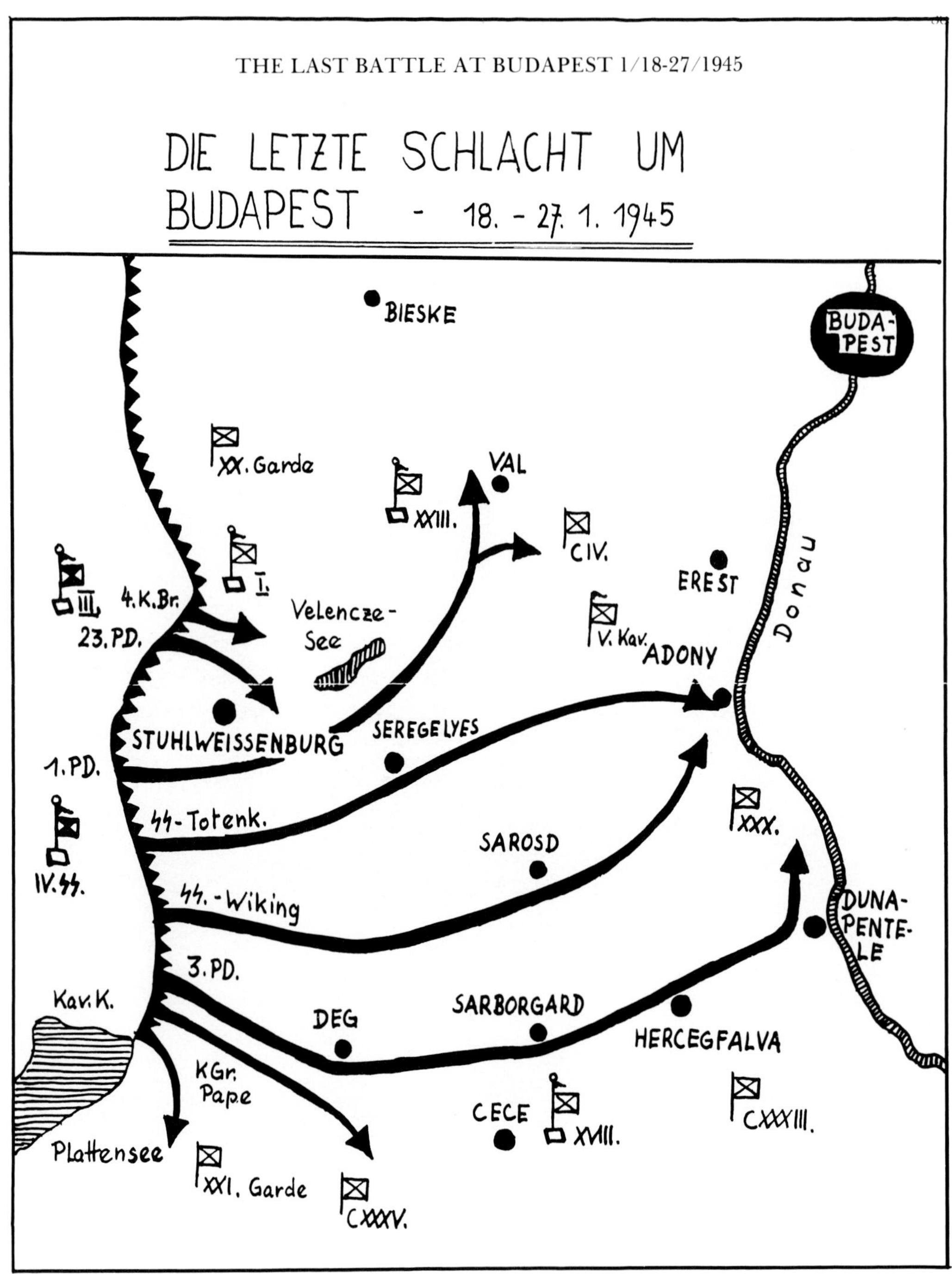

But only for three days; then the Red Army struck back. The reverses began at the south end of the front; at the same time, the major Soviet attack from the Baranov bridgehead broke the front of the central army group. Here (from right to left) the 8th and 20th Panzer Divisions, Panzer Brigade 103, and combat units of the 19th, 16th and 17th Panzer Divisions, and the 178th Reserve Panzer Division were fighting. In February the hard-pressed front was strengthened with the 21st Panzer Division from the west, the 25th Panzer Division and the newly formed Panzer Division *Jüterbog*.

After the Soviet units had succeeded in tearing up the central front and breaking through from central Poland across the Vistula and to the Oder, East and West Prussia were practically separated from the Reich. The 7th and *Holstein* Panzer Divisions were fighting in West Prussia, the 5th and 24th Panzer Divisions in East Prussia. The Army Group Courland, left to its own devices since October, still included the 12th and 14th Panzer Divisions; the 4th Panzer Division was being moved to the mouth of the Vistula.

A "Panther" tank of the 24th Panzer Division comes to the front south of Braunsberg, East Prussia, early in March of 1945, along with the last combat reserves — infantry and Waffen-SS.

The last "Panthers" of the 4th Panzer Division, carrying shock troops of the Panzer-grenadiers, were still making counterattacks west of Gotenhafen in mid-March of 1945.

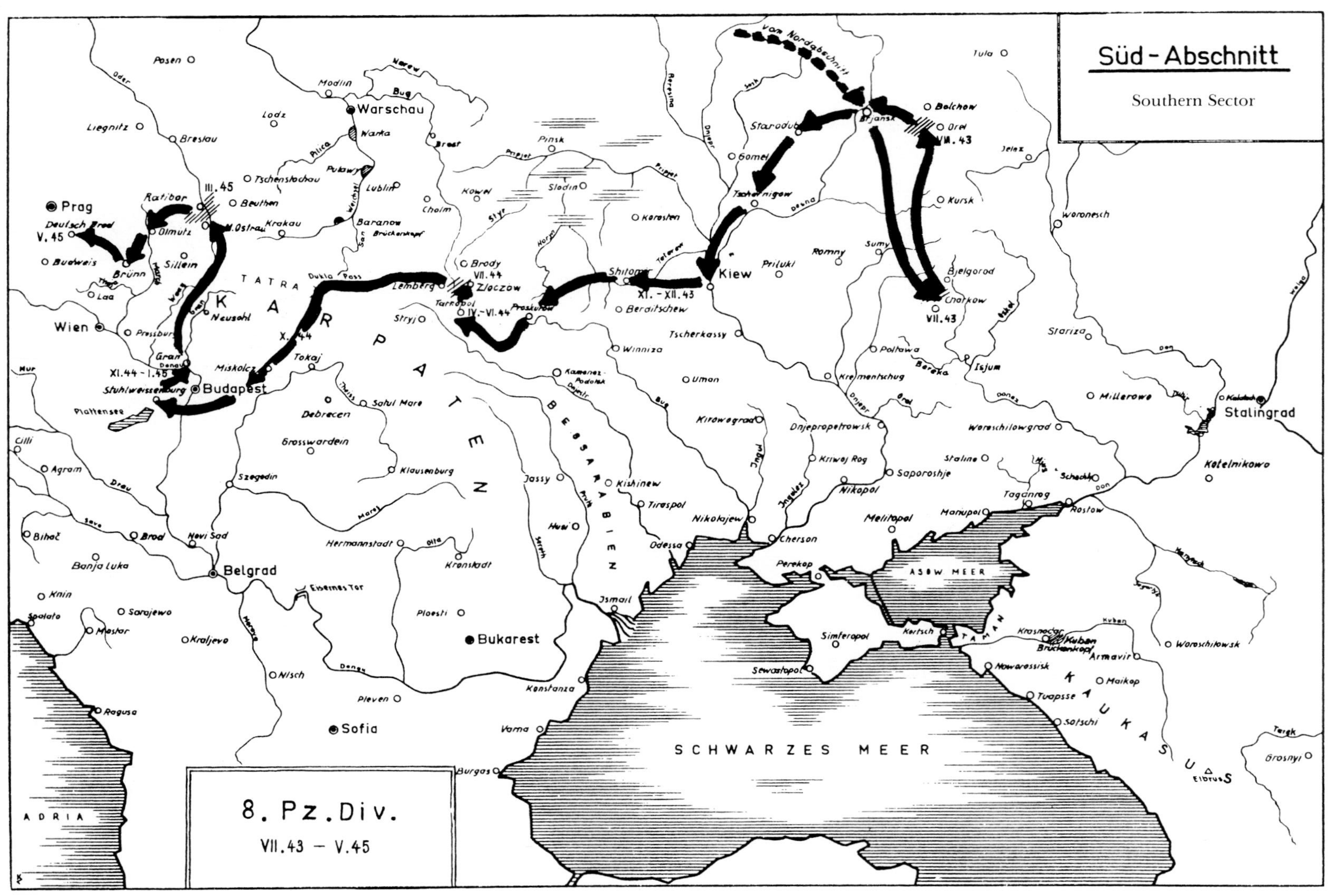

Süd-Abschnitt
Southern Sector
8. Pz.Div.
VII.43 – V.45
von Nordabschnitt
Brjansk
Bolchow
Orel
VII.43
Starodub
Gomel
Tschernigow
Kiew
Charkow
VII.43
Kursk
Bjelgorod
Shitomir
XI.–XII.43
Berditschew
Proskurow
IV.–VI.44
Tarnopol
Zloczow
VII.44
Brody
Lemberg
Dukla Pass
X.44
Tokaj
Miskolcz
Budapest
Stuhlweissenburg
XI.44–I.45
Gran
Plattensee
Wien
Pressburg
Neusohl
Sillein
Brünn
Olmütz
Ratibor
III.45
M.Ostrau
Prag
Deutsch Brod
V.45
Budweis
Warschau
Krakau
Breslau
Lodz
Lublin
Posen
Liegnitz
Tschenstochau
Beuthen
Baranow
Pinsk
Kowel
Kowel
Korosten
Priluki
Romny
Sumy
Poltawa
Tscherkassy
Winniza
Uman
Kirowograd
Dnjepropetrowsk
Kriwoj Rog
Saporoshje
Nikopol
Melitopol
Mariupol
Taganrog
Rostow
Stalingrad
Woronesch
Tula
Jelez
Isjum
Millerowo
Woroschilowgrad
Staline
Kotelnikowo
Cherson
Nikolajew
Odessa
Kishinew
Tiraspol
Jassy
Ismail
Perekop
Simferopol
Kertsch
Sewastopol
Noworossisk
Krasnodar
Armavir
Maikop
Tuapsse
Sotschi
Woroschilowsk
Grosnyi
Elbrus
ASOW MEER
SCHWARZES MEER
KARPATEN
TATRA
BESSARABIEN
KAUKASUS
TAMAN
Debrecen
Grosswardein
Klausenburg
Szegedin
Hermannstadt
Kronstadt
Ploesti
Bukarest
Konstanza
Varna
Burgas
Sofia
Pleven
Nisch
Belgrad
Novi Sad
Kraljevo
Sarajewo
Mostar
Ragusa
Spalato
Knin
Banja Luka
Bihač
Agram
Cilli
ADRIA

A "Tiger" company advances through mud and snow in Lusatia, February 1945.

One of the last German tanks still intact — a P-V — in the surrounded Silesian capital of Breslau, early in March 1945.

The last successful battle took place in the Lauban area of Lower Silesia. Here the 17th Army, with the XXXIX Panzer Corps (including the 19th Panzer Division) and the LVII Panzer Corps (with the 8th Panzer Division and Panzer Brigade 103) were able to encircle the entire Russian LXXXXIX Motorized Army Corps early in March. The 16th Panzer Division that followed did not need to go into battle.

The last weeks of the war began. Of the former Panzer regiments there were now only Panzer units at best, or only Panzer companies, still intact. While the 5th and 24th Panzer Divisions shed their blood in East Prussia, the 7th Panzer Division fought near Elbing and Danzig. In the war zone around Berlin the men of the *Müncheberg* and *Kurmark* Panzer Division held fast. The 21st Panzer Division was fighting west of Spremberg, and the 20th Panzer Division led the last tank attack in the history of the war in the Bautzen area. The 6th, 8th, 16th, 17th and 19th Panzer Divisions were in Moravia, while the 1st, 3rd, 23rd and 25th Panzer Divisions were retreating toward Austria.

The last German tank attack — including the "Panther" shown here — took place on April 21, 1945 when the *Grossdeutschland* Panzer Corps, with the 20th Panzer Division leading the way, recaptured Bautzen and drove the Soviet 52nd Army back to the northeast.

The OKW reports of 1945 mentioned "Panther" Unit I/26, Heavy Panzer Unit 509, the I./Panzer Regiment 33, the 7th Panzer Division, and the OKW report of April 26, 1945 named Panzer units for the last time:

> "In the Silesian war zone the Panzer Regiment 27 of the 17th Panzer Division destroyed or captured 103 tanks or assault guns and 104 guns between March 15 and April 10. These successes are attributable above all to the I. Unit of this regiment, under the leadership of Hauptmann Büchs."

The Surrender Dates and Places of German Panzer Divisions

Panzer Division and Commander	Surrender Date and Place
Pz. Lehr	
Ob. von Hauser	4/16/45, Altena/Ruhr
FHH-1	
Ob. Wolff	5/8/45, NW of Brünn
FHH-2	
Generalm. Bäke	5/8/45, east of Brünn
Müncheberg	
Generalm. Mummert	5/3/45, Berlin
Clausewitz	
Generallt. Unrein	4/20/45, Elm Mountains
1st, Generallt. Thunert	5/9/45, Liezen, Styria
2nd, Ob. Stollbrock	5/7/45, west of Pilsen
3rd, Ob. Schöne	5/9/45, Liezen, Styria
4th, Ob. Hoffmann	5/8/45, Vistula mouth
5th, Generalm. Herzog	4/17/45, Samland
6th, Generallt. Baron von Werdenfels	5/8/45, west of Brünn
7th, Ob. Christern	5/3/45, Hagenow, Mecklenburg
8th, Generalm. Hax	5/8/45, Olmütz
9th, Ob. Sperling	4/17/45, Iserlohn
11th, Generallt. v. Wietersheim	5/4/45, Furth im Wald
12th, Ob. von Usedom	5/8/45, Courland
14th, Ob. Grässel	5/8/45, Libau, Courland
16th, Ob. Treuhaupt	5/8/45, north of Olmütz
17th, Generalm. Kretschmer	5/8/45, Mähr, Ostrau
20th, Generalm. von O.-Bronikowski	5/8/45, Tharandt, Saxony
21st, Generallt. Marcks	4/29/45, Königswusterhausen
23rd, Generallt. von Radowitz	5/8/45, Mauterndorf
24th, Generalm. v. Nostitz-Wallwitz	5/4/45, Frische Nehrung
25th, Generalm. Audörsch	5/9/45, Moldautheinau
26th, Generalm. Linnarz	5/3/45, Bozen
116th, Generalm. von Waldenburg	4/17/45, Iserlohn
232nd, Generalm. Back	3/23/45, on the Raab
233rd, Generallt. Fremery	5/3/45, southern Jutland

The OKW report of May 9, 1945 said:

"Since midnight the weapons have been silent on all fronts."

Thus the history of the Panzer troops of the German Reich came to an end — and when, ten years later, German tanks rolled once again over the roads and through the training camps, they belonged to two German states . . .

APPENDICES

1. List of Panzer regiments, independent units and companies 141
2. Commanders of the Panzer troops — January 3, 1939 146
3. Numbers of tanks in World War II 147
4. High Command Office of the Panzer Troops 148
5. Instructions for the Inspector General 149
6. General Command of the Panzer Corps — 1943 151
7. Officers of the Panzer divisions — 1942 152
8. Panzer brigade staffs 153
9. Panzer Troop School Wünsdorf - 1939 154
10. Commanders of the Panzer Troop and Panzer Gunnery Schools 155
11. Selection of daily orders of Panzer group/army commands, 1941 156
12. Operations of the Panzer divisions 160
13. Battle reports of the Eastern Campaign, 1941-45 163
14. The emblems of Panzer divisions, 1941-42 178
15. German tanks in the Eastern Campaign 179
16. Organization, structure and action of the - by number - first and last Panzer divisions 183
17. Panzer units in action against partisans 186
18. Panzer workshop and recovery units 187
19. Workshop companies and supply depots 188
20. Full weapons complement of a Panzer regiment — 1944 190
21. Full vehicle complement of a Panzer regiment — 1944 191
22. Tanks lost in the Eastern Campaign 192
23. German tanks in the last war year 193
24. Holder's of the Oak Leaves to the Knight's Cross in the Panzer troops (to regimental commanders) 194
25. Holder's of the Knight's Cross of the War Service Cross 195
26. Field newspapers of the Panzer troops (selection) 196
27. Generals of the Panzer troops who died in battle 197
28. The Panzer units of the Luftwaffe 199
29. The Panzer units of the Waffen-SS 200
30. The appearance of the German tank 201

List of Panzer Regiments, Independent Units and Companies

Number	Repl. Dist.	Subordinate to	Notes
Lehr Reg.	III	Army Troop	
Lehr Abt.	III	Army Troop	1940 II./Pz.Reg. 33
Reg. *Brandenburg*	III	Pz.Gren.Div. *Brandenburg*	1944-45 with Panzer Assault Unit
Reg. Führer Begleit Div.		Führer Begleit Gren.Div.	1945; later III./Pz.Gren. R FG
Abt./Reg. FHH	XX	Pz.Gren.Div. *FHH*, Pz. Corps *FHH*	
Reg. Grossdeutschland	III	Pz.Gren.Div. *GD*	3rd Abt., 1 "Tiger"
(Abt.)		Pz.Corps *GD*	of Pz.Abt. 100
Reg. *Kurmark*	XI	Pz.Gren.Div. *Kurmark*	1945
Reg.1	IX	1st Pz.Div.	see also 116
Reg.2	IX/VI	1st, 16th Pz.Div.	as of 1941; 1943 III.(Stu.G.) Abt.
Reg.3	XVII	2nd Pz.Div.	
Reg.4	XVII	2nd Pz.Div.	
	XI	13th Pz.Div.	as of 1941; 1943II. & III. Abt.; I. Abt. became Pz.Abt. 507
Reg.5	III	3rd Pz.Div, 5th Lt.Div.,	until Jan. 1941;
		21st Pz.Div.	ended in Tunis, May 1943
Abt.5	X	20th Pz.Gren.Div.	1943 Stu.G.; became Abt.190
Reg.6	III	3rd Pz.Div.	1941-42 3 Abt.
Reg.7	V	4th Pz.Brig./Army	1939
		10th Pz.Div.	lost 1943
Abt.7	XIII	10th Pz.Gren.Div.	1943 Stu.G., later Pz.Abt. 110 (?)
Reg.8	V	4th Pz.Brig/Army,	1939
		Pz.Brig.E.Prussia	1939
	XII	15th, 10th? Pz.Div.	1939/1943
Abt.8	V	25th Pz.Gren.Div.	1943 Stu.G.
Abt.9	VI	25th Pz.Div.	1942-43 Pz.Reg.202 later Pz.Abt.2104
Abt.I/10	I	AOK 3/Army	1939
Reg.10	I/III	8th Pz.Div.	as of 1940, some-times 3 Abt. with Pz.Abt. 67 & I./ Pz.Reg. 10
Reg.11	VI	1st Lt.Div., 6th Pz.Div.	1941 Pz.Abt.65 as III.Abt.
Abt.z.b.V. 12	III	Army Troop	became II./Pz.Reg. *Brandenburg* 1944
Reg.15	VIII	5th Pz.Div,	to 1941
		11th Pz.Div.	1942-43 3 Abt. III., 1943 in 4th Pz.Div.
Reg.16	VI	116th Pz.Div.	from Pz.Abt. 116
Reg.17	VII	17th Pz.Div.(?)	1944-45(?), from Pz.Reg. 39
Reg.18	XI	18th Pz.Div.	3 Abt at times; disbanded 1943; I.-Pz.Abt. 160
Reg.21	IX	20th Pz.Div.	3 Abt.
Reg.22	III	21st Pz.Div.	from Pz.Reg. 100 (?)
Abt.I./23	XII	2nd Lt.Div.	1939, became II./ Pz.Reg. 25
Reg.23	V	23rd Pz.Div.	from Pz.Reg. 201
Reg.24	I	24th Pz.Div.	1942 from parts of 1st Cav. Div.(R.R.2), 3 Abt. at times; Co's called Squadrons, I. with Pz. Lehr Div. at times
Staff, I./25	XIII	2nd Lt.Div.	1939
Reg.25	IX	7th Pz.Div.	1940 from I./Pz.Reg. 23 & I./Pz.Reg. 25, 3 Abt. at times
Reg.26	III	26th Pz.Div.	from Pz.Reg. 202; I. Abt 1943, with 25th Pz.Div. Staff - Staff of Pz.Reg. *Brandenburg*
Reg.27	XI	19th Pz.Div.	from Pz.Reg. 11, 3 Abt. at times
Abt.28		Army Troop	joined Pz.Reg. 6
Reg.29	II	12th Pz.Div.	3 Abt. at times
Reg.31	VIII	5th Pz.Div.	
Abt.32		Army Troop	
Abt.33	XVII	4th Lt.Div.	1939, Pz.Abt.(trucked)

Reg.33	XVII	9th Pz.Div.	*Prinz Eugen*, 1940 with Pz. Trng.Abt. of Pz.Abt. 33; 3 Abt. at times; II. Abt. became Pz.Abt. 51 in 1943 and III. Abt. became Pz.Abt. 506
Reg.35	XIII	4th Pz.Div.	
Reg.36	XIII	4th Pz.Div.	until early 1941
	IV	14th Pz.Div.	as of early 1941; gave parts to Pz.Abt. 509
Abt.37		Army Troop	
Reg.39	XVII	17th Pz.Div. Pz.Brig.10	3 Abt. at times; became Pz.Reg. 17 (?) 1944
Abt.z.b.V.40		Army Troop	
(Comp.z.b.V. I./40)		11th Inf.Brig. AOK Norway	1940; became Pz.Abt. Norway (?) 1943
Abt.51	XVII	Army Troop, Pz.Brig.10	Panther Abt., from II./ Pz.Reg. 33
Abt.52		Army Troop, Pz.Brig. 10	Panther Abt.
Abt.55	V	255th Pz.Div.	from Reserve Pz.Abt. 5
Abt.60		Army Troop	
Abt.65	VI	1st Lt.Div. 6th Pz.Div.	Abt.(trucked) at first; became III./Pz.Reg. 11 in 1941
Abt.66	IX	2nd Lt.Div.	Pz.Abt.(trucked) 1939, to
	V	10th Pz.Div.	Pz.Reg. 25
Abt.67	III	3rd Lt.Div.	Pz.Abt.(trucked) 1939, to Pz.Reg. 10
Reg.Staff 69		Army Troop	became staff/Pz.Reg. 16
Comp.72		Army Troop	
Comp.81		Army Troop	
Comp.82		Army Troop	
Reg.100		Army Troop	French tanks, became Pz. Reg. 22
Abt.100 (F)	XII	Army Troop	Flame Pz.Abt.(1941); sp.*GD*
Abt.101(F)	IX	Army Troop	same as above (1941)
Abt.102(F)			Army Trooplater Pz.Abt. 2102
Abt.103	III	3rd Pz.Gren.Div.	Assault guns
Abt.104		Army Troop	Tiger (?)
Abt.110	XIII	10th Pz.Gren.Div.	from Pz.Abt.7 (?)
Abt.115	XII	15th Pz.Gren.Div.	from Pz.Abt.215
Abt.116	VI	16th Pz.Gren.Div.	from I./Pz.Reg. 1; became Pz.Reg.16
Abt.118	VIII	18th Pz.Gren.Div.	Assault guns
Abt.120	X	20th Pz.Gren.Div.	from Pz.Abt.5 (?)
Abt.125	V	25th Pz.Gren.Div.	from Pz.Abt.8 (?)
Abt.129	IX	29th Pz.Gren.Div.	Assault guns
Reg.130	XI	Pz.Trng.Div.	
Comp.157		Army Troop	
Abt.160	XX	60th Pz.Gren.Div. *FHH*	ex-I./Pz.Reg. 18, lost Jan. 1943
Abt.190	III	90th Pz.Gren.Div.	ex-II./Pz.Reg. 202; became II,/Pz.Reg.5
Staff, II./190	III	21st Pz.Div.	
Comp.200		Army Troop	
Comp.201	IX	201st Sich.Div.	Captured tanks
Reg.201		Army/8th Pz.Brig. 23rd Pz.Div.	French tanks; became Pz.Reg.23
Reg.202		Army/8th Pz.Brig. 26th/25th Pz.Div.	French tanks; became 26 & 29; II became Pz.Abt.190
Reg.203		Army Troop	Given low # in a Pz.Div; Staff became staff of Pz.Reg. *GD*
Comp.203	III	203rd Sich.Div.	Captured tanks
Reg.204	XII	22nd Pz.Div.	as Abt. in Ruhr, 1945
Abt.205		Army Troop	
Abt.206		Army Troop	
Comp.207	II	207th Sich.Div.	Captured tanks

Abt.208		Army Troop	
Abt.211		Army/XXXVI.Geb.K.	
Abt.213		Army Troop	
Comp.213	VIII	213th Sich.Div.	Captured tanks
Abt.214			Army Troop
Abt.215		Army/15th Pz. Gren.Div.	with 4th (Assault) Co.; became Pz.Abt. 115
Abt.216		Army Troop	Assault tanks
Abt.217		Army Troop	as above
Abt.218		Army Troop	as above
Abt.220	IV	164th *Afrika* Div.	
Comp.221	VIII	221st Sich.Div.	Captured tanks
Abt.223		Army Troop	
Comp.224		LXXXVIII. A.K.	Captured tanks
Test Co.258		Army Troop	
Comp.281	II	281st Sich.Div.	Captured tanks
Comp.285	II	285th Sich.Div.	as above
Abt.300		Army Troop	
Abt.301		Army Troop	French tanks 1941; formed anew of III./Pz.Reg. 10 as Pz.Abt. (FKL)
Abt.302 (FKL)		Army Troop	
Comp.305 (FKL)		Army Troop	
Abt.306		Army Troop	
Comp.311 (FKL)		Army Troop	with Pz.Reg. *GD* 1943
Comp.312 (FKL)		Army Troop	
Comp.313 (FKL)		Army Troop	
Comp.314 (FKL)		Army Troop	
Comp.315 (FKL)		Army Troop	
Comp.316 (FKL)		Army Troop	
Comp.317 (FKL)		Army Troop	
Comp.318		Cmdr. Army Gp.South	Captured tanks
Abt.330		Army Troop	
Abt.339		Army Troop	
Abt.345		345th Pz.Gren.Div.	
Comp.351 (F)		Army Troop	Flamethrowing tanks
Comp.352 (F)		Army Troop	as above
Comp.353 (F)		Army Troop	as above
Comp.354	VIII	442nd Sich.Div.	Captured tanks
Comp.377		Army Troop	
Abt.386		386th Pz.Gren.Div.	
Comp.387		Army Troop	
Comp.445		Army Troop (445th Sich.Div.?)	Captured tanks?
Ind.Abt.500	VI	Army Troop	"Tiger" tanks
Reg.Staff/Mot. Mot. Troops 501	I	A.O.K.3	with Pz.Abw.Abt. 511 & 521 5./Fla.Btl. 31 in 1939
Ind.Abt.501	VI	Army Troop	"Tigers", in Tunis 1943; later A.O.K.4
Ind.Abt.502	VI	Army Troop	"Tiger" tanks
Ind.Abt.503	VI	Army Troop	"Tiger" tanks
Ind.Abt.504	VI	Army Troop	"Tigers", in Tunis 1943
Ind.Abt.505	VI	Army/5th Pz.Div.	
Ind.Abt.506	VI	Army Troop	"Tigers", from III./ Pz.Reg. 33 in 1943
Ind.Abt.507	VI	Army Troop	"Tigers", from I./Pz.Reg.4
Ind.Abt.508	VI	Army Troop	"Tigers", from III./Pz.Reg.4
Ind.Abt.509	VI	Army Troop	"Tigers", from Pz.Reg. 35; in Führer Esc.Div. 1944-45
Ind.Abt.510	VI	Army/14th Pz.Div.	"Tiger" tanks
Ind.Co.513 (FKL)		Army Troop	"Tiger" tanks
Abt.567		Army Troop	Jagd-Panzer (?)
Ind.Abt.583		Army Troop	"Tiger" tanks
Abt.653		Army Troop	Jagd-Panzer
Abt.654		Army Troop	Jagd-Panzer

Abt.656		Army Troop	Jagd-Panzer
Abt.661		Army Troop	Jagd-Panzer
Abt.664		Army Troop	Jagd-Panzer
Abt.700		Army Troop	
Abt.745		Army Troop	
Lehr Reg.900		Army Troop	later Pz.Lehr Brig.
Comp.1000		74th Sich.Brig.	Captured tanks
Abt.2101		101st Pz.Brig.	
Abt.2102		102nd Pz.Brig.	ex-Pz.Abt. 102
Abt.2103		103rd Pz.Brig.	
Abt.2104		104th Pz.Brig.	from II./Pz.Reg. 9
Abt.2105	VIII	105th Pz.Brig.	
Abt.2106	XX	106th Pz.Bg.,	*FHH* later in Pz.Corps *FHH*
Abt.2107	V	107th Pz.Brig.	
Abt.2108	XIII	108th Pz.Brig.	
Abt.2109		109th Pz.Brig.	
Abt.2110		110th Pz.Brig.	
Abt.2111	VI	111th Pz.Brig.	
Abt.2112	V	112th Pz.Brig.	later Pz.Brig. FHH & Pz. Jäger Abt. *Brandenburg*
Abt.2113	XIII	113th Pz.Brig.	
Abt.2202		102nd Pz. Brig.	
Pz.Abt. *Rhodes*			Sturmdiv. Rhodes 1943
Pz.Abt. *Norwegen*		Pz.Div. *Norwegen*	
Pz.Comp. *Paris*			
Pz.Comp. *Prague*		539th Div.	

Code:
Military Districts:

I. Königsberg	X. Hamburg
II. Stettin	XI. Hannover
III. Berlin	XII. Wiesbaden
IV. Dresden	XIII. Nürnberg
V. Stuttgart	XVII. Vienna
VI. Münster	XVIII. Salzburg
VII. Munich	XX. Danzig
VIII. Breslau	XXI. Posen
IX. Kassel	

Sich.Div. = Sicherungsdivision (The Panzer companies of the Sicherungsdivisionen were officially listed as "light Panzer securing companies" or light Panzer companies "East.")
(F) = Flamethrowing Tank Unit
(FKL) = Unit with radio-controlled tanks

COMMANDERS OF THE PANZER TROOPS January 3, 1939

Brigades & Regiments	Garrison	Commander
1st Panzer Brigade	Erfurt	Generalm. Schaal
1st Panzer Regiment	Erfurt	Oberstlt. Nedtwig
2nd Panzer Regiment	Eisch	Oberstlt. Keltsch
2nd Panzer Brigade	Vienna	Oberst von Prittwitz
3rd Panzer Regiment	Mödling	Oberst Harpe
4th Panzer Regiment	Korneuburg	Oberst Baessler
3rd Panzer Brigade	Berlin	Oberst Stumpff
5th Panzer Regiment	Bernau	Oberst Nehring
6th Panzer Regiment	Neuruppin	Oberst Crüwell
4th Panzer Brigade	Stuttgart	Oberst Kempf
7th Panzer Regiment	Vaihingen	Oberst Landgraf
8th Panzer Regiment	Böblingen	Oberstlt. Elster
5th Panzer Brigade	Bamberg	Generalm. von Hartlieb
35th Panzer Regiment	Bamberg	Oberstlt. Eberbach
36th Panzer Regiment	Schweinfurt	Oberstlt. Breith
6th Panzer Brigade	Paderborn	Generalm. Ritter von Radlmaier
11th Panzer Regiment	Paderborn	Oberst Philipps
25th Panzer Regiment	Erlangen	Oberst Irmisch
I./23rd Panzer Regiment	Mannheim	Major Ilgen
8th Panzer Brigade	Sagan	Oberst Haarde
15th Panzer Regiment	Sagan	Oberst Streich
31st Panzer Regiment	Jägerndorf	Oberst Schuckelt
Independent Units:		
I./10th Panzer Regiment	Zinten	Major Sieberg
Pz.Abt.33	St. Pölten	Major von Köppen
Pz.Abt.65	Iserlohn	Major Thomas
Pz.Abt.66	Gera	Major Sieckenius
Pz.Abt.67	Spremberg	Oberstlt. Goerbig

Numbers of Tanks in World War II

(Data from Müller-Hillebrand, *Das Heer*, Volume 3)

Typ	I	II	(F)	35 (t)	38 (t)	III	III	IV	IV	IV	V Panther	VI Tiger I	VI Tiger II	Flak-Pz.	Pz. Befw.	Berge-Pz.	Summen der	
Fahrgestell	I	II	II/III	35 (t)	38 (t)	III	III	IV	IV	IV	V	VI	VI	38 (t) u. IV	I-VI	38 (t), III, IV, V	Zeilen 1 bis 16	„front-fähigen" Pzkpfw.
Waffe	M.G.	Kw.K. 2 cm	Flammöl	Kw.K. 3,7 cm	Kw.K. 3,7 cm	Kw.K. 3,7 u. 5 cm L 42	Kw.K. 5 cm L 60 u. 7,5 L 24	Kw.K. 7,5 cm L 24	Kw.K. 7,5 cm L 43 u. L 48	Pak 7,5 cm L 70	Kw.K. 7,5 cm L 70	Kw.K. 8,8 cm L 56	Kw.K. 8,8 cm L 71	Flak 2 cm, 2 cm-Vierling, 3,7 cm, 3 cm-Zwilling	versch.	—		
Nr. d. Zeile	1	2	3	4	5	6	7	8	9	10	11	12	13	14	15	16	17	18
Datum: 1. 9. 1939	1445	1223	3	—	—	98		211							215		3195	3195
1. 4. 1940	1062	1079	7	143	238	329		280							243		3381	3381
1. 9. 1940	957	920	61	142	320	537		300							183		3420	3420
1. 1. 1941	1079	955	87	(190)	476	918		419							244		4368	4178
1. 2.	1028	984	85	(170)	520	1015		453							232		4487	4317
1. 3.	1044	994	85	(175)	570	1110		476							260		4714	4539
1. 4.	(786)	1019	85	(179)	636	1200		459							286		4650	3685
1. 5.	(829)	1042	85	(184)	686	1323		499							308		4956	3943
1. 6.	(877)	1072	85	(187)	754	1440		517							330		5262	4198
1. 7.	(843)	1067	85	(189)	763	1501		531							331		5310	4278
1. 8.	(771)	985	85	(189)	661	1479		488							331		4989	4029
1. 9.	(642)	900	85	(191)	543	1571		470							335		4737	3904
1. 10.	(681)	896	86	(191)	547	1646		499							328		4874	4002
1. 11.	(717)	887	86	(191)	528	1784		485							315		4993	4085
1. 12.	(728)	868	87	(192)	434	1866		511							318		5004	4084
1. 1. 1942	(723)	(837)	89	(197)	(381)	1849		513							307		4896	2758
1. 2.	(708)	(800)	89	(201)	(424)	1723	64	530							289		4828	2695
1. 3.	(693)	(810)			(491)	1656 *)		534							278		4462	2468
1. 4.	(702)	(860)			(522)	1893		552							273		4802	2718
1. 5.	(708)	(907)			(521)	2068		609 *)							269		5082	2946
1. 6.	(701)	(979)			(454)	2306		681							264		5385	3251
1. 7.	(692)	(1021)			(479)	2482		723							266		5663	3471
1. 8.	(692)	(1029)			(479)	2457		761							255		5673	3473
1. 9.	(692)	(1039)			(436)	2628		842				9			257		5903	3736
1. 10.	(690)	(1014)			(375)	2630		863				11			256		5839	3760
1. 11.	(692)	(1006)			(334)	2767		901				16			257		5973	3941
1. 12.	(687)	(996)			(309)	2704		957				30			248		5931	3939
1. 1. 1943		(997)	Fahr-		(287)	2944		1077				65			278		5648	4364
1. 2.		(950)	gestell III:		(252)	2762		1130			4	85			280		5463	4261
1. 3.		(730)	64		(242)	1757		975			21	108			252		4149	3177
1. 4.		(350)	97		(161)	(564)	1102	(182)	836		61	127			317		3797	2540
1. 5.		(304)	100		(186)	(485)	980	(164)	913		22	165			324		3643	2504
1. 6.		(265)	108		(197)	(475)	932	(164)	1047		263	191			359		4001	2900
1. 7.		(236)	109		(204)	(477)	946	(167)	1305		428	240			412	12	4536	3452
1. 8.		(218)	105		(212)	(462)	(782)	(158)	1216		524	261			430	11	4379	2547
1. 9.		(209)	93		(201)	(450)	(639)	(157)	1203		601	284			461	30	4328	2672
1. 10.		(433)	75		(255)	(473)	(658)	(186)	1388		675	299			509	40	4991	2986
1. 11.		(419)	62		(260)	(464)	(603)	(184)	1488		783	349			507	38	5157	3227
1. 12.		(408)	44		(249)	(443)	(517)	(186)	1503		912	373			483	40	5158	3355
1. 1. 1944		(399)	30		(227)	(438)	(482)	(176)	1492		1084	395			477	66	5266	3544
1. 2.		(400)	27		(227)	(433)	(448)	(167)	1543		1205	414		121	484	74	5543	3868
1. 3.		(394)	27		(227)	(433)	(455)	(167)	1657		1339	499	5	140	466	74	5883	4207
1. 4.		(413)	18		(227)	(431)	(429)	(163)	1969		1617	556	6	141	475	74	6519	4856
1. 5.		(419)	12		(227)	(431)	(404)	(164)	1955		1649	551	12	141	488	115	6568	4923
1. 6.		(426)	11		(229)	(433)	(406)	(166)	2138		1898	615	31	141	520	127	7141	5481
1. 7.		(445)	11		(232)	(430)	(374)	(159)	2177		2105	631	55	141	549	138	7447	5807
1. 8.		(385)	11		(229)	(431)	(367)	(161)	1967		2067	511	101	141	541	147	7059	5486
1. 9.		(386)	11		(229)	(435)	(366)	(159)	1873	34	2160	441	175	141	573	197	7180	5605
1. 10.						(515) *)		(80)	1459	94	1794	283	142	185	326	311	5189	4594
1. 11.						(523) *)		(80)	1525	211	1729	245	145	207	307	424	5396	4793
1. 12.						(533) *)		(80)	1630	382	1966	243	166	243	327	466	6036	5423
1. 1. 1945						(534) *)		(80)	1604	575	1982	245	183	256	320	505	6284	5670
1. 2.						(534) *)		(80)	1491	665	1964	185	219	228	299	526	6191	5577
1. 3.						(534) *)												

*) = keine Trennung nach Typen, daher großer Anteil ().

*) = ohne Pzkpfw. III mit Kw.K. 3,7 cm

Erläuterung: Zahlen in ( ) bedeutet, daß diese Typen nicht mehr frontfähig sondern nur noch zur Verwendung im Sicherungsdienst hinter der Front, bei Besatzungskräften und zur Ausbildung geeignet waren

High Command Office of the Panzer Troops
Last Peacetime and last Wartime Officers

Chief of the Mobile Troops in Army High Command — 1939
(In parentheses: rank and office at war's end)

Chief of the Mobile Troops:	General of the Panzer Troops Guderian (Generaloberst and Chief of the Army General Staff)
Adjutant:	Major Riebel (Generalmajor and Commander Panzer Regiment 24, fell before Stalingrad 8/23/1942)
Staff Officers:	Major i.G. Roettiger (General of the Panzer Troops and Chief of the General Staff of Army Group C) Major i.G. von Le Suire (General of the Mountain Troops and Commanding General of the XXXXIX. Mountain Corps) Haupamann Dr. Luther (Oberst and Unit Leader, Army Personnel Office)

Inspector General of the Panzer Troops — 1945
(In parentheses: rank and office in peacetime, 1939)

Inspector General:	Generalleutnant Thomale (Major in Weapons Department of the OKH)
Adjutant:	Major i.G. Heick (Leutnant in Antitank Unit 41)
Dept. Leader for Company Organization:	Oberst d.G. Freyer (Hauptmann and Chief of Antitank Unit 8)
Dept. Leader for Training:	Major d.G. Baron v. Woellwarth-Lauterburg (Leutnant in Cavalry Regiment 17)
Staff Officer:	Major d.G. Petsch (Leutnant in Motorcycle Rifle Battalion 3)

To differentiate: Officers on the Army General Staff were designated i.G. after their rank; officers in the Wehrmacht High Command were designated d.G.

Instructions for the Inspector General of the Panzer Troops

1.) The Inspector General of the Panzer Troops is answerable to me for a further development of the Panzer troops appropriate to its decisive significance in the war. The Inspector General of the Panzer Troops is directly subordinate to me. He holds the position of a high commander of an army and is the highest superior officer of the Panzer troops.[1]

2.) The Inspector General of the Panzer Troops is responsible for the organization and training of the Panzer troops and the large Mobile Units of the Army in cooperation with the Chief of the Army General Staff. He also has the right to advise the Luftwaffe and the Waffen-SS in my name in the area of organization and training of the Panzer troops.

I reserve the right to make basic decisions.

His requests concerning the technical development of his weapons and the plans for manufacturing them will be submitted to me in close cooperation with the Reich Minister for Armament and Ammunition.

3.) In his capacity as commander of the service arm he is also commander of the reserve troops of his service arm. It is his responsibility to assure constant, fully usable replacements of personnel and tanks for the field army, regardless of whether it is a question of individual vehicles, refreshment or new establishment of units.

The apportioning of tanks and armored vehicles to the field and reserve armies is his responsibility, based on my instructions.

4.) The Inspector General of the Panzer Troops assures the planned and punctual completion of the ordered new establishment and refreshment of Panzer troops and fast units. In cooperation with the Army General Staff, he assures a purposeful utilization of the non-armored personnel of the field army.

5.) The Inspector General of the Panzer Troops has the war experience for the evaluation of combat leadership, armament, training and organization of the Panzer troops. In this respect he has the right to visit and inspect all Panzer troop units of the Wehrmacht and the Waffen-SS. The Panzer troops of the field army will inform the Inspector General of the Panzer Troops directly of experiences of all kinds. He will make his awareness and experience known to all concerned offices, including that of the Reich Minister for Armament and Ammunition.

The Inspector General of the Panzer Troops directs the preparation of all regulations for the Panzer troops. In this respect, before regulations that concern the leadership of units and cooperation with other service arms are announced, the agreement of the Chief of the Army General Staff is to be obtained.

6.) To the Inspector General of the Panzer Troops as service arm commander there are permanently subordinated:

a) The replacement and training troop units of the *Schnelle Truppen* (mobile troops — except the cavalry and cycle replacement troop units), which can be united under special command offices.

b) The schools for mobile troops (not including cavalry and cycle training facilities) of the field and reserve armies with the training troops belonging to them.

7.) The Inspector General of the Panzer troops is empowered to issue binding instructions to all offices of the Army within the area of his jurisdiction. All offices are required to place at the disposal of the Inspector General of the Panzer Troops whatever he requires.

Führer's headquarters, February 28, 1943

THE FUHRER
ADOLF HITLER

[1] The designation "Panzer Troops" in these instructions includes: Tank troops, armored grenadier and motorized infantry, armored reconnaissance troops, armored pursuit troops and heavy assault gun units.

General Commands of the Panzer Corps — 1943

General Command Units	Artillery Cdrs. Units	Map Units Units	Intel-ligence Units	Corps Supply	Field Police	Field Mail
III	3	403	43	403	403	403
XIV	414	414	60	414	414	414
XXIV	143	424	424	424	424	424
XXXIX	140	439	439	439	439	439
XXXX	128	440	440	440	440	440
XXXXI	35	441	441	441	441	441
XXXXVI	101	446	446	446	446	446
XXXXVII	130	447	447	447	447	447
XXXXVIII	144	448	448	448	448	448
LVI	125	456	456	456	456	456
LVII	121	457	457	457	457	457
LXXVI	476	476	476	476	476	90

The Artillery Commander was responsible within the Panzer Corps for command and utilization of all artillery units.

The Map Unit provided for the preparation of location maps and small printing jobs.

The Intelligence Unit consisted of a staff, three motorized companies, an armored radio company and a light intelligence column.

The Commander of the Panzer Corps Supply Troops was responsible for a 120 ton Motor Vehicle Company and a Motor Vehicle Workshop Column.

In the XXIV. and LVII. Corps, on the other hand, there were two small 30 ton motor vehicle columns, one large fuel column and one motor vehicle workshop unit; in the XXXXI., XXXXVI., XXXXVII. and LVI. Panzer Corps the Motor Vehicle Company was responsible for 90 ton vehicles, and in the III. Panzer Corps there was, in addition to the normal facilities, the East Motor Vehicle Column 403 (60 tons). The LXXVI. Panzer Corps had only a 90 ton Motor Vehicle Company.

OFFICERS OF THE PANZER DIVISIONS AS OF MARCH 1, 1942

Panzer Division Commander	1st General Staff Officer(Ia)
1st Generalm. Krüger	Oberstlt. i.G. Irkens
2nd Generalm. Baron v. Esebeck	Oberstlt. i.G. Reinhard
3rd Generalm. Breith	Oberstlt. i.G. Pomtow
4th Generalm. Eberbach	Oberstlt. i.G. Heidkämper
5th Generalm. Fehn	Major i.G. Engels
6th Generalm. Raus	Mjr. i.G. Count von Kielmannsegg
7th Generalm. Baron von Funck	Mjr. i.G. Count von Nostitz
8th Generalm. Brandenberger	Oberstlt. i.G. Berendsen
9th Generallt. Hubicki	Oberstlt. i.G. von Necker
10th Generalm. Fischer	Oberstlt. i.G. Bürker
11th Generalm. Scheller	Major i.G. Selmayr
12th Generalm. Wessel	Major i.G. Bergengruen
13th Oberst Herr	Major i.G. Kraemer
14th Generalm. Kühn	Oberstlt. i.G. Hörst
15th Generalm. von Vaerst	Major i.G. Müller, H.
16th Generallt. Hube	Oberstlt. i.G. Müller, W.
17th Generalm. Licht	Major i.G. berlin
18th Generalm. Baron v. Thüngen	Major i.G. Estor
19th Oberst Schmidt	Major i.G. von Unger
20th Generalm. Ritter von Thoma	Major i.G. Staedtke
21th Generalm. von Bismarck	Major i.G. von Heuduck
22nd Generalm. von Appell	Major i.G. Schulz
23rd Generalm. v. Boineburg-Lengsfeld	Major i.G. Reichel
24th Generallt. Feldt (in position in Norway)	Major i.G. Menges
25th Generallt. Haarde	

Panzer Brigade Staffs

The following list includes the staffs of the Panzer brigades in the Panzer divisions. These staffs were gradually disbanded until 1943.

The independent Panzer brigade staffs that were newly formed after 1943 and subordinated to the Army High Command are not listed.

The brigade staffs also included a light tank column and an intelligence column.

Pz.Brig.	Dist.	Subordinate to	Notes
1	IX	1st Panzer Division	became 18th Pz.Brig.
2	XVII	2nd Panzer Division	disbanded 1942
3	III	3rd Panzer Division	disbanded 1940
4	V	Army Troop, 2nd Lt. D, 10th Panzer Division	disbanded 1943
5	VIII	Army Troop, 4th Panzer Division in 1938, 3rd Panzer Division in 1940	disbanded 1942
6	VI	Army Troop, 1st Lt. D, 6th Panzer Division in 1939	disbanded 1940
8	VIII	5th Panzer Division, Army Troop 1941	Staff Pz.Brig.100 1942
10	none	Army Troop	Pz.Brig. Strachwitz
17	none	Army Troop	disbanded 1943
18	IV	18th Panzer Division, Army Troop 1943	disbanded 1943
19	none	19th Panzer Division	disbanded 1943
20	none	20th Panzer Division	disbanded 1943
21	none	21st Panzer Division	disbanded 1943
100	IX	Army Troop	Ind.Pz.Brig.8

Panzer Troop School Wünsdorf - 1939
Structure and Officers

Staff:

Commander	Oberst Kühn
Adjutant	Hauptmann Jansa
Staff Officers	Oberstleutnante von Holtzendorff, Theiss, Majore Borowietz, Volckheim, Hauptleute von Hülsen, Rahneberg, Hennecke, von Zerzschwitz
Weapons Officer	Oberleutnant Gabriel

Tactical Training:

Director	Major Fronhöfer
Instructors	Hauptleute Goinka, Hildebrand, Teege, von Mutius, Oberleutnant von Flotow

Technical Training:

Director	Oberstleutnant Spaeth
Instructors	Hauptleute Gröbke, Dr. Hoffmann

Panzer Training Section:

Commander	Major von Lewinski
Adjutant	Leutnant Felix
Company Chiefs	Hauptleute Peffer, Wolf, Oberleutnante Edlervon der Planitz, Düwel

COMMANDERS OF THE PANZER TROOP SCHOOL

1925-1929	Oberstleutnant Stottmeister
1929-1931	Oberst Genée
1932-1934	Oberst Fessmann
1934-1937	Oberst Haarde
1937-1938	Oberst Ritter von Radlmaier
1938-1940	Oberst Kühn
1940	Oberst Harpe
1941-1943	Oberst Nedtwig
1943	Oberst Kraeber
1944-1945	Oberst Munzel

COMMANDERS OF THE PANZER GUNNERY SCHOOL

1934-1938	Oberstleutnant Baumgart
1938-1943	Oberstleutnant Kraeber
1943	Oberstleutnant Bonatz
1943	Oberst von Koeppen
1943-1944	Oberst von Bodenhausen
1944-1945	Major Fechner

Excerpt from Daily Orders of the Panzer Groups
Army High Commands in 1941

The High Commander
Panzer Group 1

Gr.Hq., August 12, 1941

Soldiers of Panzer Group 1!

After vigorous advances despite all flank attacks and after turning at the right time, the Panzer groups of the Russian 6th and 12th Armies have made their way across the Dniepr and thus have alone created the conditions for the great enclosing battle of Uman.

In the ten-day enclosing battle, the XXXXVIII. and XIV. Army Corps have turned back all attempted break-throughs and shattered strong enemy units, while the III. Army Corps protected the flanks and rear of the Panzer Group and reached the Dniepr at Krementschug in a bold advance.

Thus 25 enemy divisions could be destroyed. Both commanders were captured.

The victorious conclusion of this great encircling battle is the culmination of seven weeks of hard fighting by the Army Group South against numerically superior enemy forces. The enemy has suffered a defeat that will contribute much to the decisive final victory.

The High Commander of the Army and the High Commander of the Army Group have expressed their best wishes and highest recognition to all participating troop units.

I am happy to be able to share this with my Panzer group and express my thanks and my recognition to the leadership and troops for the tremendous achievements of the past weeks.

My sentiments of thanks and loyalty are also extended to the fallen comrades and to our wounded men in the hospitals.

Now on to the final victory.

Hail our Führer

(signed) von Kleist

The High Commander of the 2nd Panzer Army — Army HQ, October 18, 1941

ARMY DAILY ORDERS

Soldiers of the 2nd Panzer Army!

The breakthrough and encircling battle in the Orel-Briansk area is finished. The enemy positions between Putivl and Novgorod- Seversk were penetrated on 9/30, the enemy thrown back across the Orel-Briansk road by ceaseless pursuit, and these two important cities were taken. By doing this, the 3rd and 13th Russian Armies south of the road and the 50th Russian Army north of it were attacked from the rear, enclosed and destroyed, mainly in cooperation with our neighbor army. Only the survivors thereof could save themselves.

Our booty since the beginning of the attack adds up to:

80,044 prisoners
236 tanks
539 heavy guns
66 antitank guns
87 anti-aircraft guns
16 aircraft.

The onset of winter with its rain- and snowstorms turned the roads to mud and made marching and fighting uncommonly difficult and time-consuming. When such great and decisive results can be achieved nevertheless, this is attributable to the unqualified dedication and readiness for action of the troops and the capability of the leadership. I feel a fervent desire to express my heartiest thanks and my particular recognition for this.

We are not yet at the end of our path. To complete our victory, the enemy must be smashed completely. Therefore I call upon you again to fight on with your proved loyalty and power.

For Germany and our Führer!
Guderian

The Commander
of Panzer Troop 3

Gr.Gef.St., August 6, 1941

Soldiers of the Panzer Group!

Seven weeks of the most vital historical events lie behind us. Stalin's essential armies are shattered, his powerful Panzer army is for the most part smashed. The door to Moscow has been forced open, though the Reds still push against it in desperation: they will not succeed in closing it again.

The Niemen-Merkino, Olita, Vilnia, Smolovitze, Zeslav, Pleszczenice, the Duna-Dzisna, Ulla and Beschenkowitzi, Vitebsk, Gorodok, Nevel and Velikiye Luki, Senno, Dobromysl, Demidov, Velish, Jartzevo and Ratschino are the milestones of your victory. The closing of the basin of Minsk in the north, the shattering of the Red Armies advancing to the upper Düna and toward Vitebsk, and the barring of their path from the east at Smolensk are your achievements. Finally I had to order you to turn from attacks in full swing to fight off enemy efforts to free themselves. You were equal to this task too. You leave your positions on the Vop and southwest of Byeloi as victors.

The Führer has ordered our replacement and a short rest. When he told me at the Army Group Headquarters on 8/4/41 that our quick advance across the Düna had exceeded his expectations and shook my hand with both of his, I accepted his handshake as thanks for you, his soldiers. I too thank you with all my heart for your dedication, your endurance, your bravery and your confidence in my leadership. My thanks also go to all the soldiers deep in the mighty front lines.

In a well-earned rest we want to gather new strength, both spiritual and physical, and prepare our weapons and equipment, in order to arm ourselves for the conclusion of the struggle against the Red military might. The sacrifice of our dead and wounded, whom we remember in honor, shall not have been in vain.

Long live the Führer!

(signed) Hoth
Generaloberst

The Commander Gr.Gef.St., 7/9/1941
of Panzer Group 4

Group Command

1. The enemy's attempt to set up a new defense front on the former Russian border has been shattered. It has been penetrated.

2. Army Group North is to move onward in the direction of Leningrad and capture Leningrad.

3. . . .

4. Army Group 4 is in position between Ilmensee and Pleskau, ready to advance toward Leningrad. . . .

a) It is to cut off Leningrad between Lake Ladoga and the
Cronstadt Bay.

b) Until the arrival of the 16th Army, it must protect its
rear from the enemy east of the Ilmensee itself.

c) It is to prevent, by occupying the Narva crossings, . . .
a retreat of the enemy from Estonia.

5. In detail . . .

6. . . .

Long live the Führer!
(signed) Hoepner
Generaloberst

OPERATIONS OF THE PANZER DIVISIONS

(Brief Histories)

1st Panzer Division: June 1940 in the west, as of September 1940 on the border of German and Russian spheres of interest, as of June 1941 in the east, as of January 1943 in the west, as of June 1943 in the southeast, as of November 1943 in the east.

2nd Panzer Division: June 1940 in the west, as of July 1940 in the Reich, as of September 1940 in the Vienna area, as of January 1941 in Rumania, as of March 1941 in Bulgaria, April 1941 in the Yugoslavian-Greek campaign, as of July 1941 in the Reich, as of September 1941 in the west, as of October 1941 in the east, as of January 1944 in the west.

3rd Panzer Division: June 1940 in the west, as of July 1940 in the Reich, as of May 1941 in the East.

4th Panzer Division: June 1940 in the west, as of December 1940 in the Reich, as of February 1941 in the west, as of May 1941 in the east.

5th Panzer Division: June 1940 in the west, as of July 1940 in the Reich, as of September 1940 on the border of German and Russian spheres, as of January 1941 in Rumania, as of March 1941 in Bulgaria, April 1941 in the Yugoslavian-Greek campaign, as of July 1941 in the Reich, as of October 1941 in the east.

6th Panzer Division: June 1940 in the west, as of July 1940 in the Reich, as of September 1940 on the border of German and Russian spheres, as of July 1941 in the east, as of June 1942 in the west, as of December 1942 in the east.

7th Panzer Division: June 1940 in the west, as of February 1941 in the Reich, as of May 1941 in the east, as of June 1942 in the west, as of January 1943 in the east.

8th Panzer Division: June 1940 in the west, as of January 1941 in the Reich, as of March 1941 in the west, April 1941 in the Yugoslavian campaign, then in the Reich, as of June 1941 in the east.

9th Panzer Division: June 1940 in the west, as of July 1940 in the Reich, as of September 1940 in the Vienna area, as of February 1941 in Rumania, as of March 1941 in Bulgaria, April 1941 in the Yugoslavian-Greek campaign, as of May 1941 in the Reich, as of June 1941 in the east, as of April 1944 in the west and integration into the 155th Reserve Panzer Division.

10th Panzer Division: June 1940 in the west, as of March 1941 in the Reich, as of May 1941 in the east, as of April 1942 in the west, as of December 1942 in North Africa, lost May 1943.

11th Panzer Division: June 1940 in the west, as of July 1940 in the Reich, as of February 1941 in Rumania, as of March 1941 in Bulgaria, April 1941 in the

Yugoslavian campaign, then in the Reich, as of June 1941 in the east, as of June 1944 in the west.

12th Panzer Division: December 1940 founded in the Reich by restructuring of the 2nd Infantry Division (motorized, q.v.), as of May 1941 in the east, at war's end in Courland.

13th Panzer Division: October 1940 founded in Rumania by restructuring of the 13th Infantry Division (motorized, q.v.), instructional troop in Rumania, as of May 1941 in the east, February 1945 renamed Panzer division *Feldherrnhalle* 1 (see and compare with Panzer division *Feldherrnhalle.*

14th Panzer Division: October 1940 founded in the Reich by restructuring of the 4th Infantry Division (q.v.), April 1941 in Yugoslavian campaign, then in the Reich, as of June 1941 in the east, February 1943 lost at Stalingrad. March 1943 founded anew in the west, as of October 1943 in the east, at war's end in Courland.

15th Panzer Division: October 1940 founded in the Reich by restructuring of the 33rd Infantry Division (q.v.), as of May 1941 in North Africa, lost May 1943. Rest of division used to form the 15th Panzer-grenadier Division in Italy.

16th Panzer Division: October 1940 founded in the Reich by restructuring of the 16th Infantry Division (q.v.), as of late December 1940 as instructional troop in Rumania, April 1941 in Bulgaria, as of June 1941 in the east, February 1943 lost at Stalingrad. March 1943 founded anew in the west, as of June 1943 in the east.

17th Panzer Division: October 1940 founded in the Reich by restructuring of the 27th Infantry Division (q.v.), as of May 1941 in the east.

18th Panzer Division: October 1940 founded in the Reich from parts of the 4th and 14th Infantry Divisions, as of May 1941 in the east, disbanded October 1943, Div. Command became that of the 18th Artillery Division.

19th Panzer Division: October 1940 founded in the Reich by restructuring of the 19th Infantry Division (q.v.), as of May 1941 in the east, as of June 1944 in the west, as of August 1944 in the east.

20th Panzer Division: October 1940 founded in the Reich from parts of the 19th Infantry Division, as of May 1941 in the east.

21st Panzer Division: July 1941 founded in North Africa by renaming and restructuring of the 5th Light African Division (q.v.), lost May 1943. July 1943 New 21st Panzer Division founded in the west by expanding the *Schnellen* Brigade West, as of February 1945 in the east.

22nd Panzer Division: September 1941 founded in the west, as of March 1942 in the east, September 1942 gave about half the division to found the 27th Panzer division (q.v.), disbanded 2/4/1943.

23rd Panzer Division: September 1941 established in the west, as of April 1942 in the east (southern sector).

24th Panzer Division: End of 1941 founded in the west by restructuring of the 1st Cavalry Division (q.v.), as of June 1942 in the east, February 1943 lost at Stalingrad. As of March 1943 formed anew in the west from recovered and former members of the division, as of August 1943 in northern Italy, as of October 1943 in the east.

25th Panzer Division: Spring 1942 founded in Norway, as of September 1943 in the west, as of November 1943 in the east, April 1944 hit hard, integrated into the Panzer Division *Norwegen* in Denmark (q.v.), as of August 1944 in the east.

26th Panzer Division: October 1942 founded in the west of parts of the 23rd Infantry Division (q.v.), as of August 1943 in the southwest.

27th Panzer Division: September 1942 founded in the east by division of the 22nd Panzer Division (q.v.) and strengthened by army troops, January 1943 disbanded.

116th Panzer Division: April 1944 founded in the west by restructuring of the 179th Reserve Panzer Division (q.v.) and using the remains of the beaten 16th Panzer-grenadier Division (q.v.), served in the west.

232nd Panzer Division: February 1945 founded in the east of Field Training Panzer Division Tatra (q.v.), disbanded March 1945.

233rd Panzer Division: March 1945 founded in Denmark by renaming of the 233rd Reserve Panzer Division.

Panzer Lehr Division: May 1944 founded in the west of Reserve Panzer Lehr Division.

Panzer Division *Norwegen:* September 1943 founded in Norway, June 1944 disbanded and mostly integrated in the 25th Panzer Division (q.v.).

Panzer Division *Feldherrnhalle 1:* February 1945 founded in the east by renaming the 13th Panzer Division.

Panzer Division *Feldherrnhalle 2:* 11/27/1944 founded in the east by restructuring of the Panzer-grenadier Division *Feldherrnhalle* (q.v.), February 1945 renamed Panzer division *Feldherrnhalle 2* and united with Panzer Division ***Feldherrnhalle 1*** as ***Panzer Corps Feldherrnhalle.***

Panzer Division *Holstein:* February 1945 founded in Denmark of parts of the 233rd Reserve Panzer Division, as of late February 1945 in the east, late March 1945 disbanded.

Panzer Division *Schlesien:* February 1945 founded in the Reich, as of February 1945 in the east, late March 1945 disbanded.

Panzer Division *Jüterbog* February 1945 founded, as of February 1945 in the east.

Panzer Division *Müncheberg:* February 1945 formed, as of March 1945 in the east.

Battle Reports of the Eastern Campaign 1941-1945

(Extracted from previously published divisional histories)

Advance in 1941

At 4:43 A.M. the first Panzer III and IV forded the river after going into it along two ruts in the sand, towing trailers that carry 400 liters of spare fuel that can be pumped out from inside, under the leadership of the Commander of the 1st Unit of the 18th Panzer Regiment, Major Count Manfred von Strachwitz, the first column being that of Oberfeldwebel Wierschin. His tanks were completely closed, with air brought in through long pipes instead of rubber buoys, equipped for a fording capability of 4 to 5 meters. Since it did not take long to find a shallow place that was about 2 meters deep, the other tanks could wade through the water with open turrets. Generaloberst Guderian was present and was pleased that the maneuver was carried out so quickly.

This river crossing with wading tanks, the first in military history, was reported on later by the then Chief of the 2nd Company, 18th Panzer Regiment, Oberleutnant von Grolman: "The radio contact with the regiment on the other side of the bend was lost at first, so I followed the prescribed advance course independently, accompanied by a reconnaissance pilot who gave us good assistance. Shortly before the bridge over the Lessna, Guderian passed us in his tank with two drivers and was first to cross the undestroyed bridge."
(18th Panzer Division, 6/22/1941)

—

The 10th Panzer Regiment arrived at Dünaburg in the early morning hours. It was able to take possession of the bridge at Zarasai in a surprising advance after hard but brief fighting, penetrate the Russian security there and move steadily forward to the Düna bridges.

One unit each of Regiment 800 was placed on them under the leadership of Oberleutnant Knaak, who had been wounded in a similar action at Kedainiai but stayed with the troops.

The group of Regiment 800 placed on the railroad bridge to the left moved past five enemy armored scout cars and, at the bridge, attacked the other enemy scout cars standing there, since they could not attack with their machine guns. As a result they soon decided to turn onto the big road to the south toward the highway bridge and took up positions there. In the process Feldwebel Krückeberg was able to cut an ignition cable which, it was thought, was one of the cables that had been prepared for blowing up the bridge.

The second group of Regiment 800 was positioned on the highway bridge, where its leader, Oberleutnant Knaak, was in the foremost tank. The Russian guards, talking with civilians on the west side of the bridge were completely taken by surprise and shot down, and Group 800 drove across the Düna bridge to the opposite side. There an antitank gun crew had meanwhile taken notice and fired a shot at the foremost tank, which put it out of commission and fatally wounded Oberleutnant Knaak. At the same time, a murderous fire began from the Düna shore, which was heavily occupied, and from all the houses on both sides of the

bridge. It was thanks to the far-seeing leadership of Oberstleutnant Fronhöfer that the tanks of the 10th Panzer Regiment followed right behind the groups of Regiment 800."
(8th Panzer Division, 6/26/1941)

—

On June 25 the attack was continued via Smorgon and Molodeczno. The breakthrough of the fortifications on the former Polish-Russian border north of Minsk succeeded, so that in the evening the so-called Minsk-Moscow Autobahn (highway) was reached near Sloboda. On June 27 the Panzer Regiment reported after destroying or capturing a tank column and other armored units, "Victory all along the line," though suffering heavy losses of their own. By the evening of June 28 Minsk could be taken. In the course of Russian counter-attacks and defensive fighting, Oberst Rothenburg was severely wounded while at the head of his Panzer Regiment, and while being brought back to the hinterlands, which had not been secured from the enemy, he was shot by the Russians.

The division honored the memory of this exemplary troop leader; the 25th Panzer Regiment was known from then on as Panzer Regiment *Rothenburg*.

On July 2-3 the Panzer Regiment advanced to the Beresina. The bridge at Lepel was destroyed later. But SR 7 was able to take possession of an unharmed bridge and form a bridgehead on the eastern shore. On July 4 the division set out to open the narrows of the lake east of Beshenkovitshi. The enemy defended the narrows and the surrounding area bitterly. Enemy advances, supported by tanks and artillery from the dominating heights, could be turned back. During the following days heavy fighting occurred over and over in this sector.

After the way was opened for the rest of the division and all the artillery of the Panzer Corps was made ready on July 10, an attack, planned to the last detail, was prepared for. Through bold and determined action by the II. Battalion of SR 7 the narrows of the lake could be taken.
(7th Panzer Division, June-July 1941)

—

The advance of the Panzer Regiment from the bridgehead, ordered for 9:00 A.M. on June 23, was delayed because of a missed delivery of fuel. At noon there was a fight against enemy tanks and infantry at Eigirdony, in which AR 92 also took part. Yet the division — now constantly in contact with the enemy — continued its advance, though slowed by road and bridge problems. The unpaved stretches of road through sand and swamp, especially between Rudziski and Warka, developed into a considerable hindrance and necessitated reinforcing work by the engineers, and later the construction of a makeshift bridge. In the darkness the troops pushed and pulled the vehicles laboriously across the soft ground one by one. When a Soviet 40-ton tank fired on a battery of AR 92 at Omuskis and seriously damaged two guns, the 2./AR 92 destroyed this tank. On account of the fire in Omuskis, the town had to be avoided via swampy meadows. Marching groups toward the rear were fired on by enemy units that had been left behind in the flanking woods.

On June 24 the 21st Panzer Regiment crossed the Varka and drove back enemy tanks near Vilna. The regiment secured the area on the other side of the Varka to the

north and east. The incredibly bad roads caused increased fuel consumption. Since the tank trucks still had not arrived on account of the road conditions, the troops suffered from a fuel shortage. The parts of the division that had gradually fallen behind along the advance route raised dust clouds visible from far away on the unpaved roads dried by the summer heat, making inviting targets for attacking bombers. The troops experienced six such attacks on the very first day, in which the planes dropped their bomb loads from great heights. They stopped the advance for the time being, but caused no noteworthy damage. In the last attack, when four German fighters shot down four of a pack of seven enemy bombers without suffering any losses themselves, no more enemy planes were seen in the skies for a long time.
(20th Panzer Division, June 1941)

The 1942 Advance

According to orders, the 22nd Panzer Division, which had been brought forward, was to advance through the gap and then turn to the north to encircle and destroy the enemy. But a storm that broke late in the afternoon of May 9 turned the battleground into a swamp, so that the 22nd Panzer Division and the motorized advance unit of the corps got completely stuck and the movements of the infantry divisions were slowed considerably. Only with the greatest effort was it possible for the 22nd Panzer Division, without their artillery regiment which had not yet arrived, to push northward and try to achieve the encirclement. The division commander did not want to attack during the night. His division, which had arrived some six weeks before and been trained further in fast action by the corps in the Crimea, had never before carried out a night attack. But I insisted on my request to move forward as far as possible during the night. As soon as a further advance was no longer possible on account of total darkness, the division should halt, in order to move farther to the north at the first light of morning. That was necessary, for otherwise the enemy, a master at retreating, would have slipped out of the trap. The 22nd Panzer Division was indeed able to advance deep into the enemy flank. Then it settled down and was able at daybreak the next morning to make a surprise attack on Soviet tank positions. In the tank battle that now ensued, the division scored high numbers of kills, and the enemy opposition collapsed completely. They were able to break through to the north shore of the Kertsch, so that the intended surrounding of considerable enemy troops succeeded."
(22nd Panzer Division, 5/9/1942)

—

In the morning twilight of August 21, 1942 the II./Pz.Reg.201 moved ahead, passed through Novo Ivanovski and crossed the Urvany. At 5:15 A.M. enemy troops were driven out of positions at Kolchose, south of Pravurganski, and some were taken prisoner. About 8:00 the Panzer unit reached the Naltshik-Maisij railroad line and brought the locomotives of two freight trains arriving at Naltshik to a stop by firing on them.

Accompanying engineers blew up the railroad line at numerous positions; then the II./Pz.Reg.201 was ordered back to Kolchose, where it prepared for an attack on the highway bridge at Maiskij as part of the Burmeister Battle Group. At 10:00 A.M. the battle group attacked; the I. and III./Pz.Art.Reg.128 supported the attack. Under heavy defensive fire from Soviet artillery the tanks fought their way to within 600 meters of the bridge. Four antitank guns of two antitank nests were put out of commission. The enemy artillery employed barrage fire before the bridge. At 4:00 P.M. the enemy blew up the bridge. The attack was broken off.

At 5:45 P.M. the II./Pz.Reg.201 advanced again. The goal this time was the railroad bridge over the Tscherek to the south. The 23rd Motorcycle Battalion followed. With artillery and mortar support, the attack got within 500 meters of the bridge. Against heavy enemy opposition and mass antitank and artillery fire, the attacking group pushed to within 100 meters of the bridge; then it too was blown up. The attack was halted. The Burmeister group went back to its original positions.
(23rd Panzer Division, 8/21/1942)

Our target is visible before us: Ordshonikidze.
The way to it led exclusively across a coverless flatland.

According to prisoners' statements, the whole city was protected by the strongest fortifications, surrounded by concrete bunkers, antitank positions under steel bunkers, the usual mine fields and then some.

After overcoming enemy resistance in the Gisel area, the leading battalions reached one of the tank traps near the airfield. In the truest sense of the word, our Panzer grenadiers pushed themselves farther and farther ahead and came within about 1800 meters of the eastern edge of the city.

Ordshonikidse was an important armory of the Soviet Caucasus Army. In addition, the Grusin Military Road leading to the city was also an important pass route over which the Soviets delivered their supplies from Transcaucasia via Tiflis. In positions were the II./93 at right, the II./66 at left and the I./66 at the left rear. Kr.43, reinforced by the III./Pz.Reg.4, was in charge of covering the left flank, I./ and II./Pz.Reg.4 were available as a shock-troop reserve.

To cover the right flank near the mountains, the I./99th Mountain Jäger Regiment, subordinate to us, was fighting along with the 203rd Assault Gun Battery and a company of the 626th Engineer Battalion. To help achieve the desired success of the attack, this unit was to thrust onto the Grusin Military Road.
(13th Panzer Division, 11/1/1942)

Battles of 1941

"Then it (the rifle battalion) breaks into the southern part of Duderhof. Russian infantry with antitank guns, which had pushed toward Duderhof-Vilosi again behind the 36th motorized Infantry Division, is smashed by the leading tanks. Thereupon Major Eckinger turns his battalion, in which tanks and armored rifle vehicles replace each other depending on the situation and teragain, toward the "bald mountain" southeast of Duderhof. From its highest point an old church, part of a cloister, looks far out across the land. Moving quickly through Duderhof, then around to the east and then snaking its way between enemy bunkers, the break through the line of bunkers staffed with naval riflemen succeeds! . . .

Through this attack with a turned front it is possible to take the commanding heights at Point 167 southeast of Duderhof. They are taken about 12:00 frontally from the northeast by the reinforced I./113th Rifle Regiment (Hauptmann von Berckenfeldt) and the reinforced 6./1st Pz.Reg. (Oberleutnant Darius). Unteroffizier Fritsch storms field positions and gun emplacements on the ridge with engineer shock troops and flamethrowers. The decisive heights were firmly in German hands by 12:30. The Chief of the 6./1st Pz.Reg. radioed to his group leader at that moment: I see Leningrad and the sea!"
(1st Panzer Division, 9/11/1941, Leningrad)

—

Through! The vehicles roll farther and farther through sunken roads, swamps, through woods and fields and over many a crumbling wooden bridge. In the vicinity of Titshi the column crosses the Ssula and is halfway there! Suddenly radio contact with the division is lost. Our own trucks are in a ravine, but when they have made their way back out of it, radio contact is made again, and behind us in Romny General Model and Major i.G. Pomtow heave a sigh of relief when they hear: "At 4:02 P.M. on the heights of Luka." The sun has long since set in a red-gold glow. But finally the battle group can stop at a high spot and camouflage the trucks under haystacks. The men look at the silhouette of the city, still visible against the evening sky, through telescopes. Clouds of smoke and steam rise over the houses; between them the machine-gun bullets whine and the artillery shells crash. There is no more doubt that the shock troops are just behind the Russian front and the van of the Army Group South is waiting just a few kilometers farther!

Oberleutnant Warthmann gives the command: "Tanks - march!" The battle group rolls on, passes through a ravine, fires on Russians who suddenly appear out of the darkness, and they hurry away, surprised. Then a brook blocks the route. The vehicles look for a crossing. There is a bridge. The Oberleutnant's P-III drives up to it — the bridge is blown up. Gray figures pop up, covered with cement, stubble-bearded, waving and waving. They are men of the 2./Eng.16 of the 16th Panzer Division! It is exactly 6:20 P.M.

The soldiers point out a passable ford through the brook. Oberleutnant Warthmann drives his vehicle across and turns toward Lubny. A short time later he reports to Generalmajor Hube. The tank of the 3rd Panzer Division with the big "G" (Guderian) on its steel walls is next to a tank with the letter "K" (Kleist). The leaders of the two army groups have united! The circle around Kiev is completed!
(3rd Panzer Division, 9/14/41, Kiev)

"When the mud season came on, the enemy had gained an ally who achieved what the Russian leadership and the bitterly fighting troops had not yet succeeded in doing, despite all the blood they shed. It was not the Russian winter, but the autumn rain that brought the German advance to a standstill. It rained and snowed endlessly; in the knee-deep mud on the roads all movement came to a stop. Thus it was almost impossible to supply the troops with even the most vital supplies for fighting and living. Even on the so-called "good" roads the traffic was faced with indescribable difficulties from mid-October to early November. The drivers of the supply-truck columns achieved the superhuman. Finally there was nothing left but to bring supplies to the front with the few horse-drawn wagons available. Only when the frost set in did it gradually become possible to strengthen the front and, in particular, to think about securing orderly supplying. Until then our division units were supplied by air since November 4 by the "Old Aunt" Ju 52. Two slices of hard bread, some sausage and a few cigarettes were on the menu every day. Supplying the troops from the country was only possible to a very limited extent, as the villages along the line of advance still had supplies of potatoes, but practically no cattle any more."
(2nd Panzer Division, 10/26/1941, Moscow)

—

"Since 4:00 A.M. the enemy, after heavy artillery fire in the last few days, has made several strong attacks from the southwest, with the focal points on both sides of the Krujukovo railroad line. Five enemy batteries and Stalin units, firing the rocket salvos that we have come to dread, have recently appeared on the scene. Plus numerous tanks of the heaviest type. But all the enemy attacks have been turned away. The enemy has only succeeded in temporarily putting pressure on our securing measures east of Krujukovo, but the old situation can be restored again with one counterstroke.

The ensuing cessation of fire is used to bury our own dead. But we have a hard job doing that, because the ground is frozen so hard that it can't be broken with shovels or even pickaxes. With hand grenades placed in holes dug in advance it is finally possible to blow out a few shallow trenches for our fallen comrades. But that is all that can be done for them."
(11th Panzer Division. 12/3/1941, Moscow)

Battles of 1942

In thick swarms the Stukas carried their bombs to Stalingrad and flew low on the return trip, their sirens howling proudly just above the turrets of the tanks that rolled forward. After a hard fight, the 16th Panzer Division crossed the Tartar trenches and crossed the Frolov-Stalingrad railroad line south of Kotluban. Railroad trains went up in smoke. The enemy seemed completely taken by surprise. The advance went on smoothly. Early in the afternoon the tank commanders saw the imposing skyline of the city of Stalingrad to the right on the horizon, stretching along the Volga for 40 kilometers. Grain elevators and smokestacks, skyscrapers and towers rose above the smoke and fire. Very far to the north and cathedral tower rose above the formless clouds of smoke.

Enemy fire began about 3:00 P.M. Before the northern suburbs, Spartakovka with its tractor factory, Rynok and Lataskinka, were Russian anti-aircraft guns, manned by women. They greeted the attackers with their shells. Gun by gun, 37 emplacements had to be fought down by Pz.Abt. von Strachwitz and II./64. And then the first tanks were on the commanding west shore of the Volga. Quietly and majestically, the wide dark river flowed past, carrying towboats downstream, and beyond it the Asiatic steppes extended to infinity, and pride and joy and awe were seen on the men's faces. The division settled down for the night near the river on the northern edge of the city. The battle groups prepared feverishly for the next days' battles. The Russian antitank and anti-aircraft fire was already flying. The harsh glow of the shots flashed like heat lightning in the clear night sky.
(18th Panzer Division, 8/23/1942, Stalingrad)

—

September 15, 1942. Today I must spread out and relieve the squadron that has been to our right. The Panzer Unit von Lanken is moving through the southern part of the city toward the "Garrison Heights" today, but isn't making progress. The terrain over there, which we can't see from here, is full of bunkers, emplacements and dug-in tanks.

September 16, 1942. We are being pulled out of here too, in order to attack the city with tanks again and finally wipe out this nest of resistance. We move in marching order along the tracks into the city, where the von Heyden unit has just reached the main railway station and pushed on to the Volga shore. Then we turn around and move westward toward "Garrison Heights." Here the city is completely burned out, the streets peppered with shell craters.

At the edge of the city we stop and, supported by fire from the tanks, set out to establish a system of strong positions on a north-south line rising to the heights. We push up to the first trenches and over them in tough close combat. Thirty meters in front of us is the second trench, and behind it is scrub speckled with bunkers and tanks. In one concerted plunge we take the second trench and mop it up. Strong artillery fire meets us now; it is impossible to tell whether it is ours or the enemy's. After the second trench is firmly in our hands and the last Russians have been hauled out of their holes or shot down with pistols, we push into the brush like shock troops. Before us is a small group of houses; a road leads to the left and there is thick brush to the right, in which numerous T-34 tanks can be seen at a distance of 50 to 100 meters.
(24th Panzer Division, 9/16/1942, Stalingrad)

In the first light of morning the Quentin Battle Group (6th Panzer Reconnaissance Unit) and the Hünersdorff Panzer Group move out to win a crossing over the Aksay," it says in the war diary for December 13. "The Quentin Battle Group already encounters stubbornly fighting enemy tanks at Point 90.7, along with strong artillery and Stalin units."

And from the war diary of the 11th Panzer Regiment: "The advance is slowed by two ice-covered ravines. At the bend of the railway line there is a brief firefight with enemy tanks east of the tracks. The Quentin Group moving forward east of the tracks asks for support against these tanks. But the Commander decides not to be drawn off to the east by these tanks and orders us to go on to the northwest toward Salivski."

The crossing of the Aksai at Salivski is accomplished by the tanks at 8:00, almost without enemy opposition.

From the war diary of the 11th Panzer Regiment:

"First Unit moves northward and prepares to attack Verchne-Kumski. While being crossed by the tank of the Regimental Commander following the First Unit, the bridge caves in and the Commander's tank blocks the way for all following vehicles. Additional forces cannot be sent after the First Unit. For the attack by the whole regiment, the 114th Armored Infantry Battalion and artillery had been added. After a heavy Stuka attack on Verchne-Kumski, the Commander decides to attack with the First Unit. Verchne-Kumski is taken about 12:00 after weak enemy resistance. At this time the building of a bridge over the Aksai begins, as the tank that broke through cannot be removed from the bridge."

(6th Panzer Division, 12/13/1942, relief of Stalingrad)

—

The advance of the Panzer divisions was delayed, since the Commander had chosen the wrong way and thus arrived at a slope down which the tanks, especially those of the 4th Panzer, threatened to slide on the slick ice. Only after the unit had turned to the more northerly advance route chosen by me on the spot, could the attack be carried out through the planned cooperation of the three main units. Around the Kolchos a full hour was spent in a bitter tank battle before the enemy gave way. The Kolchos fell around 11:00. In the process, 15 enemy tanks, most of them immobile and built into the defenses, were destroyed! It could not be determined whether these tactics were caused by lack of fuel or orders to halt. The mobile tank battle was joined by tanks coming in from the north. Our own tanks moved out to the west, then attacked to the northeast and forced a withdrawal. Fortunately the enemy had not chosen the effective tactics of a tank attack from the northwest, which would have been most sensitive for the division. During the battle, the reinforced group of the 40th Panzer-Grenadier Regiment, having come up behind the Panzer group, took over the protection of the open left flank.

The corps reported that the enemy, under the pressure of the attack, was forming a new defense front on his right flank, on the heights north of Verchne-Kumski. Thus the original plan of taking the town of Verchne-Kumski by the frontally attacking 6th Panzer Division was given up and an attack against the heights north of the town was commenced. It was not to be carried out, because it got dark too early (about 3:00 P.M. In the afternoon hours the enemy again tried to attack with

tanks from the northeast, but we were able to turn them back with scarcely any trouble.
(17th Panzer Division, 12/16/1942, relief of Stalingrad)

Battles of 1943

The preparations for the "Citadel" summer offensive were taken by the OKH as an occasion to restructure the Panzer divisions according to the concepts of the Inspector General of the Panzer Troops, Generaloberst Guderian. As early as December 1942 the staff of the 9th Panzer-Grenadier Brigade had been removed; now two units of the 33rd Panzer Regiment were given up, the IV. Unit of the 102nd Panzer Artillery Regiment was made into the independent 287th Anti-Aircraft Artillery Unit, the subsequent 59th Motorcycle Battalion was integrated into the 9th Panzer Reconnaissance Unit. Thus as of the end of June 1943, the following units were ready for action:

Division Staff

Pz.Reg.33 (1 unit)	Pz.Art.Reg.102 with	Pz.Eng.Btl.86
Pz.Gren.Reg.19 (2 btl.)	2 light + 1 heavy units	Pz.Nachr.Abt.85
Pz.Gren.Reg.11 (2 btl.)	sFlak Art.Abt.287	Pz.Div.Na.Tr.60
Pz.Reconn.Abt.9	Pz.Jäger-Abt.50	Feld.Ers.Btl.60

On 7/5/1943 the 9th Panzer Division, subordinate to the XXXXVII. Panzer Corps, advanced to from the Orel bend in the direction of Fatesh at the focal point of the 9th Army (Model). The betrayed offensive, which did not get through, forced the OB to stop the attack on July 13 on account of unanswerable losses. The 9th Panzer Division was at once assigned to stop the Soviet breakthrough in the rear of the 9th Army north of Orel, in the XXXXI. Panzer Corps; in mid-August it was put under the command of the Panzer AOK 2, with which it went into action north of Kirov with the LVI. Panzer Corps. With that the division took part in two important relocating moves into the "Hagen position" east or Briansk, until it was rushed by rail into the sector of the 6th Army on August 22, to join the XXIX. AK on the Mius front.
(9th Panzer Division, June-July 1943, Citadel/Orel)

—

5:00 AM: German infantry and tanks move out of the Butovo-Gerzovka line with assault guns and 4./Pz.Stu.Pi.Btl. *GD* with the attacking grenadier battalion, the III. Battalion under Hauptmann Senger.

9:00 AM: Point 237.8 west of Cherkasskoye is reached! —The 12th Corps turns westward. — Our tanks have trouble with tank traps in the Gerzovka lowlands. — Neighbor to the right — 11th Panzer Division — is on hill 237.8. — Neighbor to the left — Armored Fusiliers — on the same hill with us. Heavy enemy aircraft activity.

9:15 AM: Direct bomb hit on regimental battle station —casualties: Regimental Adjutant Hauptmann Beckendorff, Leutnant Hofstetter IV. Btl. (Adj.), Leutnant Stein, Panzerjägerabteilung *GD* fallen.

10:00 AM: Command from Iz Division to Panzer Brigade: Push forward to Point 210.7 — I. and II. Battalions join in. — Delayed by stop before tank traps. — II. Battalion has a hard time coming through, as Panzer Unit is blocking the way.
11:00 AM: Bridge built over the Gerzovka lowlands — about in themiddle of the division's attack area.
1:50 PM: Soviet attack with 7 tanks toward Korovino (at the Fusiliers), our III. Battalion is there too.
1:53 PM: All 7 attacking Russian tanks are shot down by our own tanks. Enemy air activity increases at times.
2:30 PM: The I. Battalion and "Panther" Brigade begin action atthe tank traps. The II. and IV. Battalions in the lead south of Point 229.8 and in Mulde.
3:30 PM: Makeshift bridge over the Beresovy lowlands smashed by Panthers.
5:50 PM: Regimental battle station relocated to western border of Yamnoye.

(Panzer-Grenadier *Grossdeutschland,* 6/6/1943. "Citadel")

Withdrawal in 1944

On the next day, April 5, the attack was to be continued at the first light of morning. Generalleutnant von Saucken had thus ordered the Mühlenkamp Panzer Battle Group to attack the heights south of Dubova, which were heavily occupied by the enemy; the rest of the 33rd Panzer-grenadier Regiment, along with the Panzer Regiment of the 5th Panzer Division, which was making a sweeping attack from the north, was to bring about the fall of Dubova, also heavily occupied, and then, with its flank andrear secured by the 5th Panzer Division, advance to attack the northern edge of Kovel on a broad front.

It was a complete success and created the long-sought connection with the "strong point" of Kovel. In the night before April 5 the reconnaissance men of the 33rd Panzer-grenadier Regiment had made a temporary connection with the foremost support points of the Pol.Reg.Goltz of the Kovel fortress troops. By the attack of the reinforced 4th Panzer Division, this was finally accomplished during April 5.

About 3:15 A.M. the attack began. Two wedges of shock troops moved to the southeast, the Mühlenkamp Panzer Battle Group at the right with the heights 2 kilometers south of Dobrova as their goal, at left the 33rd Panzer-grenadier Regiment moving on "do Dubrowei." After a hard fight, the first goal of the attack was attained in a short time. Now the fight for the enemy's outer bastion at the northern edge of Kovel, which was liberally supplied with antitank guns, began. Now the Mühlenkamp Panzer Battle Group moved forward under constant fire, with one tank column to the right toward the railroad bend northwest of the city, with the left column along the Brest-Litovsk-Kovel railway line, and after a stubborn firefight destroyed the tank barricades there, while the attack unit of the 4th Panzer Division pushed directly into the northern part of Kovel from the north.
(5th Panzer Division, 4/5/1944)

—

On the 26th we march on. We cannot follow the planned course via Toubovka, since this town is already occupied by strong Russian forces. At Nikolaievka the marching column of the division, and General Källner with it, is suddenly attacked by strong Russian tank forces from Toubovka. At once the division takes a circular position around the town. The Schneider Panzer Group of the 27th Panzer Regiment is able again to destroy 20 enemy tanks.

The I./Pz.Gren.Reg.73 is put in the lead to fight the way through to Yelisavetivka. The edge of the forest there is already occupied by strong Russian forces; the battalion is soon stopped cold. Meanwhile General Källner has found a new march route. Via Maschina he pushes the division over 40 kilometers on a marching route all their own through the Ukrainian forests. Darkness falls, but the men go on tirelessly over the bad forest road, through gigantic water holes. What is accomplished here by the exhausted soldiers is superhuman. So many stuck vehicles are gotten loose, but the men must march. And the regiment is the rear guard. As soon as the column stops, one hears loud rattling of Russian tank tracks from the north.
(19th Panzer Division, 12/26/1944)

"12th Panzer Division: Experienced, proved Panzer division with numerous energetic, outstanding commanders. Tough leadership that thinks of everything."
(12th Panzer Division, evaluated by the Army Group, 1944)

Retreat in 1945

The Hoffmann Group drives (12:20 P.M.) the enemy off Hill 78.7 and at the same time out of Ileni. The town is partly in our hands. The enemy draws back between Ileni and Muldeini.

At 2:20 P.M. Panzer Engineer Battalion has also reached Ileni.

At 3:00 P.M. an enemy counterattack succeeds. Our own units are partially driven back into the woods to the west.

The von Gaudecker Group, along with the I./Pz.Gren.Reg.12, cannot reach the HKL after four tries, because of too-heavy enemy opposition.

The I./12 is brought out at 5:45 A.M. and the Panzer-grenadier Regiment 12 sent in. II./33rd Pz.Gren.Reg. shifts the HKL backward (west of the "Egg Woods") and sets up for defense there.

Attacks led by Panzer Engineer 79, the 32nd Panzer Engineer Battalion and I./273, trying to win back the old HKL on both sides of Hill 78.7, do not reach their goal despite hard close combat.

The 12th Panzer-Grenadier Regiment takes over (6:00 A.M.) the command over the 4th Panzer A.A., 79th Panzer Engineer, 32nd Panzer Engineer Battalion and I./273.

During the day the enemy moves into the "Egg Woods" group by group, with our artillery steadily firing on them. Heavy enemy artillery, grenade-thrower and antitank fire are directed at our position, and often salvos of gunfire as well.

The HKL of the von Gaudecker Group's sector is closed (5:00 P.M.), barrage fire is laid down by artillery — In the evening the battalions call on their few reserves for counterattacks. A second position is occupied by the heavy company and parts of the Machine Gun Battalion "Stettin." Despite the complete exhaustion of the men in the trench, the defense appears to have accomplished as much as possible.
(4th Panzer Division, 1/5/1945)

—

The division's report on the events of the first day's fighting shows strikingly successful statistics: 63 enemy tanks had been destroyed, eleven of them with the "Panzerfaust" alone. Numerous antitank guns, grenade launchers and handguns were captured. The engineers succeeded in rescuing two still driveable "Sherman" tanks from no man's land and bringing them back behind their own lines. On the other hand, success was won that cannot be expressed in statistics. The Red Infantry — not overly secure in their positions in any case — had suffered heavy losses and largely lost the momentum of their attack. Even their tasks of defending themselves were carried out only to some degree, despite sufficient artillery and salvo support. Their trust in the American "Sherman" tanks, which had shown themselves to be unequal to either the "Tiger" and "Panther" or the weaker Panzer IV and assault guns, had vanished. The tank crews themselves had become more cautious. They delayed where they should have moved energetically, and it showed over and over that they tried hard to avoid tank-versus-tank fighting, even when they were definitely in the majority. In addition, the 14th Panzer Division seemed to be an opponent that simply would not give up. A radio message had begun that even on the morning of 1/25, after quite significantly successful Russian attacks,

sounded like a cry for help from a defender driven into a bad spot: "Send tanks and antitank guns! We're stuck! The 14th is attacking!" What answer the Red troop leader gave to that is not known. But it was unmistakable that from now on the attacking pressure was increased by the use of fresh infantry forces, and that the whole operational reserves of tanks and heavy weapons were thrown into the battle gradually. The combat activity of the tactical air units also increased in extent and impact, made easier by clearing weather.
(14th Panzer Division, 1/25/1945)

—

The towns in the Mark Brandenburg glow tonight like burning torches in the spring sky. Buckow, Strausberg, Altlandsberg, Fredersdorf are the flaming guideposts for the leading Soviet tank units. The few German units still able to fight are not in any condition to offer energetic opposition. Aside from the fact that they are completely exhausted and do not have great quantities of ammunition, they are stuck between columns of refugees on the destroyed roads or in the burning forests of the Mark. The vehicles much constantly avoid new bomb craters. Shot-up trucks and tanks are everywhere; others lie motionless because they ran out of fuel or their axles broke. These trucks are often loaded with things that were urgently needed at the front. Now, of course, nobody finds the time any more to bother about the loads of ammunition boxes, food supplies or clothing. Volkssturm personnel have set up tank obstacles that are no problem for the heavy Russian tanks, but are for the fleeing population with their horsedrawn wagons and handcarts. Now the columns stop until they are blown apart by tank guns and rolled over by T-34s.

The men of the *Müncheberg* Division get caught in the tangle of overlapping events. The tanks are the corset stays of the division; they keep the unit from breaking up, though with great difficulty. Feldwebel Hartmann and his Panzer crew are constantly on the move to put down small Soviet breakthroughs, haul shattered groups out and protect late columns of refugees.
(Panzer Division *Müncheberg*, 4/21/1945)

Emblems of the Panzer Divisions, 1941-42

1. Panzerdivision
Wehrkreis IX Kassel
Pz.-Grenadierregiment 1, 113
Panzerregiment 1
Pz.-Artillerieregiment 73

2. Panzerdivision
Wehrkreis XVII Wien
Pz.-Grenadierregiment 2, 304
Panzerregiment 3
Pz.-Artillerieregiment 74

3. Panzerdivision
Wehrkreis III Berlin
Pz.-Grenadierregiment 3, 394
Panzerregiment 6
Pz.-Artillerieregiment 75

4. Panzerdivision
Wehrkreis XIII Nürnberg
Pz.-Grenadierregiment 12, 33
Panzerregiment 35
Pz.-Artillerieregiment 103

5. Panzerdivision
Wehrkreis VIII Breslau
Pz.-Grenadierregiment 13, 14
Panzerregiment 31
Pz.-Artillerieregiment 116

6. Panzerdivision
Wehrkreis VI Münster
Pz.-Grenadierregiment 4, 114
Panzerregiment 11
Pz.-Artillerieregiment 76

7. Panzerdivision
Wehrkreis IX Kassel
Pz.-Grenadierregiment 6, 7
Panzerregiment 25
Pz.-Artillerieregiment 78

8. Panzerdivision
Wehrkreis III Berlin
Pz.-Grenadierregiment 8, 28
Panzerregiment 10
Pz.-Artillerieregiment 80

9. Panzerdivision
Wehrkreis XVII Wien
Pz.-Grenadierregiment 10, 11
Panzerregiment 33
Pz.-Artillerieregiment 102

10. Panzerdivision
Wehrkreis V Stuttgart
Pz.-Grenadierregiment 69, 86
Panzerregiment 7
Pz.-Artillerieregiment 90

11. Panzerdivision
Wehrkreis VIII Breslau
Pz.-Gren.-Regiment 110, 111
Panzerregiment 15
Pz.-Artillerieregiment 119

12. Panzerdivision
Wehrkreis II Stettin
Pz.-Grenadierregiment 5, 25
Panzerregiment 29
Pz.-Artillerieregiment 2

13. Panzerdivision
Wehrkreis XI Hannover
Pz.-Grenadierregiment 66, 93
Panzerregiment 4
Pz.-Artillerieregiment 13

14. Panzerdivision
Wehrkreis IV Dresden
Pz.-Gren.-Regiment 103, 108
Panzerregiment 36
Pz.-Artillerieregiment 4

16. Panzerdivision
Wehrkreis VI Münster
Pz.-Grenadierregiment 64, 79
Panzerregiment 2
Pz.-Artillerieregiment 16

17. Panzerdivision
Wehrkreis VII München
Pz.-Grenadierregiment 40, 63
Panzerregiment 39
Pz.-Artillerieregiment 27

18. Panzerdivision
Wehrkreis IV Dresden
Pz.-Grenadierregiment 52, 101
Panzerregiment 18
Pz.-Artillerieregiment 88

19. Panzerdivision
Wehrkreis XI Hannover
Pz.-Grenadierregiment 73, 74
Panzerregiment 27
Pz.-Artillerieregiment 19

20. Panzerdivision
Wehrkr. IX Kassel XI Hann.
Pz.-Grenadierregiment 59, 112
Panzerregiment 21
Pz.-Artillerieregiment 92

21. Panzerdivision
Wehrkreis VI Münster
Pz.-Gren.-Regiment 125, 192
Panzerregiment 100 (22)
Pz.-Artillerieregiment 155

22. Panzerdivision
Wehrkreis XII Wiesbaden
Pz.-Gren.-Regiment 129, 140
Panzerregiment 204
Pz.-Artillerieregiment 140

23. Panzerdivision
Wehrkreis V Stuttgart
Pz.-Gren.-Regiment 126, 128
Panzerregiment 23
Pz.-Artillerieregiment 128

24. Panzerdivision
Wehrkreis I Königsberg
Pz.-Grenadierregiment 21, 26
Panzerregiment 24
Pz.-Artillerieregiment 89

25. Panzerdivision
Wehrkreis VI Münster
Pz.-Gren.-Regiment 146, 147
Panzerregiment 9
Pz.-Artillerieregiment 91

26. Panzerdivision
Wehrkreis III Berlin
Pz.-Gren.-Regiment 9, 67
Panzerregiment 26
Pz.-Artillerieregiment 93

116. Panzerdivision
Wehrkreis VI Münster
Pz.-Gren.-Regiment 60, 156
Panzerregiment 16
Pz.-Artillerieregiment 146

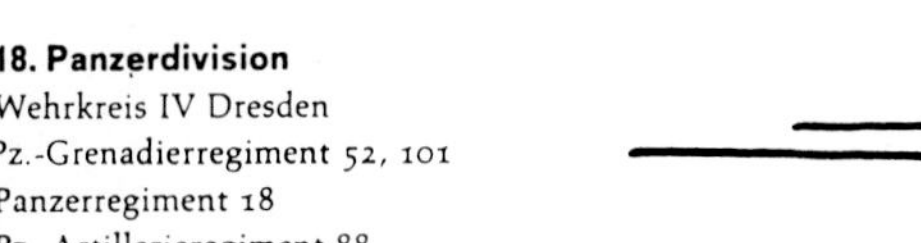

German Tanks in the Eastern Campaign

With the beginning of the offensive against the Red Army, the german tanks, thanks to their technical superiority, the tactical ability and firing discipline of their crews, gained great success. Here Type P-III tanks attack across the White Russian steppes. Note the white markings on the turret, by which one can recognize the unit. (Picture taken 6/29/1941.)

The Advance, 1941

A Panzer unit in battle at a town near Smolensk. At right a P-II, in front of it a P-III, farther ahead the riflemen's vehicle. (Picture taken July 17, 1941.)

After the battle of Kiev in September of 1941, German tanks — passing Russian prisoners of war — move ahead into battle near Moscow.

Defense on all Front Sectors - 1942-43

As the autumn rain poured down on Russian roads and fields, they turned into mud and mire. Now it was hard to go further. (Picture taken 10/28/1941.)

Things became even worse when the winter came. Not only did coldness and ice freeze the motors, but the tanks got stuck in the snow. Here is a P-III before Tula, December 2, 1941.

The greatest and most dangerous enemy in the fall and winter of 1941 was the Russian "T-34" tank. The German medium tanks could not match it. In the front are two T-34s (Picture taken August 10, 1942.)

The war's events often required a fast and improvised transfer of the Panzer units, which were applied as "firemen" where there was a "fire." Then the tank became a transport vehicle on which weapons, ammunition, spare parts and supplies were loaded. (Picture taken March 24, 1942.)

Once again German tanks rolled eastward. As here on September 15, 1942, in the direction of Stalingrad. But then when the winter came, they could only go back. The bottom picture shows a unit with P-IV tanks on January 18, 1943, withdrawing from the Caucasus in the direction of Rostov.

Retreat and Final Battle - 1944-45

After the failure of "Operation Citadel" in 1943, the tanks were used only for defense, countermoves or rear guard. Here the "Tiger" tanks of the *Grossdeutschland* Division roll past armored gun cars to get ready for a counterattack.

In the northern sectors of the eastern front too — here tanks of a "Tiger": unit on the Latvian Baltic coast - they moved back. Courland was cut off from the rest of the front, and the last winter of the war has come.

The last large-scale German tank attack took place in the Hungarian war zone. Here "King Tigers" go to take up positions at the Gran bridgehead, north of Budapest. (Picture taken March 5, 1945.)

Organization, Structure and Operations of the — by number — first and last Panzer divisions

1st Panzer Division
(Zone IX, E 1 Erfurt)

Created 10/15/1935 by renumbering the Weimar Light Division (ex-3rd Cavalry Division). Mobilized 8/18/1939 with:

1st Rifle Regiment, Weimar
  1st Rifle Regiment, Weimar, I., II.
  1st Motorcycle Battalion, Langensalza
1st Panzer Brigade, Erfurt
  1st Panzer Regiment, Erfurt, I., II.
  1st Panzer Regiment, Eisenach, I., II.
73rd Artillery Regiment, Weimar, I., II.
Various Units 37, but Reconnaissance Unit (mot.) 4
Various Troops 81

On 10/30/1939 the III./69th Infantry Regiment came from the 20th Infantry Division (mot.) to become the III./1st Rifle Regiment of the division. On 10/20/1940 the 2nd Panzer Regiment left to join the newly formed 16th Panzer Division. The 1st Panzer Division gained a second Rifle Regiment 113 on 11/6/1940, out of the III./1st Rifle Regiment (ex-III./69) and a II. Battalion made of men from the 1st Rifle Regiment. On 2/15/1941 the II./1 and I./113 exchanged places, so that the former III./69 was now the II./1st Rifle Regiment. The 73rd Artillery Regiment gained a III. Unit from the II./56th Artillery Regiment.

1st Rifle Regiment, I., II.
113th Rifle Regiment, I., II.
1st Motorcycle Battalion
1st Panzer Regiment, I., II.
73rd Artillery Regiment, I. to III.
Various Units 37 (Reconnaissance Unit 4 disbanded 1942)
Various Troops 81

On 7/11/1942 the 1st and 113th Rifle Regiments were renamed the 1st Panzer-grenadier Regiment. Men from the I./1st Panzer Regiment, as the 116th Panzer Unit, joined the 16th Panzer-Grenadier Division. The Division retained only the II. Unit until 1/15/1943, which became the I/ Unit when the Division was refreshed in France, and the II. Unit was formed of the I./203rd Panzer Regiment. The 299th Army Anti-Aircraft Unit joined the Division. Motorcycle Battalion 1 was temporarily renamed the 91st Panzer Reconnaissance Regiment (with I., II., 7) on 3/1/1943, then on 4/29 it became Panzer Reconnaissance Unit 1. The Artillery Regiment gained an additional unit.

1st Panzer-Grenadier Regiment, I., II.
113th Panzer-Grenadier Regiment, I., II.
1st Panzer Reconnaissance Unit
1st Panzer Regiment, I., II.
73rd Artillery Regiment, I. to IV.
299th Army Anti-Aircraft Unit
Various Units 37, Various Troops 81

On 9/28/1944 the Grenadier Training Battalion (mot.) 1009 joined the Division as the Panzer Division Tatra. This was given completely new numbers in February 1945 without being recognizably restructured.

Service:

1939	Sept.	XVI	10. Armee	Süd	Osten	Radom, Warschau
	Dez.	z. Vfg.	–	„B"	Westen	Eifel, Hunsrück
1940	Jan.	z. Vfg.	–	„B"	Westen	Eifel, Hunsrück
	Mai	z. Vfg.	16. Armee	„A"	Westen	Luxemburg, Somme
	Juni	XXXIX	Guderian (12.)	„A"	Westen	Frankreich (Aisne)
	Juli/Aug.	XXXIX	2. Armee	„C"	Westen	Frankreich
	Sept./Dez.	XVI	18. Armee	„B"	Osten	Ostpreußen
1941	Jan./Febr.	XVI	18. Armee	„B"	Osten	Ostpreußen
	März/Apr.	z. Vfg.	4. Pz.Gru.	„B"	Osten	Ostpreußen
	Mai	z. Vfg.	4. Pz.Gru.	„C"	Osten	Ostpreußen
	Juni/Sept.	XXXXI	4. Pz.Gru.	Nord	Osten	Dünaburg, Leningrad,
	Okt./Dez.	XXXXI	3. Pz.Gru.	Mitte	Osten	Wiasma, Moskau
1942	Jan.	XXXXI	3. Pz.Gru.	Mitte	Osten	Welish
	Febr.	XXXXVI	9. Armee	Mitte	Osten	Welish, Rshew
	März/Apr.	XXIII	9. Armee	Mitte	Osten	Rshew
	Mai	XXVII	9. Armee	Mitte	Osten	Rshew
	Juni/Juli	XXIII	9. Armee	Mitte	Osten	Rshew
	Aug.	z. Vfg.	4. Armee	Mitte	Osten	Rshew
	Sept./Nov.	XXXIX	9. Armee	Mitte	Osten	Rshew
	Dez.	XXXXI	9. Armee	Mitte	Osten	Rshew
1943	Jan.	z. Vfg.	–	„D"	Westen	Frankreich
	Febr.	z. Vfg.	15. Armee	„D"	Westen	Frankreich
	März/Apr.	z. Vfg.	7. Armee	„D"	Westen	Frankreich
	Mai	z. Vfg.	–	„D"	Westen	Frankreich
	Juni	z. Vfg.	–	„E"	Südosten	Balkan
	Juli/Aug.	LXVIII	–	„E"	Südosten	Griechenland
	Sept.	LXVIII	11. ital. Armee	„E"	Südosten	Griechenland
	Okt.	LXVIII	„E"	„E"	Südosten	Griechenland
	Nov.	z. Vfg.	8. Armee	Süd	Osten	Nordukraine
	Dez.	XXXXVIII	4. Pz.Armee	Süd	Osten	Shitomir
1944	Jan.	XXXXVIII	4. Pz.Armee	Süd	Osten	Winniza
	Febr.	XXIV	4. Pz.Armee	Süd	Osten	Winniza
	März	z. Vfg.	1. Pz.Armee	„A"	Osten	Brody
	Apr.	LIX	1. Pz.Armee	Nordukr.	Osten	Brody
	Mai	z. Vfg.	4. Pz.Armee	Nordukr.	Osten	Brody
	Juni	z. Vfg.	1. Pz.Armee	Nordukr.	Osten	Brody
	Juli	III	1. Pz.Armee	Nordukr.	Osten	Zloczow
	Aug.	XXXXVIII	4. Pz.Armee	Nordukr.	Osten	Brody
	Sept.	XXIV	1. Pz.Armee	Nordukr.	Osten	Karpathen
	Okt.	III	6. Armee	Süd	Osten	Ungarn
	Nov.	LVII	6. Armee	Süd	Osten	Ungarn
	Dez.	IV	6. Armee	Süd	Osten	Ungarn
1945	Jan.	Kav.K.	6. Armee	Süd	Osten	Ungarn
	Febr./März	III	6. Armee	Süd	Osten	Ungarn
	Apr.	IV. SS	6. Armee	Süd	Osten	Ungarn
	Mai	IV. SS	6. Armee	Ostmark	Osten	Ostalpen

233rd Panzer Division

In April 1945 the 233rd Reserve Panzer Division was renamed the 233rd Panzer Division. It then (as of May 7, 1945) consisted of:

42nd Panzer-Grenadier Regiment, 3 battalions
50th Panzer-Grenadier Regiment, 2 battalions
(ex-3rd Reserve Grenadier Regiment)
82nd Panzer-Grenadier Regiment, 2 battalions
233rd Panzer Reconnaissance Unit
(ex-3rd Reserve Panzer Reconnaissance Unit)
1033rd Panzerjäger Unit (ex-Reserve Pz.Jäg. Unit 3)
1233rd Artillery Regiment (Staff) with Artillery
Unit 1233 (ex-59th Reserve Artillery Unit)
1233rd Panzer Engineer Battalion
(ex-208th Reserve Engineer Battalion)
1233rd Panzer Intelligence Company
(ex-1233rd Resereve Panzer Intelligence Company)
1233rd Supply Unit

Missing are the I. and III./42, 50th Staff and I./83. The 42nd Panzer-grenadier Regiment was supposed to be transferred, by command of April 6, 1945, to join the Panzer Division *Clausewitz* in the Lauenburg/Elbe area; its last listed location, though, is Aarhus.

Service:
1945 March (remainder) WBefh. Denmark
April WBefh. Denmark

Panzer Units in Action against Partisans

The Panzer units of the troops at the front were generally not used in action against partisans in the hinterlands. Only in exceptional cases (see below), or when a Panzer unit was in refreshment quarters behind the front, could it be used in action against Soviet partisan groups in appropriate military situations.

The commanding generals and commanders of securing troops in the hinterlands of the army groups, for example, had the following Panzer units in their areas in September of 1943:

Army Group North:
3rd Panzer Company Cycle Securing Regiment
918th Panzer Workshop Company

Army Group Center:
2nd Light Panzer Company Cycle Securing Regiment

Army Group South:
221st and 318th Panzer Companies

(These Panzer companies were equipped only with captured Russian light tanks.)

Some examples of action of Panzer units against partisans:

1.) March-April 1943:
8th Panzer Division against partisans in Gorodok-Orel area;

2.) May 1843:
5th Panzer Division against partisans in area northwest of Briansk;

3.) June 1943:
4th and 18th Panzer Division against partisans in Briansk-Trubchevsk;

4.) August 1944:
Pz.Abt.302 (radio-controlled tanks) and I./Paratroop-Panzer Regiment *Hermann Göring* against Polish opposition groups in Warsaw etc.

Panzer Workshop and Recovery Units

Each of the Panzer regiments had a Panzer Workshop Company (at first called simply "Workshop Company"). The independent Panzer units likewise had a Panzer Workshop Company of Column.

Special units for recovering and repairing tanks were set up in 1940 within the supply services that belonged to the army troops. These units were assigned to the Panzer troops as of April 1, 1943.

There were individual:

Panzer Repair Units with Panzer Workshop and Tank Recovery Companies,
independent Tank Recovery Companies or Columns,
Tank Spare Parts Depots OKH A-E,
Panzer Workshop Command Paris,
Panzer Supply Depots (1941 only),
Panzer Workshops in Vienna and Pschelautsch, Moravia,
Panzer Spare Parts Column No. 1,
spare parts units,
tire and spare parts depots,
Panzer Workshop Company No. 918 with Army Group North,
tank track depots of the OKH,
Panzer Repair Groups at Army motor pools on the front and in Germany.

Workshop Companies and Supply Depots

Without the men of the workshop companies, the tanks would not have been able to run and fire. Yet these companies were never mentioned in the reports of the Wehrmacht High Command. Here the tracks of a P-III are being examined and remounted. (Picture taken 8/22/1941.)

The drive wheel of the tracks of a "Tiger" has to be changed. With the help of a crane truck of the workshop company, the new drive wheel has to be moved into the right position for mounting.(Picture taken 11/1/1943.)

New Type P-II tanks have left the assembly line and are to be painted in camouflage colors. (Picture taken 10/24/1942 at a delivery depot of the MAN firm.)

In the ammunition and fuel depot of a Panzer division in the central sector of the eastern front. (Picture taken 3/27/1944.)

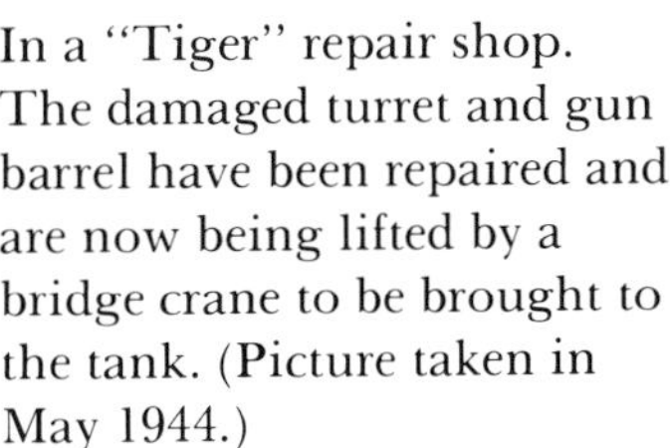

In a "Tiger" repair shop. The damaged turret and gun barrel have been repaired and are now being lifted by a bridge crane to be brought to the tank. (Picture taken in May 1944.)

Full Weapons Complement of a Panzer Regiment, 1944

Rifles	626
Pistols	911
Machine pistols	109
Machine pistols on armored vehicles	170
Light machine guns	29
Light machine guns on armored vehicles	334
20mm quadruple anti-aircraft guns on armored vehicles	6
37mm anti-aircraft guns on armored vehicles	8
75mm KwK 40 or 42 tank guns79 or 81	

Full Complement of Vehicles of a Panzer Regiment, 1944

Armored Vehicles:	
P-IV tanks	86
P-V tanks	73
P-IV armored command vehicles	3
P-V armored command vehicles	6
P-III armored recovery vehicles	2
Armored rifle vehicles	10
Unarmored Vehicles:	
Light motorcycles	13
Motorcycles with sidecars	3
Halftrack motorcycles	41
Light cars (normal)	3
Light cars (cross-country)	61
Medium cars (cross-country)	6
Light trucks (normal)	3
Medium trucks (normal)	9
Heavy trucks (normal)	28
Light trucks (cross-country)	22
Medium trucks (cross-country)	47
Heavy trucks (cross-country)	78
Chain-drive trucks ("mule")	12
Ambulances	2
Omnibus	1
Trailers	17
Special Vehicle 100	3
Towing tractors (Zgkw) 1 ton	17
Towing tractors 8 tons	6
Towing tractors 18 tons	8
Towing tractors 35 tons	4
Special Vehicle 9/1 (18 tons)	2

Losses of Tanks in the Eastern Campaign

(Data from Müller-Hillebrand, *Das Heer*, Volume 3)

Typ	I	II	(F)	38 (t)	III	III	IV	IV	IV	V Panther	VI Tiger I	VI Tiger II	Flak-panzer	Pz. Befw.	Berge-Pz.	Summe der Zeilen 1 bis 15
Fahrgestell	I	II	II/III	38 (t)	III	III	IV	IV	IV	V	VI	VI	38 (t) u. IV	I-VI	38 (t), III, IV, V	
Waffe	M.G.	Kw.K. 2 cm	Flamm-öl	Kw.K. 3,7 cm	Kw.K. 3,7 u. 5 cm L 42	Kw.K. 5 cm L 60 u. 7,5 cm L 24	Kw.K. 7,5 cm L 24	Kw.K. 7,5 cm L 43 u. L 48	Pak 7,5 cm L 70	Kw.K. 7,5 cm L 70	Kw.K. 8,8 cm L 56	Kw.K. 8,8 cm L 71	Flak 3,7 cm, Flak 2 cm, 2 cm-Vierling, 3 cm-Zwilling	versch.	—	
Nr. der Zeile	1	2	3	4	5	6	7	8	9	10	11	12	13	14	15	16
Mai 1941	—	—		—	—		1							—		1
Juni	34	16		33	27		16							1		127
Juli	109	107		175	219		108							18		736
August	141	96		173	90		70							12		582
September	7	24		62	98		21							17		229
Oktober	15	34		84	35		52							14		234
November	25	27		144	105		36							6		343
Dezember	14	89		102	208		65							28		506
Summe 1941	345	393		773	782	—	369							96		2758
Januar 1942	18	76		31	181	—	48							28		382
Februar	15	40		8	157		49	—						16		285
März	1	3		7	32		10	—						8		61
April	1	12		11	50		22	—						4		100
Mai	8	6		6	14		30							2		66
Juni	5	22		4	110		41							3		185
Juli	—	28		5	235		61							16		345
August	2	27		20	130		37				—			2		218
September	4	21		24	179		48				—			4		280
Oktober	1	11		37	87		54				3			3		196
November	5	29		25	266		57				—			9		391
Dezember	—	12		18	60		45				—			4		139
Summe 1942	60	287		196	1501		502				3			99		2648
Januar 1943	—	49	—	30	231		93				11			17		431
Februar		207	—	13	988		345				3			40		1596
März		51	—	30	242		136				16			27		502
April		22	—	4	80	165	19	117			4			5		416
Mai		25	1	2	13	90	4	152			17			2	—	306
Juni		12	—	—	—	2	1	4		—	—			—	—	19
Juli		26	4	—	18	171	19	271		83	33			17	3	645
August		4	11	1	14	163	11	269		41	40			18	—	572
September		1	9	1	7	1	1	136		123	65			9	—	353
Oktober		2	13	5	10	55	6	193		107	32			26	1	450
November		5	11	10	21	84	2	260		79	28			22	2	524
Dezember		4	14	—	5	35	12	301		92	58			26	1	548
Summe 1943		408	63	96	2395		2352			525	307			209	7	6362
Januar 1944		3	3		5	37	10	264		128	53			28	—	531
Februar		2	1		1	26	3	149		116	13			28	—	339
März		1	8		1	—	1	120		19	28			13	—	191
April		2	6		2	38	1	276		242	96			26	1	690
Mai		1	1		—	—	—	83		114	20			7	—	226
Juni		1	—		6	8	8	262		133	89			19	2	528
Juli		46			—	4	—	426		347	191			46	8	1068
August		4				2	3	365		278	91			21	5	769
September		1				—	—	292	—	298	142		16	23	3	775
Oktober		—						141	20	283	39	10	19	27	7	546
November								81	5	105	19	11	18	12	3	254
Dezember								158	28	234	2	30	38	21	6	517
Summe 1944		61	19		15	115	26	2617	53	2297	783	51	91	271	35	6434
Januar 1945								287	93	237	62	6	22	46	11	764
Summe Mai 1941 bis Januar 1945	405	1149	82	1065	4808		6153		146	3059	1155	57	113	721	53	18966

Bem.: Panzerkampfwagen des Typs 35 (t) waren ab 1941 nicht mehr im Feldheer vorhanden.

THE GERMAN TANKS IN THE LAST WAR YEAR

Type	Fighting Weight (tons)	Weapons	Speed on road, cross country, kph	Armor plate front, sides turret front
P-IV	23.6	75mm KwK	42 15-20	50mm 30mm 50mm
P-V/I	44.8	75mm KwK 42 L/56	55 30-40	80-100mm 45mm 80mm
P-V/II	(Same, but with narrow turret)			
P-V/I	54	88mm KwK 42 L/56	40 20-30	100mm 60-80mm 120mm
P-VI/II	68	88mm KwK 42 L/71	38 15-20	150mm 80mm 150mm
P-III (Flame)	23	2 MG	40 18-20	50mm 30mm 50mm

HOLDERS OF THE OAK LEAVES TO THE KNIGHT'S CROSS IN THE PANZER TROOPS

(Ranks only to regimental commander)

No.	Date of Award	Rank & Name & Unit	Position
44	12/31/1941	Oberleutnant Buchterkirch	Chief II./6th Panzer Regiment
47	12/31/1941	Hauptmann Schulz	Cmdr. I./25th Panzer Regiment
133	10/11/1942	Hauptmann Kümmel	Cmdr.I./8th Panzer Regiment
144	11/13/1942	Oberstlt. Count Strachwitz	Cmdr.I./2nd Panzer Regiment
219	4/2/1943	Hauptmann Hudel	Cmdr. I./7th Panzer Regiment
236	5/10/1943	Hauptmann Stotten	Cmdr. I./8th Panzer Regiment
262	8/1/1943	Major Bäke	Cmdr. II./11th Panzer Regiment
285	8/29/1943	Major von Cossel	Cmdr. I./35th Panzer Regiment
348	12/7/1943	Oberstleutnant Langkeit	Cmdr. 36th Panzer Regiment
385	2/8/1944	Major Löwe	Cmdr. Pz.Abt.501
396	2/12/1944	Oberst von Lauchert	Cmdr. 15th Panzer Regiment
425	3/13/1944	Hauptmann Rettemeier	Cmdr.Pz.Abt.5
436	3/26/1944	Hauptmann Grüner	Cmdr. I./2nd Panzer Regiment
485	6/4/1944	Oberfeldwebel Strippel	Zugf. 4./1st Panzer Regiment
513	6/26/1944	Hauptmann Count v. Kageneck	Cmdr. Pz.Abt.503
535	7/27/1944	Leutnant Carius	Fhr.2/Pz.Abt.502
536	7/27/1944	Oberst von Oppeln-Bronikowski	Cmdr.22nd Panzer Regiment
538	7/28/1944	Major Schulze	Cmdr.Pz.Abt.21
581	9/10/1944	Leutnant Bölter	Fhr.1/Pz.Abt.502
590	9/21/1944	Major Haen	Cmdr. Pz.Abt.103
604	10/4/1944	Oberleutnant Burg	Fhr. 7./Panzer Regiment *GD*
636	10/28/1944	Major Schultz	Cmdr. 35th Panzer Regiment
649	11/16/1944	Major Weidenbrück	Cmdr. Pz.Abt.104
729	2/5/1945	Oberst Sander	Cmdr. 31st Panzer Regiment
754	2/24/1945	Leutnant von Rohr	Fhr. 2./25th Panzer Regiment
795	3/23/1945	Oberstleutnant von Meyer	Cmdr. Panzer Regiment *Coburg*

Of the soldiers listed above, the following subseqneutly received the "Oak Leaves with Swords...": Oberst Count Strachwitz, Oberstleutnant Schultz, Oberstleutnant Bäke, Major General von Oppeln-Bronikowski; the first two officers were also decorated with the "Oak Leaves with Swords and Jewels. . ."

HOLDERS OF THE KNIGHT'S CROSS OF THE WAR SERVICE CROSS

Oberleutnant (Eng.) Römer	101st Panzer Brigade
Leutnant (Eng.) Schlegel	Pz.Abt.103
Army Works Master Benoit	31st Panzer Regiment
Army Works Master Sextel	35th Panzer Regiment
Senior Radio Master Hoelck	6th Panzer Regiment
Oberfeldwebel Reuschel	3rd Panzer Regiment
Overfeldwebel Schwarz, A.	201st Panzer Regiment
Oberfeldwebel Schwarz, F.	23rd Panzer Regiment
Oberfeldwebel Wassner	36th Panzer Regiment

Senior Master Hahne of the Alkett firm in Berlin, who had already served in the German Panzer training facility in Kama, USSR, and who did outstanding work in tank construction until the war ended, received the "Golden Knight's Cross of the KvK." (This decoration was given only twice.)

Field Newspapers of the Panzer Troops
(Selection)

Armee-Zeitung' (2nd Panzer Army)
Blücher. Frontzeitung einer Panzerarmee
Die Feuerwehr. Grabenzeitung der Panzer-Grenadier Division "Grossdeutschland", later Panzer Corps *Grossdeutschland*
Frontnachrichtenblatt der Armeezeitung 'Der Sieg'
Grabenzeitung des 'Panzer voran'
Die Oase. Feldzeitung der deutschen Truppen in Afrika
Panzer am Balkan. Nachrichtenblatt unserer Panzergruppe
Panzer voran! Frontzeitung einer Panzerarmee im Osten
Panzerfaust. Feldzeitung für die Soldaten einer Panzerarmee
Panzerfunk. Nachrichtenblatt einer Panzerarmee
Der Panzer-Kamerad. Nachrichtenblatt einer Panzerdivision, (6th Panzer Division)
Raupe und Rad. Frontzeitung einer Panzerarmee, (2nd Panzer Army)

Various Panzer divisions had information sheets and field newspapers printed for members of the division by their map units during the course of the war. The edition of the 6th Panzer Division is listed above as an example of this type.

Generals of the Panzer Troops who Died in Battle

Rank & Name	Position	Year and Place of Death
Glt. Angern	Cmdr. 16th Panzer Division	1943, Stalingrad
Gm. von Bernuth	Ch.Gen.Staff Pz.AOK 4 1942,	East Front, Ctr.
Glt. von Bismarck	Cmdr. 21st Panzer Division	1942, Tobruk
Gen. of Inf. Block	Comm.Gen. LVI. Pz.C.	1945, Oder Front
Gm. Büchting	Höh.Nachr.Fhr., Panzer Army Africa	1942, El Alamein
Gm. Baron Digeon von Monteton	Cmdr. Weapons School 3rd Panzer Armee	1944 Gorodez/Witebsk
Gen. Edler von Dawans	Chief General Staff, Panzer Group West	1944, La Caine,
Gen. of Inf. Eibel	Comm.Gen. XXIV.Pz.C.	1943, NW of Stalingrad
Gm. Baron von Elverfeldt	Cmdr. 9th Panzer Division	1945, Cologne
Glt. Fischer	Cmdr. 10th Panzer Division	1943, Tunis
Gm. v. Hünersdorff	Cmdr. 6th Panzer Division	1943, S. of Stalingrad
Gm. Jacob	Höh. Art. Officer, XXIV. Panzer Corps	1942, Stalino
Glt. Källner	Comm.Gen. XXIV. Pz.C.	1945, Sokolnica
Gen. Dr. Kern	Doctor, Pz.AOK 1	1945, Brno
Gm. Knebel	Cmdr. Weapons School, 3rd Panzer Army	1945, Pomerania
Gen.Pz.Tr. Baron von Langermann und Erlencamp	Comm. General, XXIV. Panzer Corps	1942, Storoshevoie
Gm. Mack	Cmdr. 23rd Panzer Division	1942, S. of Piatigorsk
Gen. of Artillery Martinek	Comm. General, XXXIX. Pz. Corps	1944, Beresinov
Gm. Michalik	Cmdr. Pz.Attack Unit, A.Group S.Ukraine	1944, on the Pruth
Gm. Neumann-Silkow	Cmdr. 15th Panzer Division	1941, Derna, N. Africa
Gm. Count von Nostitz-Wallwitz	Cmdr. 24th Panzer Division	1945, Eckernförde
Glt. von Prittwitz und Gaffron	Cmdr. 15th Panzer Division	1941, Tobruk
Glt. von Randow	Cmdr. 21st Panzer Division	1942, Tripoli
Gm. Riebel	Cmdr. 24th Panzer Reg.	1942, Stalingrad
Glt. Schilling	Cmdr. 17th Panzer Division	1943, Dolyenhaya
Gm. Schmidhuber	Cmdr. 13th Panzer Division	1945, Budapest
Gen. Dr. Scholl	Corps Doctor, XXXX. Panzer Corps	1942, Caucasus
Glt. Schünemann	Comm. General, XXXIX. Panzer Corps	1944, Pagost

Gm. Schulz, A.	Cmdr. 7th Panzer Division	1944, Shepetovka
Gen. Dr. Schulz, J.	Cmdr. 9th Panzer Division	1943, Krivoi Rog
Gm. von Seckendorff	Cmdr. Pz.Brig.113	1944, Lagarde
Glt. Sieberg	Cmdr. 14th Panzer Division	1943, Kirovgrad
Gen. Pz.Tr. Stumme	Füh. Pz. Army Africa	1942, El Alamein
Gen. of Artillery Wandel	Comm. General, XXIV. Panzer Corps	1943, Chilino
Gm. Ritter v. Weber	Cmdr. 17th Panzer Division	1941, Krassnyi
Gen. of the Panzer Troops Zorn	Comm. General, XXXXVI.Pz. Corps	1943, Krassnaya-Rostsha

Abbreviations:	Gen. = General	Inf. = Infantry
	Glt. = Generalleutnant	Art. = Artillery
	Gm. = Generalmajor	Pz.Tr. = Panzer Troops

Other generals died of other causes during World War II:

Illness (including in imprisonment)	8
Accidents	4
Suicide	5
Death sentence of German courts	1

The Panzer Units of the Luftwaffe

After the paratroopers of the Luftwaffe were not supposed to be used in parachute action, according to the highest command, after their service on Crete in 1941, the divisions were ordered to service on the front. In the course of this restructuring, the Paratroop Panzer Division *Hermann Göring*, consisting of two regiments, was formed near Berlin in November 1942.

(In the following years the Army assigned officers, non-commissioned officers and enlisted men to it; for example, Generalmajor von Necker and Generalmajor Lemke, as army officers, were commanders of this division.)

Service dates and places of Paratroop Panzer Division *Hermann Göring*:

1943	January-April	Training in Bordeaux area
	May-July	Service in Sicily
	August-December	Service in Calabria, near Salerno and on the Volturno
1944	January-February	Service in Nettuno area
	March-April	Refreshment in Tuscany
	June-July	Service in and near Rome
	August	Transfer to the eastern front
	September	Combat in and near Warsaw
	October	Retreat action toward East Prussia
	November-December	Service in Gumbinnen area
1945	January	Service in southern Polen (Lodz)
	February	Combat around Breslau
	March-April	Service in Lower Silesia and East Saxony
	May	Surrender in central Germany

The Panzer Units of the Waffen-SS

SS-Panzer-Armee-Oberkommando 6:

Formed 10/26/1944 in the west for the Ardennes offensive, service in Hungary and Austria as of 3/3/1945.

Subordinate to SS-Führ.-Nachr.Reg. (mot.) 500.

Officers of the Army also belonged to the staff of SS-Pz.AOK 6.

Likewise, Army or Panzer Corps of the Army with their divisions were also subordinated to the SS-Pz.AOK 6.

SS-Panzer Corps:

No.	Notes	Formed
I	*Leibstandarte Adolf Hitler*	1943
II		1942
III	Germanic Panzer Corps	1943
IV		1944
VII		1944
XIII		1944

SS-Panzer Divisions:

No.	Name	with SS-Panzer Reg. No. & Name
1	*LAH*	1 *LAH*
2	*Das Reich*	2
3	*Totenkopf*	3 *Danmark*
5	*Wiking*	5
9	*Hohenstaufen*	9
10	*Frundsberg*	10 *Langemarck*
12	*Hitlerjugend*	no SS-Panzer Regiment

SS Divisions with SS Panzer Units:

No.	Name	with SS-Panzer Unit No. & Name
4	*SS-Polizei Division*	4
11	*Nordland*	11 *Hermann von Salza*
16	*Reichsführer-SS*	16
17	*Götz von Berlichingen*	17
18	*Horst Wessel*	18
26	Hungarian No.3	26
27	*Langemarck*	27
28	*Wallonia*	28
31	Bohemia-Moravia	31

The Appearance of the German Tank

Assault Tank "A7V" of World War I; 9 tons, 100 HP, two 57mm rapid-fire guns, two machine guns.

Panzer I, Version A, 5.4 tons, 60 HP, two machine guns.

Panzer II, Version F, 9.5 tons, 20mm KwK 38 L/55, one MG 34.

Panzer III, Version J, 22.3 tons, 265 HP, 50mm KwK L/60, two machine guns.

38(t), 10.5 tons, 125 HP, 37mm KwK (t) L/40, two machine guns.

Panzer IV, Version H, 25 tons, 300 HP, 75mm KwK L/48, two machine guns.

Panzer V, version G, 44.8 tons, 700 HP, 75mm KwK L/70, three machine guns.

Panzer VI-II "King Tiger", 69.7 tons, 700 HP, 88mm KwK L/71.

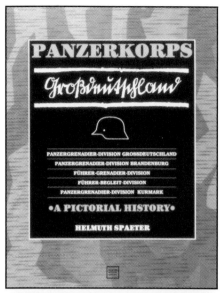

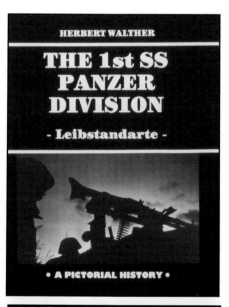

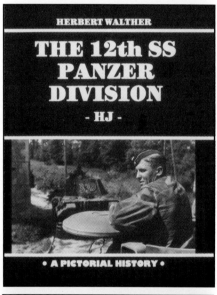

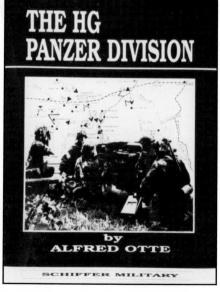

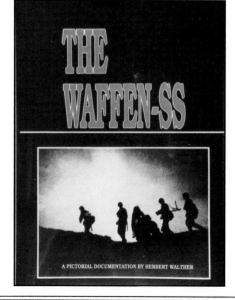